Anonymous

Irish Local Legends

Anonymous

Irish Local Legends

ISBN/EAN: 9783744734769

Printed in Europe, USA, Canada, Australia, Japan

Cover: Foto ©ninafisch / pixelio.de

More available books at **www.hansebooks.com**

IRISH
Local Legends.

BY
LAGENIENSIS.

Dublin:
JAMES DUFFY AND CO., Ltd.,
15 Wellington Quay.

1896.

Printed by
EDMUND BURKE & CO.,
61 & 62 GREAT STRAND STREET, DUBLIN.

PREFACE.

THE collecting and preservation of Folk-lore Tales have engaged the attention and interest of many national writers, especially during the present century. Such compositions have been presented in all known languages, while they have an undoubted ethnological value in historical and romantic literature. Fantastical or visionary though the topics may appear to be, still their record is pleasing to the imagination, and even inviting to philosophic reflection. Let not our readers suppose that fables are solely based on idealism. Subjectively to our ancestors, several were realistic ; while objectively, their themes are frequently traced from, if not found within, the domain of fact. This is more especially true of many Irish Local Legends. Their original forms have undergone various changes during the lapse of time. Popular and oral narrative often becomes an alembic of transmission, which serves to draw forth their spirit and essence, while flavoured or coloured with fantasy and invention, to supply the loss of historic or traditional incidents.

However, the term Legend has an application to narratives and relations, not even remotely bordering on romance ; and therefore, in connection with the subject matter of the present little work are introduced themes only intended to revive some reminiscences of customs and incidents, that are fast fading from a knowledge of the present generation. It seems to the writer, that many a trivial recollection of past times, if noted and transmitted by contemporaries, should be of greater interest and value as illustrations of manners and usages now unknown, than are the facts of more importance related by many chroniclers, and thus rendered notorious for all time. Entertaining such a view, some anecdotes and descriptions are here introduced, that may serve to amuse if not instruct several of our readers.

The following "Irish Local Legends" were received, mostly from accidental and familiar intercourse with the peasantry, and set down in substance at various times, while visiting different parts of Ireland. Sometimes they were fashioned at a way-side inn, in a *memoranda* book, and sometimes on an Irish hill-side, while fresh in the writer's recollection. They represent, indeed, but a small part of many such national romances, now hardly remembered; for the author had not in view the object of becoming a professed gleaner, and it amused an occasional disengaged hour to shape them into a form, not always according—it must be acknowledged—with the stories as at first related to him. They have for the most part appeared already in successive numbers of *The Irish Builder*, and with some inconsiderable changes they are here collected and re-issued.

When the "Wizard of the North" deemed it desirable to introduce Mottoes for the various chapters of his inimitable Waverley Novels, he found a ready resource in composing a few poetical lines, to which he appended the words, "Old Play," "Old Ballad," or some other equally enigmatical reference. This appears to have been one of the humorous caprices, which often seize on a man of genius, and it was a device which saved him many an hour of tedious library search. Finding the range of English and Classical literature sufficiently copious and accessible, as also sufficiently appropriate, for selection; the following Legends are severally headed with quotations from the works of renowned writers, who stand sponsors for their own genuine compositions. The Mottoes have been culled as flowers to cover those plain, unvarnished sketches and descriptions, that are veiled and nestle beneath the adornment; so that, like darker shadows of the clouds, our homely tales may be mantled in some measure with the borrowed radiance of a silver lining.

Those pleasant days are now past and gone, when a few weeks of vacation could be snatched from other duties and occupations, to spend them in a selected locality, and to enjoy, besides the hospitality of many a kind friend, that accommodation supplied in a hostelry of some considerable Irish town. There a posting establishment was always readily available, to furnish a cab or outside car for reaching rather distant places almost unknown to ordinary tourists, and which, nevertheless, had a scenic or historic interest, within their circuit, specially appreciated by the well informed antiquary as also delightful to the lover of rural and homely landscapes. Greater still was the desire of describing or sketching on the spot some mouldering ruin, or the outlines of some traditional site, neglected alike by artist and writer; yet, having a record in olden chronicles, and with difficulty traceable, or to be identified, owing to a lost or altered nomenclature. But, above all, when a pedestrian excursion was alone practicable and at the same time desirable for exhilaration and exercise, the greatest enjoyment was experienced to ascend the higher hills and gaze with rapture over the level, diversified plains, or to track the windings of lovely glens and valleys, there to search for particular objects of exploration, while accompanied by some intelligent peasant. He had only the Local Legends to communicate, but he was invariably obliging, and anxious enough to repeat those fire-side narratives of his fathers that had been preserved to his time.

Like our monuments that have survived the wreck of ages, and the still more destructive ravages of man, yearly crumbling to decay, and seldom engaging the aid of a competent restorer to save them from utter annihilation, are the traditional stories of Ireland. In a similar manner, the grand heroic songs, the lively dance tunes, and the tender, plaintive airs, that charm the ravished ears and elevate the souls of persons possessing the most refined musical genius, and even of our peasant circles, still remain uncollected and unpublished; while deteriorated taste has usurped the operatic stage, filled the concert programme, and countenanced the vanity of too many modern composers, who produce intricate scores, difficult of execution, but devoid of melody, sentiment or inspiration for all true vocalists and admirers of old lyric songs. Would that some systematic and effective efforts should be made, to rescue from oblivion such prized national memorials, and to preserve them as pearls of great price. An earnest, well-directed endeavour of the sort ought richly reward the patriotic feeling and cultured intelligence of societies or individuals, capable of appreciating their varied extent and inherent beauty as compositions. The harvest is still great, but the labourers unhappily are few, in the luxuriant fields of Irish romantic literature; nor should a moment be lost, while those waifs yet survive, in gathering up our derelict fragments ere they entirely perish.

December, 1896.

CONTENTS.

No.   PAGE

I. THE RIVAL PROFESSORS.
    Legend of Howth, County of Dublin .   1

II. THE GOBBAN SAOR AND HIS CRITICS.
    Legend of Ardmore, County of Waterford 7

III. THE BABOON'S RESCUE.
    Legend of Woodstock Castle, County of Kildare 10

IV. ROMANTIC BIRTH OF ST. FURSEY.
    Legend of Inchiquin or Inisquin. County of Galway . . . 13

V. THE GARRAN BAWN.
    Legend of Moghia, near Lismore, Queen's County . . . 22

VI. CONLA THE ARTIST AND THE DEAD BONES.
    Legend of Dun-Cruithne, Innishowen, County of Donegal . . . 23

VII. THE TYRANT CHIEFTAINESS AND HER PUNISHMENT.
    Legend of Lios Na Eiblin Oge O Coille Mor, County Cork . . . 24

VIII. THE WATER MONSTER.
    Legend of the River Lagan, County Down 26

CONTENTS.

No.   PAGE

IX. NAOMH GREOIHIR, OR ST. GREGORY OF THE GOLDEN MOUTH.
Legend of Inishmaan, Aran Islands, County of Galway . . . 27

X. THE BLACK MAN'S APPARITION.
Legend of Mundrehid, Queen's County   29

XI. THE SEA-SYREN'S REVENGE.
Legend of the River Delvin, County of Meath 31

XII. CONTESTS OF THE CLANS.
Legend of Mullaghmast, County of Kildare 33

XIII. THE CAPTIVE PIPER.
Legend of Knockaney, County of Limerick 39

XIV. THE PEISTHA DISCOMFITED.
Legend of Drumsna, County of Monaghan 44

XV. THE LEINSTER TRIBUTE.
Legend of Tara, County of Meath . 46

XVI. FIN-MAC-COOL'S STONE-THROW.
Legend of the Clough-Mor, County of Down 51

XVII. THE DEATH-COACH.
Legend of Timogue, Queen's County . 53

XVIII. THE BLESSED TROUTS.
Legend of the Three Wells, County of Wicklow 56

XIX. MISTAKEN IDENTITY.
Legend of Sandymount, County of Dublin 57

No.		PAGE
XX.	THE DRUID'S BETRAYAL. Legend of the River Bann, County of Londonderry	64
XXI.	THE GOBBAN SAER'S INGENUITY. Legend of St. Mullins, County of Carlow	68
XXII.	THE PEISTHA OF SAINT'S ISLAND. Legend of Lough Derg, County of Donegal	71
XXIII.	THE WITCH TRANSFORMED. Legend of Cullenagh, Queen's County	74
XXIV.	THE FOOL'S FANTASIES. Legend of Cloonfush, County of Galway	83
XXV.	TIPPERARY TACTICS. Legends of Upper and Lower Ormond, County of Tipperary	89
XXVI.	THE BATTLE OF THE CATS. Legend of Irishtown, County of Dublin	100
XXVII.	HUMOURS AND HUMORISTS. Legends of Ballyroan, Queen's County	104
XXVIII.	THE WITCH'S FATE. Legend of Antrim, County of Antrim	119
XXIX.	THE CONFEDERATE PEDDLERS. Legend of Dingle, County of Kerry	123
XXX.	THE STORM SPECTRE. Legend of the Mullet, County of Mayo	142

Irish Local Legends.

No. I.
The Rival Professors.
LEGEND OF HOWTH, COUNTY OF DUBLIN.

" Doubtless the pleasure is as great
Of being cheated, as to cheat ;
As lookers-on feel most delight,
That least perceive a juggler's sleight,
And still the less they understand
The more th' admire his sleight of hand."
—Samuel Butler's *Hudibras*, part ii., canto iii.

WHO among the residents of the Irish capital can be unacquainted with the numerous attractions adorning the Hill of Howth? With ready means of access to holiday-makers, we have now become familiar with its picturesque old town, its ecclesiastical ruins, its modern villas, its castle and demesne, its heath-covered heights, its sea-cliffs, its surrounding terrace-road, its various interesting highways and by-paths, with the charming views of land and water scenes, stretching out in every direction. Above all, what can compare in loveliness with the shore-lines of Dublin Bay, the city at the Liffey's mouth, and the back-ground of mountains swelling away in the distance? Many years ago when the tide of fashion had not set in so much, and when fewer fine mansions had been erected therein, it was our delight to visit Howth more frequently than of late, to have an invigorating walk over the heather, and to spend a social evening in pleasing converse with a friend. The herring-fishing season was especially an animated one for the colony of seamen that chiefly tenanted the village, and, when the little vessels were not out at sea, the fishermen were to be found in groups around the harbour, or taking observations from the high wall that ran along the brow of the Hill.

A

On an occasion of this sort, when the late Rev. John Francis Shearman—so greatly distinguished for his proficiency in Irish history and antiquities—was the Catholic curate of Howth, we had a ramble together through that irregularly built and situated town. My friend, as well known, was a special lover of folk-lore, and a gleaner of traditions from the narratives of his people; he knew their habits, customs and peculiarities very intimately, and often took care to elicit that store of information he desired to gather from them by familiar conversation. He then wished to show his visitor the substantial walls of the former college still remaining, and yet supporting the roofs of some tenement houses in one of the lanes opening on the lower street, not far removed from the interesting Abbey Church ruins within the enclosed graveyard.

As we ascended the steep road leading from the railway-station up the chief street, a gang of sailors dressed in their peculiar costume had already congregated at the sea-wall. Some were lounging and gazing over it; others were detached standing and engaged in conversation; while others again were in walking motion and in pairs—one of the party spinning a yarn, while his companion was evidently an interested listener. Among the latter class, it was very observable what force of habit had formed into the instinct of a slouched gait, a shrug of the shoulders, and a short turn round at the end of every ten or twelve paces, the usual length of the decks on their fishing-smacks. As we approached, they touched their caps by way of salute. Stopping for some time to inquire about the state and prospect of the fisheries, we found the men were waiting for the ebb-tide to go on board their respective vessels. After a friendly chat, addressing a fine hardy-looking fellow named Tom Breen, Father Shearman asked if, while waiting, he would have any objection to come along with us to the top of the street, so that he might show us the college, and tell us all he had heard about it. The fisherman expressed his great readiness to do so, and accordingly, taking leave of the others, we started onwards. Having had a full examination of the old buildings both within and without, well knowing Tom's powers of narrative for local traditions, and especially with regard to the still surviving fame of the college, the local curate asked him to repeat for us a story, which had not been heard for the first time. On every available occasion, Tom Breen was obliging and ready to impart his information when required, and, therefore, he willingly complied with the request. We remained attentive listeners, and he proceeded with the college story, somewhat in the order and form we shall here endeavour to reproduce.

"Well ye see it was a long time ago, since the monks lived in these ould anshent walls, and since their college was in the most flourishin' state, so that all the young gintlemin from every part of Ireland, England, and Scotland, came to study here. And soon the kerecther it had for high larnin' spread to France and all the other counthries in Europe. And by all accounts, it turned out fine shcolars, long afore Maynooth or Thrinity College was in bein'. Every where else the monks and schoolmasthers were doin' their very best to keep up their schools to compare widh Howth College, but none of them could hould a candle to it.

"Now there was a fine university in Paris at the same time, and the professors there began to fear that their young stugents would lave them and go over to finish their coorses in Howth. Soon they grew jealous of the Father Abbot and the monks that were here, and the Paris Shuperior and his clargy considhered what was best to be done, to save the univarsity from complete desartion of their young min. 'Wouldn't it be well,' siz the Father Shuperior, 'to sind over the best and most ontilligent of our gintlemin, that tache Greek and Latin here, to visit that out-of-the-way place called Howth, and to find out some more correct information than we now have about the monks' larnin'. There's an ould sayin', siz he, that cows in Connaught have long horns, and maybe afther all, they're not such great shakes as they purtind to be, and maybe it's only braggin' and boastin' of their knowledge they are, as so many fellows are doin' every day, and not a bit the betther on that account.' 'Troth and for my part,' siz another of the professors, 'I don't think the Univarsity of Paris can be sunk so low, as that a *sprioshawn* of a monasthery like Howth could turn out sich cliver min, or that we hav'n't here their aiquils in all the langiges and sciences.' 'Aye,' and siz another, 'begorra, I'll hould a hundher pounds to five, that if we challenge them to meet an aiquil number of huz afore their own shcolars on the Hill of Howth, that we'll sack thim in Greek or Latin, or any other langidge than Irish, which is their own native tongue.' No sooner said nor done; half-a-dozen professors at once volunteered to dhraw up a challenge, and whin it was signed widh their names, it was put in the Frinch post office, and the letther said they were comin' afther it themselves, in a month's time. To be shure, the ship soon carried the letther to Dublin, and it kem in due course widh other parcels to the Father Abbot in Howth.

"I need hardly tell ye, whin the Riverend Father opened the letther, and read its contints, he thrimbled all over like an aspin-lafe, and then got into a brown study. Howsomediver, he thought it best to call the community together, and consult them as to what they had best do about the challenge. Whin they met, 'Now,' siz the Abbot, 'brothers, we're put in a terrible quandary,' siz he, 'for if we're cowed by the challenge, and don't accept it, we'll lose all our credit, not only in Ireland, but in England and Scotland, and if we do accept it, and are beaten in a fair stand-up fight with the Frinchmin, why our stugents will all lave huz and go off to Paris for their edication, and then we'll have to close our fine college in Howth.' Now the youngest of the masthers there, called Father Teague, was the first to offer his opinion; but his heart was shtronger than his wake judgment, and he thought that neither himself nor any of his brothers should show the white feather, as they must be more than a match for the Frinch professors. 'Well, Father Teague,' siz Father Pathrick, a vinerable and larned vice-president of the college, 'it's all very well to talk up bowld whin the inimy is far away, but whin you come to the scratch, maybe you wouldn't be so shure of winnin' the battle, and for my part, although I have been tachin' Greek and Latin double the linth of time since you were ordained, I can tell ye, those Frinch professors must be very smart chaps to be set over the Univarsity of Paris. Beat us to bruss they would, as shure as a gun. But I tell you what we can do, and I think we'll gain the day over thim. Now that we know whin they are comin' to Howth, let all the masthers in the college turn out, scatther themselves along the road-sides betuxt this and Dublin, and dhress themselves up in the most tatthered clothes we can find, with shtraw suggauns tied about their middles, ould caubeens on their heads, and coarse brogues on their feet. Besides, let thim borry all the shovels and shcrapers they can get, to clane the road. Thin, whin word is given that the Frinch ship has got into Dublin Harbour, let all our tachers begin to shcrape the roads as hard as they can, and whin the six Frinch professors come up, let aich monk bid them the time o' day in Latin, and thin ingage thim in conversation usin' only the same langidge. Thin whin axed by the Frinch their names and places of livin', let thim all say they are labourers belongin' to Howth Monasthry, and that they got their edication in the College.' Father Pathrick's advice was taken, and this is what happened :

"At the ind of the month, the six Frinch professors had larned a little Irish, and shure enough they set out and sailed over to Dublin, dhressed in grand style. Whin they landed there, they saw a poor man at the quay wall, and politely inquired if he could direct thim on the road to Howth. Now he was one of the lay-brothers of the monasthry looking out for thim, and in disguise ; and like himself, he had another confedherate there, who was to play his thricks on the thravellers. 'Begorra, gintlemin, yees are welcome to ould Ireland,' siz the first, 'and we always like to see Frinchmin comin' over among huz as towrists, and my frind here will show yees the road to Howth with great pleasure. But first of all, ye'll take a little refreshment and a glass of sperrits, to warm yees up after the say-voyage.' They did so, and thanked him kindly, and said on partin' they liked the Irish wine betther nor what grew in their own counthry, although the flavour was a little sthronger.

"Their guide to Howth with the head-professor moved a little in advance of the rest ; but whin he came up to the first of the road-shcrapers, he winked, and the labourer restin' on his shcraper took off his caubeen. Now this was Father Teague, and although he thought he was first class at the Latin, the sorra haporth too much of it he knew, with all his consate, only he was wondherfully good for a labourin' man. The head-professor returned his salute in the same langidge, and thin he was curious to know how a *spalpeen* like that could have so much larnin'. 'Whethen,' siz the road-shcraper, 'whin I was a *gorsoon*, my father and mother sint me a few quarthers to the monks' college in Howth there beant, and whatever little I know I larnt from the masthers.' 'And no masther of them all can spake it betther, I am sure,' siz the head-professor. And so they wint on to the next road-shcraper, about a quarther of a mile, and there too the guide gev a wink as he approached. The second labourer raised his ould hat as politely as any

Frinchman could do it, and agin called out in Latin, 'Good day, gintlemin, God speed ye.' No less surprised than afore. the Frinchmin stopped to spake to him, and they were towld a like story about the schoolin' he got for a few quarthers in Howth College. He was even a betther spaker of Latin than the other, and biddin' him good-bye, they thravelled farther on, wondherin' at the great edication given to the poor in Ireland. Well, to make a long story short, the Frinch professors walked along, and at every quarther of a mile, the same sort of labourers and salutes were met widh, and in aich case, the workmin seemed to be surpassin' one another in the purty way they spoke Latin, and betther nor any clargy the Frinch ever met in their own counthry.

"At last they were comin' nigh the Hill of Howth, and who was on the road but Father Pathrick in disguise. He offs with his caubeen and salutes them in the grandest way, and in the best Latin they had yet heerd. The Frinch professors questioned, examined, and crosshackled him, in every way, and for a long time on the road. He thin in turn began to put questions to them. Faix and soon they found themselves bogged and hasped for an answer. Now seein' the turret of the monasthry church not far distant, and bleevin' that the abbot and monks were all there, and ready to meet them on the public platform, the head-professor fell back among his comerades, and held a conference widh thim. 'Boys,' siz he, 'yees have seen and heerd the poor scholars along the road, who were tached in the college there, and how highly coached they are in Latin afther a short coorse, and what must not be the larnin' of their masthers, who 'ar at it all their lives. I'm shure if we carried out our challenge, the monks of Howth would make hares and holy shows of huz all afore the Irish people, and those of the whole world. So the best of our play is to hurry back to the ship and sail away home to France.' The other professors approved his advice, and thin all of them turned their backs on Howth. I need hardly tell ye, the road shcrapers laughin' in their sleeve noticed the homeward-bound movements of the Frinch; and as the thravellers passed aich of thim on their return, 'God speed ye, gintlemin,' was the partin' salute given agin in Latin. The thravellers were so much ashamed whin they reached Paris, that they gev out an excuse for their failure by statin' that they never landed on the shores of Ireland at all, but that havin' sailed out to say, they were dhriven back to France by conthrairy winds. But the Father Abbot and monks of Howth consealed their own thrick, and belled it over the whole counthry, that the most larned min in France kem over to howld a conthravarsy wid thimselves, and whin they wint as far as the monasthry gate, they got afeerd of incountherin' the monks, and darn't carry out their challenge, but ran away like cowards."

Thus ended Tom Breen's story, we feeling greatly interested and amused while the narrative proceeded. Having thanked him for his courtesy, we bade him adieu, and walked on to the comfortable presbytery, enjoying greatly the humour of those incidents related, regarding the famous College of Howth, and the scheme of the ingenious if not ingenuous monks to preserve and propagate its literary reputation.

No. II.
The Gobban Saor and his Critics.

LEGEND OF ARDMORE, COUNTY OF WATERFORD.

" Blessed that child of humanity, happiest man among men,
  Who, with hammer, or chisel, or pencil, with rudder, or ploughshare, or pen,
Laboureth ever and ever with hope through the morning of life,
Winning home and its darling divinities—love-worshipped children and wife,
Round swings the hammer of industry, quickly the sharp chisel rings,
And the heart of the toiler has throbbings that stir not the bosom of kings."
—Denis Florence MacCarthy's *Bell-Founder*, part i.

EVERYBODY knows, that a celebrated artist, the Gobban Saor, was the greatest builder of churches in Ireland. Among other great works, he designed and erected that remarkable group, which rises over the sea at Ardmore, in the County of Waterford. The Round Tower and the churches there are well known as objects of curiosity to the antiquary and tourist; but few are aware, that after Gobban had built them, he chose to erect a house for himself and to settle in the neighbourhood. His fame for ingenuity and good workmanship soon extended to the most distant places; and wherever a great building was desired by any of the clerics, he was ever and always consulted about its erection, and most generally employed to carry out the design. Moreover, he was skilled in all branches of the fine arts; especially in wood and metal work. He also kept a number of tradesmen and apprentices at the carpenters' bench, and quite as many at the smiths' forge. All of these he taught their respective trades, so that many of them became famous, and when they set up on their own account they got sufficient employment from the kings, and chiefs, and bishops, in various parts of Ireland.

Although one of the most clever artists, however, the Gobban Saor found that whatever piece of work he executed, some captious individuals had objections to it. At length, like many an astute politician, he hoped to gage the tendency of popular opinion, and to steer his bark accordingly; for as he reasoned, that two heads being admittedly wiser than one, by a still juster conclusion, the more opinions he heard expressed, and by a still greater number of people, the more hints he should receive, and therefore profit most by such suggestions. He thought over a plan, which he deemed to be a capital expedient to put his theory to the test. Then setting to work with a will, and sparing no labour or skill on the object which engaged his attention for many weeks, the Gobban Saor made a grand box, in what he thought the best of taste, ornamented with fine carving, and painted in the most attractive tone of colouring. Afterwards, he placed it on the middle of a cross-road, which the people would have to pass by on their way to Mass, it being the Sunday he chose for that exhibition. Getting inside the box, he locked it, and waited to hear what comments might be made on it, by the people going by to attend their devotions.

A crowd soon gathered round the box, when the general opinion prevailed, that it was the "finest" box ever they saw; only some thought that the legs were a little too long. Hearing this, Gobban waited until they were all gone into the church, when he got out, and, having his tools with him, he cut a small portion off the feet. "Now it must certainly please them," thought he to himself. Getting into the box again, he waited to hear what should be said by the people on their way from Mass. Then another crowd, collecting round the box, gave it as a pretty general opinion, that it was the "grandest box" ever made, only the legs were then too short; and others thought that it should look much better if these were removed altogether. Whereupon, Gobban took away the legs, to gratify his critics, and to learn again what effect that might have on the public taste and judgment.

He resolved to try the experiment for another Sunday. Then he found the criticisms had taken quite another turn. Every one seemed to be of opinion, that the box was too long for its width, and that its proportions were not very good. Whereupon, the Gobban Saor, set himself anew to the task of shortening it considerably, and once more he ensconced himself within it. The following Sunday, he heard a different class of objections; for all then agreed, that the box now looked too short, and that the sides should be narrowed to make it more shapely. The artist again remodelled his box, and once more he subjected it to inspection. He heard the first person that arrived state, that the box then looked worse than before, for its height was out of all proportion to its length and breadth, and that the lid ought to be lowered very considerably. This too seemed to be the opinion very generally entertained by all the bystanders. More disappointed and disconcerted than ever, the Gobban Saor spent that week in taking off several inches from the top, and now the box became so small, that he had barely room to squeeze himself into it, to learn what judgment the people might form of himself and his workmanship on the next Sunday. "Although there were faults in the box before," said one of the farmers, "the Gobban Saor might have let well enough alone; for what with sawing it here, and hacking it there, scraping of the paint, and patching it together, every change has been for the worse." "I quite agree with you, neighbour," said one who was present, "and besides it is labour lost, nor does it increase the Gobban Saor's credit as an artisan." Several voices were then heard expressing various conflicting opinions, but all of these of a fault finding character, and hardly any were qualified in a favourable point of view.

On hearing the foregoing remarks, Gobban could no longer restrain his patience, and got out of the box. Then, breaking it up, he said he would never try to please everybody for the future, but should have reliance on his judgment alone to plan and execute his own work.

No. III.
The Baboon's Rescue.

LEGEND OF WOODSTOCK CASTLE, COUNTY OF KILDARE.

"The lone tower dark against a heaven all glowing,
Like seas of glass and fire—I saw the sweep
Of glorious woods far down the mountain side,
And their still shadows in the gleaming tide,
And the red evening on its waves asleep ;
And 'midst the scene—oh ! more than all—there smiled
My child's fair face, and hers, the mother of my child ! "
—Mrs. Felicia Hemans' *The Forest Sanctuary*,
part ii., stanza xi.

IN the early part of this century, a Mrs. Mary St. John lived in Stradbally, Queen's County, and she was an industrious collector of stories, related by the townsfolk and country people. That lady and her companion, a Mrs. Bradshaw, occupied a handsome and convenient private house near the bridge, which spans the Beauteogue River running through the village. Both were favourites among the townspeople, and especially beloved by the poor old beggar women, who were always to be found assembled before their front door, during the hour for dinner; as soon afterwards the maid servant appeared, and distributed a portion of broken meat and of vegetables to each expectant of the compassionate ladies' charities. An afternoon walk usually preceded their dinner-hour, and their return home was the signal for the trooping after them of their poor *clientele*, who were always profuse in their praises, and with blessings on them, loudly and fervently expressed.

Each Sunday in the village there were different hours for service, both in the Protestant church, and in the old Catholic chapel, when their respective bells tolled the signal for the different congregations to enter. In a village community, observations are made that cannot well be avoided; and when the various families in town turned out to attend their devotions, some were remarked as going forth at the first tap of the bell, and walking leisurely, since they were sure to be in good time. Others again were noticed leaving their homes only at the last moment, and sometimes after the last toll of the bell, then moving at a striding pace, or even running, and always in time to be late. In the little square outside the chapel gate, a crowd of country people was usually collected, at an early hour, but rather to engage in conversation or to discuss the current social and political subjects of the day. Sometimes these debates waxed warm, as voluble orators of differing opinions longed for the opportunity of engaging in contests, which were only adjourned as the bell ceased ringing, and a general rush was made for the gate, when Mass was about to commence. The square tower of the Protestant church had two bells, but these were of different tones: the first bell rung was pitched in a slow and deep measure, and it was called "Solemn Bob"; while at its close, and for about five minutes before the service began, a much smaller bell sent forth a quick and jingling sound, supposed to express "Come or Stay," and therefore so called by the townspeople. Then only were the numerous Protestant laggards on the run. Now Mrs. St. John and Mrs. Bradshaw were invariably out of their house, dressed in a most matronly and becoming fashion, the very moment "Solemn Bob" gave the first note. With the Book of Common Prayer, Bible and Hymn Book, both ladies were to be seen moving towards the church, which was not far distant; while their dignified demeanour and praiseworthy punctuality in proceeding to commence their devout exercises gave edification to people of every rank, class and religious denomination. Hats were raised and courtesies were made as they passed along, and these salutes were courteously returned by the gentlewomen, who felt indeed, that they were greatly loved and respected by their neighbours, gentle and simple.

The external manner and bearing of both ladies were quite different: Mrs. Bradshaw, tall and lean, being distinguished by a reserved and distant mien in her intercourse with other persons, yet withal condescending and approachable enough, however puritanical she might seem; while Mrs. St. John, rather full and portly in figure, was ever cheery and good humoured, social and agreeable in conversation, knowing nearly all people in the village by name and occupation, having a kindly word for each in passing, and often stopping to inquire about themselves and families. She had ready wit, in a remarkable degree, and a knowledge of the world, for she had travelled to the East and lived for some time abroad. Yet, her exile altered not her truly Irish nature, and when she returned to her native country, the scenes of childhood had special attractions for her.

Being a student of village and peasant life, she loved to

meet some eccentric character, and have a linguistic passage at arms in good humoured fashion with him or her, as the case might be. Such opportunities were often afforded, and several stories were current of the smart things said, and the repartees which were returned on either side.

With children she felt quite at home, and loved to converse with them, inquiring about their school proficiency, putting such questions as she thought interested them, and eliciting such replies as their information or intelligence permitted them to make. Oftentimes she drew from her reticule Shrewsbury cakes, which served to ingratiate her still more in their regards, while those marks of her favour were willingly received and thankfully acknowledged. She was an elderly lady in Stradbally, about the year 1834, and then in good health, but the writer has not been able to ascertain the year of her death. Having premised so much regarding early recollections of this lady, it next becomes necessary to introduce the legend for which we are indebted to her.

To gratify her own literary taste, and as we think, chiefly for private circulation among her friends, Mrs. St. John printed a ballad poem, intituled " Ellauna," Dublin, 1815, and divided into four cantos. It is now many years past, and in our school-boy days, when we were gratified with the perusal of that little octavo book, which was all the more interesting to us, because Ellauna happened to be the heroine, and a chieftainess of the great dynast family belonging to the O'Mores of Dunamase, and who formerly ruled over all the Leix territory. The notes annexed to each canto contained some items of historical or traditional information ; and we then penned down the following narrative—probably *verbatim et litteratim*—on a scrap of paper, which, lest it might be otherwise forgotten, we deem worthy of preservation in our storied repertory.

It was stated, that Dorothea O'More, daughter to O'More of Leix, brought in dowry to Gerald, the seventh Baron of Offaly, the town of Athy, with the manor and adjoining Castle of Woodstock. The Black Castle, afterwards the County Gaol, was the defence for a bridge over the Barrow. It is related, that the O'More either built or liberally endowed two or three religious houses in Athy. Near this town, on the western bank of the Barrow, stands the old Castle ; and it has a historic interest attaching to it in the mediæval times, when the Geraldines were its occupants.

A local legend prevailed, that the Castle of Woodstock accidentally took fire. The nurse of Fitz-Gerald's heir, the son of Dorothea, perished in the flames; but, when the family and domestics looked up, they beheld a large and favourite baboon, with the child in her arms and on the highest parapet of the Castle. She clanked her chain for aid; a ladder was speedily procured, and the infant was happily restored to his despairing parents. In remembrance of this signal deliverance, the chief of Offaly had inwoven on his banners a baboon, chained proper. To the present day, this continues to be the armorial distinction borne by the illustrious House of Leinster.

No. IV.
Romantic Birth of St. Fursey.
LEGEND OF INCHIQUIN OR INISQUIN, COUNTY OF GALWAY.

" Temer si dee di sole quelle cose
　　Ch' hanno potenza di fare altrui male:
　　Dell' altre no, che non son panrose.
Io son fatta da Dio, sua mercè, tale.
　　Che la vostra miseria non mi tange,
　　Nè flamma d'esto incendio non m' assale."
　　　　—Dante Alighieri's *La Divina Commedia*,
　　　　　Inferno, Canto Secondo, ll. 88—93.

"Of those things only should one be afraid
　　Which have the power of doing others harm;
　　Of the rest, no; because they are not fearful.
God in His mercy such created me
　　That misery of yours attains me not,
　　Nor any flame asails me of this burning."
　　　　—Henry Wadsworth Longfellow's *Translation*.

In framing an Irish story, it was never deemed to be a canon of composition, that the Sanachee should keep within the limits of probability or even of consistency in the course of his narrative. Sufficient for him, if it was extravagant enough to excite the wonder of his hearers, and to mystify their intelligence. The confusion of persons and places offered no impediment in the plot, provided the commonalty for whom it had been prepared could find ingredients presented to the fancy and combined according to the taste or opinion of the individuals addressed. With such reflections premised, we shall introduce the following *romaunt* derived from popular tradition and referring to a renowned Irish saint.

A very long time ago, dating so far back as the seventh century, King Ædfind, or "Hugh the White,"—said to have been ruler over the Hy-Bruin or Breifne district—is thought to have lived in some part of the Connaught province. However, we have only a partial glimmer of traditional accounts, drawn from numerous old *codices* preserved in different libraries, with more recent comments of chroniclers, to state our present legend. It is strange, too, these records are mostly preserved abroad; and from the earlier ones, Surius, the Bollandists, Colgan, and Mabillon have furnished versions of that provincial dynast's career, in Acts of the celebrated St. Fursey. From these, James Desmay, Doctor of Theology of the Sorbonne, and Canon of St. Fursey's Collegiate Church, at Perrone, in France, published that great saint's life in French, in the sixteenth century. Therein, he not only preserves those legends referring to the subject of his memoir, but he even dilates on them with a breadth of fond imagination, yet betraying much ignorance regarding Ireland's early condition and history. We here select for the subject of a legend those circumstances related as preceding and accompanying St. Fursey's birth. These are romantic to a degree. In the action of that story, and in the sentiments there expressed, we are strongly reminded regarding the chivalry of the middle ages and the practices of knight-errantry; while there is reason to believe, nevertheless, that warlike and heroic adventures were required at a very early period, to qualify young Irish chiefs for distinction and knighthood.

When three brothers—Brendan, elsewhere called Brandubh, King of Louth or Leinster—for the narrative is varied—Feradhach, and Ædfind, King of Breifne, lived in their own parts of Ireland; King Finlog ruled over the province of Munster, and he had a distinguished son named Fintan. This prince desired much to visit the other kings, chiefs, and territorial magnates of Ireland, to engage their favour and friendship, as also to acquire a personal knowledge of local customs and laws. Among others, he sought Brandubh, King of Leinster, who received him very honourably; and, at his fort, the young prince acquired the friendship and love of the king, as also of his chiefs. His personal attractions, valour, urbane manners, and regular morals, made him everywhere a welcome guest.

Having remained some time with Brandubh or Brendan, Fintan had a favourable report of his younger brother, Ædfind, who lived away from the Leinster King, and at a considerable distance. Although a pagan, that brother was renowned for courtly manners and hospitality. Thither Fintan proceeded, and there introduced, he was received with respectful courtesy and attention. This king had an only daughter named Gelgeis, Latinized Gelghesia, or, Anglicised, "the White Swan." She had been brought up in all the exercises of piety, her mother most probably having been a Christian; besides, she was a princess of great accomplishments and beauty. Soon after the arrival of Fintan, accompanied by her lady friends, Gelgeis went to an exhibition or a spectacle. Most probably it was a military assault-at-arms or some sportive game. There the princely guest was distinguished for his accomplishments and prowess. At once the attention of Gelgeis was directed towards Fintan, and her curiosity was awakened. She felt a great inclination to learn his personal history, and soon she found that he was a pagan. From some of her attendants who were present, Gelgeis inquired who he was, for what purpose he came, and what were his peculiar qualities and rank.

While engaged in a conference of this sort, Fintan himself approached, presenting a pleasing address, air, and demeanour. He accosted the lady in these words—"O most beautiful princess, it is the custom of noble youths to seek the palm of military prowess through different parts of the world, and thus to deserve the regard of noble maidens. Wherefore, having come to this part of the country, and obtained the good opinion of your father and mother, I still desire more earnestly to ingratiate myself into your favour, and, if possible, to hold the first place in your affections. For no constrained reason, but through a voluntary impulse, I have exiled myself so long from home. I am the eldest son of Finlog, King of Munster, and, according to the laws of my country, I ought to succeed him in the kingdom. Therefore do I desire in my youth to acquire a knowledge of the various habits and customs of different countries, and to gain the favour and friendship of many kings and princes, so that, if I live to enjoy the inheritance to which I am born, I may be able to govern my principality with prudence and defend it with valour, or, if circumstances require it, to make others subject to my rule."

Then Gelgeis told him that kings were only happy when they recognised the superiority of the King of kings, and who practised the requirements of religion, who proved themselves obedient to the Divine will, and who, by exercising justice and prudence, should learn from the Almighty a true and wise order and example for the rule and government of their states. The additional words attributed to her are:—"O honourable youth, the works of Divine wisdom are variously manifested, and by their operation all things in heaven, on earth, in the sea, and beneath the depths, are directed. If faithfully and firmly believing in God, you commit to Him your hopes, the glory you desire, and the rewards you expect in the present life, doubtless in the next you will secure eternal felicity."

Her persuasive words and singular modesty of deportment gained on the affections of Fintan, and soon he desired to contract a marriage with the beautiful princess. Having resolved on the course to be taken, Fintan proposed his intentions to Gelgeis, hoping to obtain her consent for his suit. She replied, that, being a Christian, she had rather always remain a virgin than engage in a matrimonial alliance with any man of a different persuasion. She said, moreover, that, unless a prospect of some great good, or of a result agreeable to God, were afforded, she had rather not embrace the engagements and difficulties inseparable from the marriage state. The possibility of Fintan becoming a Christian and of renouncing idolatry having been established, an effort was made to learn the will of Gelgeis's father on this matter. This king was a determined enemy of Christianity, however, and he was also found adverse to the question of his daughter's marriage with a Christian.

Meantime, Ædfind had formed such a favourable opinion of Fintan, that he desired him to remain as one of his courtiers and to engage in his service. Not unwilling to live in a position, where he could enjoy the conversation and society of his beloved Gelgeis, Fintan consented, and gradually their intercourse became more impassioned; nor was this unknown or unnoticed by their confidants at court, although the father of Gelgeis did not suspect her affections had been thus bestowed on the young warrior and stranger.

The counsellors of the young couple, after mature consideration, thought it better to advise a marriage, even although the father's consent could not be obtained; and thus those friends were chiefly instrumental in procuring a matrimonial alliance between Fintan and Gelgeis. Mutual consent and faithful love blessed their union. Fintan abjured the worship of idols, and married Gelgeis, according to the prescribed rites of the Church. The parents of both parties were ignorant, however, regarding these proceedings.

In due course of time, Gelgeis was about to give birth to a child; but soon her condition became known to Ædfind, who instituted inquiries, and at last he obtained the revelation of what had occurred. Inflamed with a hatred of the Christian religion, and construing the secret marriage of Gelgeis as indicating contempt for paternal authority, King Ædfind resolved on allaying the flames of his own wrath by condemning his daughter to a most cruel death. The unnatural tyrant commanded, that she should be conducted to a pyre, which had been prepared for the purpose, and which afterwards was to be set in flames. This intelligence caused the chiefs and nobles, together with the people, to feel deepest affliction, while all orders and classes of persons greatly deplored the impending fate of their beloved princess, whose virtues and graces were so universally esteemed.

When Gelgeis heard of this fearful sentence, she deemed it right to offer an explanation of her motives, with her apologies for the secret course she had taken. Still fearing his ungovernable rage, she suppliantly approached her father to offer dutiful submission, and those reasons that induced her to engage in the matrimonial state. Notwithstanding her tears and entreaties, he scarcely allowed her a hearing, but gave orders that immediate preparations should be made for her execution. As the dynast was known to be of an implacable and a hasty temper, no one dared advocate her cause or intercede for a remission of her sentence, lest the king's anger might be excited against the intercessor. However, Ædfind's elder brother Brandubh chanced to be present at that time when Gelgeis had been condemned to the flames. Meantime, some chiefs had waited on the king's brother, and Brandubh entered completely into their views, feeling a deep compassion for the sad condition of his niece. This king is said to have used all his influence to overcome Ædfind's cruel resolution.

B

He urged remonstrances as to what judgment the neighbouring kings, all Ireland, foreign nations, and all posterity, must arrive at, in consideration of such a shocking barbarity. He besought the king not to stain his reputation and that of his family, by such an unheard-of wickedness, nor to grieve the hearts of all his subjects, by inflicting on them such a mortal wound,—in fine, that he should be ashamed to be considered as a tyrant over a woman, as an unnatural parent sacrificing his own daughter, as an unjust man acting against a just person, or as a wicked judge oppressing an innocent princess. But all these arguments were vainly urged; for neither entreaties, reason, pity, nor kindred were able to move the arbitrary tyrant. This latter even urged the executioners to obey commands given, and he warned the people to interpose no obstacle thereto, under pain of incurring his displeasure.

The time fixed for the execution of Gelgeis approached, and a vast crowd assembled. In silence, the people stood around, while Brandubh and the chiefs lamented the impending fate of the princess. Sorrow and distress were visible in the countenances of all spectators. However, when human patronage is wanting, it often pleases the Almighty to interpose His providence in an effectual manner, on behalf of injured innocence. The divine care and complacency entertained for Gelgeis were soon manifested.

The infant then carried in her womb, and who had not yet seen the light, began to plead the cause of his mother, in a clear and distinct voice. Against her inhuman parent he bitterly inveighed, because that tyrant sought the death of an innocent person, and because he pronounced an unjust sentence, without favourably hearing a daughter's justification. The king was declared guilty of an unnatural cruelty towards Gelgeis, because he had ordered executioners to satiate his blind rage, passion, and frenzy, instead of exercising the judgment of an equitable and a merciful ruler and parent. Fear and wonder took possession of those Pagans who were present, while pious impetration and hope characterised the assembled Christians. The former superstitiously imagined themselves hearing some sound or complaint of a passing spectre, and not that of a human voice; while the latter conceived, that those words proceeded from the Almighty Himself, recognising the words of inspired Scripture—" God hath done all things whatsoever He hath wished, both in heaven and on earth." Instead of being mollified by the miracle recorded, Ædfind allowed his mind to become still more obstinate and unyielding. Losing all temper at the idea of being foiled in his intentions, the king ordered his executioner to prepare three different fires.

When his daughter approached nearer to the prepared pyre, she asked one favour from her father. The object she had in view was to offer up a short prayer to the Almighty on behalf of her immortal soul. That favour he granted. She thus spoke—"My God and my hope from youth, Thou who art a protector in all anguish and tribulation, behold how I have loved Thy truths, since those who are just obtain eternal life. Before Thee, in my heart, I desire to cherish faith, and to make a true confession, in the presence of many witnesses. O Lord, in whose sight the very depths of our souls are revealed, Thou knowest that I have not sought the marriage for which I am now adjudged to the flames, on account of worldly satisfaction or honour; but, moved by Thy inspirations, and owing to the counsels of my faithful friends, I desired to win my spouse for Thee, and to bring forth an offering worthy of Thee, who should sustain Thy afflicted Church, overthrow idolatry, and the tyrannic sway of a prince, that should rule by his virtues in this quarter. Wherefore, O Lord, have mercy on me, and may my death end in life everlasting. On account of Thy glorious name, preserve the fruit of my womb; for when through Thy divine will he was conceived, I dedicated him to Thy service. O Lord God, let Thy mercy attend to Thy handmaid's supplication, now asking Thee in tears, for the safety of one I should hereafter be obliged to bring forth in pain. Protect him under the shadow of Thy wings, that he may produce fruits for Thee in Thy Church, and that his enemies may recognise him when seen; because in the day of tribulation, Thou wilt not forsake those trusting in Thee, nor wilt Thou leave unsupported those oppressed by the proud and tyrannical."

Having thus prayed, Gelgeis is said to have been brought forth by the executioners, and committed to the flames. On beholding the fire preparing to consume her, a flood of tears came from her eyes. This proved the occasion of another astonishing miracle. For when those tears watered the ground, a gushing fountain sprang up, and a heavy shower of rain fell from the skies at the same time. It pleased the Almighty, by such means, to extinguish those fires prepared for her destruction. In this manner, Gelgeis was preserved from harm, nor even was any portion of her garments consumed. The people were wonderfully rejoiced at this great triumph of innocence and justice. They also demanded with loud cries the death of her unnatural parent.

Still not becoming a convert in consequence of those miracles, yet Ædfind relented in his meditated scheme of cruelty. A popular insurrection even broke out because of this miracle, which resulted in the safety of Gelgeis. According to Saint Fursey's older Acts, the influence of ecclesiastics had been exerted in appeasing this seditious tumult ; but Gelgeis' entreaties procured her father's safety from his own subjects. Nevertheless, Ædfind resolved that Gelgeis and her husband should be banished from his territories. Then Fintan began to consider, whether he should go back to his father in Munster, or select another patron, his uncle St. Brendan, who lived still nearer that place. At this time, that distinguished and holy abbot had a monastic establishment on the Island of Inisquin, or Inchiquin, in Lough Orbsen, now Lough Corrib. Fintan thereupon resolved to seek the latter in his monastery.

Having had a revelation, that a great plenitude of divine wisdom was hereafter to dwell in St. Fursey, the holy Brendan enjoined a fast of three days on himself and upon his community. No sooner had Fintan and Gelgeis arrived on the island, than a lodging was prepared for them in the guest-house of the monastery, while every care and courtesy was lavished on them by the great abbot, known as the Navigator, who discovered the greater Ireland in the Western Ocean, and who was afterwards the Bishop of Clonfert. A great and brilliant light surrounded the house, as if promising to indicate the advent of another light, which was soon to shine upon earth ; and, when her time had elapsed, Gelgeis brought forth her son, who was destined for a high and holy mission.

The following continuation of narrative is to be found in the older Acts of St. Fursey. Nevertheless, places and persons are greatly confounded, so as to prevent any clear historic sequence or identification. Brendan received the boy, and conferred on him the sacrament of Baptism, bestowing the name Fursey at the same time. This name is said, by Desmay, to have had the signification of "Virtue," in the Irish or Scottish language. The abbot Brendan not only supplied corporal food to his spiritual son, but in course of time trained him up in monastic discipline, and in a knowledge of sacred learning, for which the boy had such a special aptitude.

It need scarcely be added, that in after time occurred those celebrated ecstasies of St. Fursey, which took place in his monastery, and that were written in a book. From this Venerable Bede transcribed them into his Ecclesiastical History of England, composed in the eighth century. One of the brothers of Bede's monastery used to relate those visions, as he heard them told by a religious man, who had learned them from St. Fursey's own lips, when he dwelt among the East Angles. That account described his transport in spirit to Hell, Purgatory, and Paradise.

The historians of general literature have hardly traced with distinctness those originals from which the finest works of imagination have been produced. Strange as it may appear, and with all the profusion of comment bestowed on the subject, few writers have been able to state the sequence of intellectual delight, which has been drawn from the "Vision of St. Fursey." That composition afterwards became the model on which was founded the visions of Adamnan, and of Tundal. It was closely imitated by Frate Alberico, a monk of Monte Cassino. It became the most widespread and popular romance of the ages preceding Dante. The latter took from it his ideas, and formed on it the plan and ground-work for his sublime poem; while various scenes and passages of the original are reproduced, but with some additions from more ancient and classical sources, in the immortal "Divina Commedia."

No. V.

The Garran Bawn.

LEGEND OF MOGHIA, NEAR LISMORE, QUEEN'S COUNTY.

"A Pack-horse turn'd his head aside,
Foaming, his eye-balls swell'd with pride.
'Good gods! (says he) how hard's my lot!
Is then my high descent forgot?
Reduc'd to drudgery and disgrace,
(A life unworthy of my race)
Must I, too, bear the vile attacks
Of ragged scrubs and vulgar hacks?'"
—John Gay's *Fables*, Part ii.

ONCE upon a time, there were two celebrated monasteries in vogue; one of those was at Aghaboe, in the Queen's County, and the other some eight or ten miles distant, at Monahincha, in the County of Tipperary. Now it happened, that the monks of one of these monasteries had a grey horse, past its labour in the field. But he was a hardy and a knowledgeable old animal, that was yet turned to good account. He had travelled so frequently in his day between Aghaboe and Monahincha, that he knew every inch of the Ballaghmore or great road.

In those times, there were no postal facilities between the religious of the two houses, and yet they were obliged to keep up a daily communication. At last it was thought, that the Garran Bawn—as the old horse was called—might be trained to travel back and forward each day, with saddle-bags slung on either side of his back to balance each other. Soon did the animal learn to jog along leisurely, with the necessaries and messages for the monks of both establishments contained in the saddle-bags, and without even a guide to direct him. Nor would any of the people along the road molest him, as they knew his office was to bear only what was useful for the monks.

However, there were three rascals living in the neighbourhood, called Deegan, Dooly, and Dullany, who had not the same respect for the old horse, nor for the requisites he was accustomed to carry. These men entered into a conspiracy to seize the poor animal one day, and to plunder the panniers. Accordingly, they waited for him on the highway, at a place called Moghia, near Lismore, where the Garran Bawn was stopped, and the robbers, emptying out the contents of the saddle-bags, decamped with their plunder. However, after this shabby transaction, they all came to misfortune and sorrow, as the story goes. They even brought a deep disgrace on all those who belonged to their families. A law was passed in both the religious houses, that no person named Deegan, Dooly, or Dullany, should be ordained a priest; nor was any monk of the name ever afterwards admitted into the Monasteries of Aghaboe or Monahincha.

No. VI.

Conla the Artist and the Dead Bones.

LEGEND OF DUN-CRUITHNE, INNISHOWEN, COUNTY OF DONEGAL.

> "Gone your abbot, rule and order,
> Broken down your altar stones;
> Nought see I beneath your shelter,
> Save a heap of clayey bones.
>
> Oh! the hardship, oh! the hatred,
> Tyranny and cruel war,
> Persecution and oppression,
> That have left you as you are!"
> —Sir Samuel Ferguson's *Lays of the Western Gael*,
> The Forester's Complaint.

IT is long ago since St. Patrick travelled through Innishowen, where lived a celebrated worker in metals, known as Conla the Artist. Not even the celebrated Harry Gow, the armourer, so famous through Sir Walter Scott's account of him in the "Fair Maid of Perth," could match him in skill. Conla lived at Dun-Cruithne or the Picts' Fort, and he wrought chiefly in bronze vessels of exquisite design and finish for St. Patrick who baptized him. The people there whenever they wished to praise a white-smith's handywork yet say, "Conla himself was not a better workman." It seems that when Conla died, he left a shrine of exceeding great beauty unfinished, and not another man could be found to complete it properly, after he had been laid in the tomb.

Many succeeding years having rolled by, St. Columkille passed that way, and saw the unfinished shrine. He asked about the artist, but the people told him Conla was in the grave. "Bring me there," said Columba, "and I shall raise him to life, so that he can finish it." This being done, the decaying bones were shown to the saint, who blessed them. To the great admiration of all who were present, flesh grew upon them, Conla came to life again, and completed his work. What is still more surprising, he lived afterwards for many years, and he was the progenitor of a numerous offspring. These were known as the Clann-Cnaimhsighe, or "the posterity of the bones," for all future time. The Cramsies are still numerous in Innishowen, and if asked to translate their name in English, they render it "Bones," and sometimes "Fairy-bones." But they are always delighted to boast their descent from Conla, a very holy man, whom they regard as the patron saint of their family. They still believe, that his skill was superhuman, and that his hands were guided by the angels.

In the sixteenth century, the remarkable shrine of Conla was kept in an ancient chapel at Screen—so called from the circumstance—in the parish of Tamlachtard or Magilligan, in the county and diocese of Derry. In our time, all trace of this remarkable relic has been lost, nor has tradition survived to give a clue for its recovery.

No. VII.

The Tyrant Chieftainess and her Punishment.

LEGEND OF LIOS NA EIBLIN OGE O COILLE MOR, COUNTY CORK.

> "All which is not pure shall melt and wither.
> Lo! the desolator's arm is bare,
> And where man is, Truth shall trace him thither,
> Be he curtained round with gloom or glare."
> —James Clarence Mangan's *German Anthology*.
> The Field of Kunnersdorf.

NOT far from the town of Charleville, and in the parish of Shandrum, is the townland of Kilmagoura. On it may be seen a large elevated Lios or Fort, where a castle is said to have formerly stood. This latter was tenanted by a masculine and tyrannical lady, belonging to the great Desmond Geraldine family; and, as an extensive wood grew around her castle, she is still traditionally remembered in the neighbourhood as Eileen Oge Fitzgerald of Kylemore or of the Great Wood. She was of a fierce and restless character, constantly leading her clansmen to make forays in all the adjoining districts. She killed all who opposed her, and then took possession of their property. This plunder she brought to and buried in the Lios, where the spoil is thought still to remain. Her death at length relieved her neighbours from the terror she inspired. But, her punishment followed afterwards, for she was often seen to wander as an evil spirit, and at night over the scenes of her former depredations. Owing to her oppressive behaviour, she was condemned to wear a thin garb, while she appeared as an old woman, shivering with cold. Her feet resembled those of a sheep, with the divided horny hoofs. Once, when a priest was out late and attending a sick call, she crossed his path. He then commanded her to stop, and inquired, why she was thus wandering, or why she appeared in that guise, with the feet of a sheep. The spirit then answered, in Irish: "Ata allus bocht do saothar ar saor ar a bocht, agus bainne a cuig caoire do caolig mo cos." This may be rendered into English, but amplified beyond a mere translation: "For my cruelty in oppressing the poor, forcing them to perform weighty tasks, and for depriving a poor widow of the milk of her five sheep, my feet are deformed, and I am thus doomed to perpetual motion, until the Day of General Judgment." With the single exception of this Eileen Oge Fitzgerald, all the local and popular traditions having reference to the Geraldines are invariably in their praise; while admiration for their worth, bravery, and noble actions is generally expressed in the fireside stories of the peasantry.

No., VIII.

The Water Monster.

LEGEND OF THE RIVER LAGAN, COUNTY DOWN.

"Flow Lagan, flow—though close thy banks of green,
Though in the picture of the world unseen,
Yet dearer to my soul thy waters run,
Than all the rills that glide beneath the sun ;
For first by thee my bosom learned to prove
The joys of friendship, and the bliss of love ;
No change of time, or place, shall e'er dispart
Those ties which Nature twines around my heart ;
Each dear association, grown more strong,
As years roll on, shall flourish in my song."
—Rev. Dr. William Hamilton Drummond's
Giants' Causeway, Book i.

NOT far from the episcopal city of Dromore, flow the lazy deep waters of the River Lagan, and often the Patron Saint, Bishop Colman, rambled along its banks in prayer and meditation. Indeed, if tradition speak the truth, often he passed over it with dry feet. But, it was well known, a great water monster lurked beneath its surface, always in quest of prey. Notwithstanding the danger of approaching him, yet, an incautious and innocent young damsel went down the bank, and stood upon some stepping-stones to beetle her linen. The wily monster sailed slowly towards her, and before she was aware of his approach, he suddenly reared his huge head from the deep, opened his tremendous jaws, and at one gulp swallowed the poor maiden alive. Although her terror was very great, yet she had presence of mind to call out, "Oh, holy Colman, save me!" Her cry was heard by the saint, and he prayed to Heaven for her release. Some of the girl's companions who stood on the bank, and who witnessed that fearful doom, set up shouts and screams. But St. Colman approached the river, and commanded the infernal beast to deliver up his prey. Then the girl he had swallowed was cast unharmed on the bank. There, to this very day, are shown the tracks of the holy bishop's feet, and that path down to the Lagan is called "St. Colman's-road." The monster of the deep was afterwards banished far off, and to the shores of the Red Sea ; but whether he survives in the shape of a modern crocodile—they are said to live for centuries—and sheds tears for his past delinquencies, or whether he has been long buried in the sands of Egypt, must furnish matter for further inquiry, as history and tradition are alike silent on the subject.

No. IX.
Naomh Greoihir, or St. Gregory of the Golden Mouth.

LEGEND OF INISHMAAN, ARAN ISLANDS, COUNTY OF GALWAY.

> "But man was born for suffering, and to bear
> Even pain is better than a dull repose,
> 'Tis noble to subdue the rising tear,
> 'Tis glorious to outlive the heart's sick throes;
> Man is most man amidst the heaviest woes,
> And strongest when least human aid is given,
> The stout bark flounders when the tempest blows,
> The mountain oak is by the lightning riven,
> But what can crush the mind that lives alone with heaven?"
> —Jeremiah J. Callanan's *Recluse of Inchidony*, stanza xxi.

THE opening between Aranmore and Inishmaan, or the Middle Island, is called Gregory's Sound. According to the Islanders of Aran, its name was derived from a certain venerable man named Naomh Greoihir, or St. Gregory. This holy penitent came originally from the mainland, lying in a south-eastern direction. There he had been guilty of committing some very grievous sin, and he almost despaired of forgiveness. In his anguish of mind, Gregory gnashed his teeth together, and in doing so happened to bite off his under lip, which gave him a frightful appearance. At this time, the holy abbot Enda lived on the Islands of Aran. Gregory took boat, and sailed over to Inishmaan, hoping to receive religious consolation, and to appease his remorse of conscience. He wished to become one of St. Enda's monks, and to spend the remainder of his days in exercises of the most rigorous penance. Yet, on revealing to St. Enny the heinousness of his crime, the great Abbot refused to admit him as a member of his religious community, lest it might prove a cause of scandal to his brethren. However, the superior promised to give him spiritual consolation and advice, if he lived in a retired place, on the north shore of Inishmaan. There was to be found a cave, in which Gregory took up his abode, and underwent a severe course of penance. To make amends for the disfigurement caused by the loss of his lip, St. Eany caused one of gold to appear in its stead. Hence, in after time, the pious anchoret was denominated, "Gregory of the Golden Mouth."

A rock and a little cove near his hermitage were called Portaich : and in after time, the place of his habitation was known as Gregory's Cave. Here the fervent penitent spent the remainder of his life in solitude and prayer. During the time of his sojourn, St. Enny and his monks often passed over from Aranmore to visit him, and to solace the hours of his voluntarily-imposed exile. Gregory lived for a long time there, and when old age came on, his declining health warned him that death was near. He sent for the monks of St. Enda, to prepare him for a final departure, and he received at their hands the last rites of the Church. But such was his great humility, that he considered it should be a sort of profanation, to have his remains interred among the saints of Aran ; and he, therefore, asked as a dying favour, that they should be towed out in a sort of coffin or tub, into the middle of the sound, and there consigned to the deep. In compliance with this request, when his breath departed, and the body was without life, his relics were taken, and placed in the tub, while stones were also added to increase the weight, so as to cause them to sink in the depths of the sound. The monks rowed over towards Killeany, after their work had, as they thought, been consummated. Yet, what must have been their surprise on landing, to find the tub, supposed to have been at the bottom of the ocean, high and dry on the beach, at a place now called Port. Again, they took back the tub or coffin containing Gregory's relics, and sunk it once more in the middle of the sound. On landing, they found a repetition of what had previously occurred. Taking back the remains a third time, these were again sunk in the sound. Yet, on landing that third time, the coffin lay before them on a bank of sand. Astonished at this spectacle, and moved, as it were, by a sudden inspiration, they cried out,—"Iongnadh, iongnadh, adlaicmaois ameasg na naomh." "A miracle, a miracle, let us bury Gregory among the saints!" The place where his remains lay was not far from the burial ground and church of Killeany, where, even then, numbers of holy monks had been interred. A grave was there opened, and in it the body of Gregory, the Recluse, was deposited.

A green mound, rising amid the drifting white sands, that are often swept by the eastern or southern winds over the burial ground, is yet shown. No family on Aranmore would encroach on this sacred site, while interments are being made among the saints reposing at Killeany, without note or distinction. Solitarily as he had lived, the bones of the penitent Gregory are isolated, on the verge of the burial ground, and his grave has no monument. Yet, still the Aran guide, Derane, and the islanders, point it out to visitors, and tell the romantic story of its occupant. It is somewhat apart from the interesting ruins of old Killeany, which, according to tradition, is the mortuary church of St. Endeus.

No. X.

The Black Man's Apparition.

LEGEND OF MUNDREHID, QUEEN'S COUNTY.

"Was never wight that heard that shrilling sound,
But trembling feare did feel in every vaine:
Three miles it might be easy heard arownd,
And echoes three did answer'd itselfe agayne."
—Edmund Spenser's *Faerie Queene*,
Book i., Canto viii., stanza iv.

ONE fine day in summer, after a walk up the southern slopes of Slieve Bloom, in company with some friends, we reached the site of Mundrehid's old ruined church, the walls of which were then nearly level with the ground. The name of this place is derived from the River Men or Mena, which runs near it, and Drehid or Drochid, the Irish denomination for "bridge," which has spanned the stream from times the most remote. The old and lonely cemetery was round it, a few rude headstones studding its surface. The scenery there was truly deserving our admiration. While our friends were resting on the site, and, after taking a few observations, we sat down on the low ruined wall. There about the sixth or seventh century, St. Laisren established his dwelling. On the 16th of September his festival is registered in the Irish Calendars. While resting there, we were soon joined by a shepherd, passing by the way, and his name was Ned Feehery. He lived near the place, and being asked for some information regarding it, he communicated very readily the following legend.

Ever since the old church fell into decay, a Druid had been known to haunt the site. Occasionally he had been seen by the older inhabitants. Before the apparition occurs, a tremendous roar is heard, so that the earth quakes all around. Immediately the ground opens, and then a small black man springs up, covered with armour, and wearing a belt, from which a sword hangs. He draws the sword, and flourishes it over his head. He next races three times around the graveyard, and in a short time he disappears from that spot whence he rose, and sinks under the earth's surface. This strange earthly visitant Ned Feehery declared he had himself once distinctly seen, and towards the dusk of evening.

The richest fields in Ossory surrounded the church, which once belonged to a monastery on that spot. Near it Gortavoragh and the Friar's Garden—where the peasantry root for money—were pointed out beside the little River Turtawn, which appears to have bounded the monastery fields. Through these, headless coachmen and headless horses driving about the paddocks have been witnessed by people, during the still hours of night.

Some twenty years later we returned to Mundrehid, but found that the gentleman farmer in possession had not only levelled the large ditches crowned with finely-grown hawthorns, which surrounded the small paddock fields, but even the stones were uprooted from the old foundations in the grave-yard, and the rude head-stones were removed. No trace of a grave now remains, while not a single vestige of the patron's historic home is left. Living memory alone preserves the site. Countless generations of the dead moulder at present under the levelled spot. Thence their bones may be raised by the future antiquary, to attest the position of that disused cemetery. The deed of the Vandal is still reprobated in that neighbourhood; but the peasants relate, how his desire to open wide pastures as a range for cattle did not prosper according to the full extent of the spoiler's wishes, as many of them were carried off by disease, while the herds of other farmers were spared such a visitation.

No. XI.
The Sea-Syren's Revenge.

LEGEND OF THE RIVER DELVIN, COUNTY OF MEATH.

"From the water smooth ascended,
Thither fast their shallop wended ;
And grouped around they joyous view
Glorious beings bright and fair,
In clusters standing, smiling there ;
Amid their number gladly trace
Many a loved and well-known face,
Long ago on earth they knew,
Mourned as dead, with sorrow true."
—Arthur Gerald Geoghegan's *Monks of Kilcrea*,
The Gleeman's Tale, canto ii., sect. xx.

A GREAT repertory of Irish folk-lore is the Dinnsheanchus, which professes to account for the origin of names applied to various celebrated places in Ireland. Doubtless it furnishes a record of the most ancient traditions still preserved. It usually asserts, that the compiler never found it difficult to solve the mystery of those local designations. Without citing any authorities, he sets off with some romantic legend—generally of the pagan times—and as imagination is allowed full play in the narrative, so are we expected to give implicit credence to the romance. There is a good copy of the Dinnsheanchus in the Book of Ballymote, a well-known manuscript kept in the Royal Irish Academy. It may be premised, that the present River Delvin, which rises in Meath, and which falls into the Irish Channel at Gormanstown, north of Balbriggan, in the County of Dublin, was formerly called in Irish Inbher Ailbine. This is how it got the latter name according to the topographer.

Long centuries ago, in that part of the country lived a prince, named Ruadh Mac Righduinn, son to the King of Fir-Muiridh, or the people of Muiredh, a plain in Bregia or Meath. He collected a crew for four currachs, to cross the sea, and in order to visit his foster-brother, the son of the King of Lochlann or Scotland. When the sailors reached the middle of the sea, however, they failed to move in any direction, but the currachs stood still, as if held by an anchor. Ruadh then went round that ship in which he sailed, to ascertain the cause for such detention. He jumped over its side, and then he went under the tide. There he saw nine women, the fairest of the Nereid race. They were seated in three canoes, each boat holding three of those beauties. They took Ruadh with them, and for a time he was lost to his companions. Those syrens had a charming territory under the waves, and abounding in all manner of delights.

The prince remained nine nights; severally one night with each of those Naiads in their submarine land. One of these sea-nymphs became pregnant by him. After that delay he was permitted to depart. However, he promised to visit them on his return, if he could. Ruadh then went to the house of his foster-brother, and remained with him seven years. Then he returned, but he kept not his appointment; and, having no desire to live under the sea, he arrived at Muiridh. The nine women then went to seek him, and having with them the son that had been born during his absence. They wished to be avenged of the father; but they met him not, and were denied access to the prince in his palace. Stung with rage and despair, the mother then killed her own and Ruadh's son. Afterwards, she flung his head on the shore; whereupon, all were terrified, and they said, as if with one mouth, "Is oilb bine," "It is an awful crime." Thence came the designation of Inbher Oillbine, or the River Oillbine.

An old Irish poem of twenty-four stanzas has been composed, and it recounts the substance of the foregoing legend. The name of Moymurthy, a manor and chapelry, in the parish of Moorchurch, near Gormanstown, preserved the traditional Muiridh territory down to a late period in the seventeenth century.

No. XII.
Contests of the Clans.

LEGEND OF MULLAGHMAST, COUNTY OF KILDARE.

" Forget not our wounded companions who stood
In the day of distress by our side,
While the moss of the valley grew red with their blood,
They stirred not but conquered and died.
The sun that now blesses our arms with his light,
Saw them fall upon Ossory's plain :
Oh ! let him not blush, when he leaves us to-night,
To find that they fell there in vain."
—Moore's *Irish Melodies.*

THE stories of Irish history are not always as legendary as they are dramatic. Nearly every circumstance of the succeeding epilogue, referring to a memorable period, is not only within the range of probability, but it is vouched for by contemporaneous record, to be found in the Wars of the Gaedhil and the Gael, edited by the Rev. Dr. James Henthorn Todd, for the Irish Archæological Society.

In old Pagan times, by the will of Olioll Olum, King of Munster, this dominion was divided between his two sons Eoghan Mor and Cormac Cas. The former was set over Desmond or South Munster, while the latter was appointed ruler of Thomond or North Munster. It also established an alternate right of supreme rule in their posterity over the whole of Munster. Thus the Eugenians or Desmondians were at one period the dominant sept, and the Dalcassians, descended from Cormac Cas, were in succession the supreme rulers. This recognized jurisdiction continued from the third to the eleventh century. Such sequence may be traced through the casual entries to be found in our Irish Annals.

Towards the close of the tenth century, the Danes had established themselves in some of the maritime strongholds around the coast of Ireland, and had chosen situations at the mouths of harbours and rivers, where arose in due course the chief cities of the Island. There likewise trade and commerce flourished in a remarkable degree for that remote period. Among those cities, Dublin and Limerick were notable. While both were surrounded with strong and high walls; in the former was established an Irish-
C

Scandinavian principality, able not only to guard against any surprise of the native princes, but even to acquire dominion over the Isle of Man, and to maintain a powerful fleet, which ensured obedience and subjection. Moreover, the civilizing influences of Christianity had dispelled the errors of pagan ancestry, and independent alliances had been formed with native Irish chiefs, whose interests and jealousies combined to assure mutual aid and force, when threatened with any encroachment from extern foes. Thus, as the foreigner was strong and secured in his maritime stronghold, the Kings of Leinster were never wholly free from excursions into their exposed domain, unless when in friendly alliance with the Scandinavians.

The invading Danes had seized upon Limerick much later, and finding its position admirably suited as a port for their vessels, they began their process of settlement in like manner; but with greater opposition from the king and men of Thomond, who did not choose to have such rivals within their territories. At that time, Mahon was king of Thomond, and his celebrated brother Brien—afterwards known as Borumha or of the Tributes—had waged war successfully with the Danes, had sacked and plundered Limerick, and had rendered the invaders tributaries to them, as a penalty for permission to live there, and to carry on the peaceful pursuits of commerce. The subsequent events are recorded in the pages of Irish history. On the death of Mahon, Brien Boroimhe had already acquired great reputation for his abilities and prowess. He was a renowned warrior, and having advanced his principality to a high degree of supremacy and pretension, among the divisional territories of Ireland, the entire sovereignty was at last obtained in a war waged between himself and the monarch Malachy, who was deposed. Then was the chief seat of power transferred from Meath to Thomond. Brien Boroimhe was acknowledged as Ard Righ of Erin, until a quarrel began between himself and Maolmurra, the King of Leinster.

This was destined to be a war, waged on a gigantic scale, and confederacies were formed on either side. The King of Leinster not only engaged the Danes of Dublin to espouse his quarrel, but messengers were sent to invite large accessions of sea-rovers from Scandinavia to unite their forces. On the other hand the Monarch of Ireland summoned to his aid the chiefs of Ulster, Munster and

Connaught; and with a large army, the aged warrior marched towards Dublin, to meet the Leinstermen and Danes, as also to stem the torrent of invasion expected from the northern shores. However, under renowned leaders, the sea-rovers landed on the Irish shore, and without delay, all his opponents were concentrated on the plains of Clontarf, even before the Monarch of Ireland could draw together all his forces.

On Good Friday, 1014, a furious battle was fought north of the City of Dublin, and it lasted from morning until night, with desperate courage and determination displayed by the leaders and their clansmen. After dreadful slaughter, in which many of the chiefs and warriors were slain, the victory of the Irish Monarch was complete and decisive. However, it was dearly purchased with his own life, that of his valorous son Murrough, and that of his grandson Turlough, then a mere youth. As nothing could be attempted against those who fled for protection within the walls of Dublin, the command of the Irish army had now devolved on Donough, the only surviving son of Brien Boroimhe. After some little delay, Donough resolved on disbanding his forces—probably the only wise course he could then adopt—and accordingly under their respective chiefs, the men of each territory directed their march homewards, well satisfied that the Leinstermen and Danes were then too demoralized for any further hostile attempt. Besides, the Leinster king and the principal Danish leaders had fallen in battle.

With greatly diminished force, the Munster bands, under the leadership of Donough O'Brien, took a south-eastern course from Dublin, and marched defiantly through the hostile territory of Leinster. No further opposition seemed to be threatened, and if it were, the army he still commanded was deemed sufficient to cope with it. However, further toil and dangers were to be encountered, before the Munster troops were destined to reach their province; while divisions and disputes arising in their ranks served to cast a cloud over that glory they had acquired in the late sanguinary engagement.

After the celebrated Battle of Clontarf, Donogh, son to Giallapatrick, King of Ossory, in conjunction with the men of Leix, formed an encampment on the plain known as Magh Chloinne Ceallaigh—probably around the present Cloney Castle, east of the Barrow River—to oppose the

Dalcassian troops then returning victorious to Munster. The exact site of that encampment we have now no means for ascertaining. The plain in question is known to have been within the territory of the O'Kellys. Their district also bore the name of Magh Dructain, and it formed one of the dependencies of Leix.

The position of this armed force barred the passage of the Munster army on their homeward-bound march. Faint and wearied, the Dalcassians rested at Athy, where they washed their wounds in the River Barrow. Intimation of opposition to be encountered had been conveyed to Donough O'Brien, who commanded the Munster forces. A very short time before this event, and soon after the decisive Battle of Clontarf had been gained, dissensions had broken out among the surviving leaders of the Munstermen. The chiefs of Desmond, taking advantage of the broken state of the Dalcassians, who had lost great numbers in the late battle, put forward a claim to sovereignty in Munster.

Full of provincial jealousy and rivalry, the dissentient bands had separately marched from Dublin to Mullaghmast, about six miles to the eastward of Athy. Here a very remarkable fort had been erected on a rising ground, while it was enclosed with a high circular rampart, and surrounded by a deep ditch, as if intended for a place of defence and security from invaders. It affords a far-reaching field of vision over all the surrounding country; and even at present, it forms an attractive object, as hawthorns and other bushes have mantled over its sides, and they serve to shade the beautiful green sward within, to which access is attainable through an opening in the mound.

Evening had now approached, and the troops wearied with their march resolved on halting for the night. They lighted fires, on which were boiled or roasted the joints of beeves and sheep intended for their meals. However, the Desmondians selected a field for their tents apart from that occupied by the Dalcassians. They formed into hostile camps—Donough O'Brien as chief of the Dalcassians, and Cian the son of Molloy commanding the Desmondians. This latter chieftain sent messengers to Donough demanding hostages, and stating that as the people of Desmond had submitted to Brien Boroimhe and to his brother Mathgamhain, the turn of Munster sovereignty then justly reverted to Cian. But Donough replied, that the Desmondians had ubmitted to his uncle and father by right of conquest, and not in recognition of any alternate right to the throne. Brien had bravely wrested Munster from Danish power, at a time when the chiefs of Desmond submitted to foreign domination and tyranny. He had also established his claim to the throne of Ireland, and owing to his prowess, had proclaimed himself as supreme Monarch. Wherefore, refusing to give hostages, Donough declared his determination of defending with the sword his right to the title of his renowned father. This was regarded as a defiant answer to Cian, who resolved to lead his men forward, and attack the diminished ranks of the Dalcassians.

Preparations for battle were not neglected on the side of Donough O'Brien. He had ordered the sick and wounded to be placed within the fort of Mullaghmast for protection. But these heroic men refused the inglorious position assigned to them. Filling their wounds with moss, and snatching up arms, they insisted on taking their place among the ranks of warriors.

Clannishness, more than a sense of enlarged national sentiment, arrayed these combatants in battle line. But, their determination caused the Desmondian troops to hesitate; especially as a subordinate chief, disappointed in his own petty scheme of ambition, refused co-operation in supporting the pretensions of Cian. The Desmondians, thus divided among themselves, again separated into distinct bodies, and then they marched homewards to their respective tribe lands.

The rumour of this dissension probably reached Donogh MacGiallapatrick, and he must have thought it a favourable opportunity to avenge a private feud and hereditary enmity. The warrior King of Munster had asserted his right to rule over Ossory, which he claimed as a dependency of his kingdom. This claim however was resisted by the dynast of Ossory, but he was unable to defend himself in an independent position by force of arms. As an enemy of Brian Boroimhe, this latter powerful monarch had kept the father of the Ossorian king in captivity for a whole year.

Having rested for some time, the men of Thomond under Donough O'Brien set out on their march, and crossing the Barrow, their most direct course lay through the plains of northern Ossory. The camp of Donogh MacGiallapatrick was broken up to intercept their homeward-bound course, and according to local tradition, he resolved to bar the Thomondian right of passage near Gortnaclea on the banks of the River Nore, which there bounded the Ossorian territory on the western frontier of Leix. Having collected a large army under his immediate command, MacGiallapatrick then thought himself in a position to assume the offensive, and to assert his supremacy. Accordingly with great insolence, he sent ambassadors to demand hostages from Donough O'Brien, or, in other words, to claim the sovereignty of Munster. These proposals were indignantly rejected, and there the wounded Thomondians again insisted on being led to battle with their comrades. Stakes were driven into the ground, against which the scarred veterans were to lean for support during the time of action. The unwounded soldiers were expected not to abandon them with life, while in this exposed condition. Such determined heroism produced once more its moral effect, and the Ossorians became intimidated, by this amazing valour of the Thomondian battalions. The men of Ossory and of Leix were withdrawn by their leader, and the Eugenians pursued their march. Yet, when all danger had passed over, one hundred and fifty of the war-worn veterans fainted away on that spot, and these soon expired. There likewise they were buried, with few exceptions; the bodies of some of the most distinguished warriors being borne to their native territories. Thus the remains of the chiefs were interred in the family burial-grounds of their ancestors.

The march of this valiant body of troops homewards seems to have been right through the level plains of Leix territory, and over the southern slopes of the Sliabh Bloom Mountains, by the old Ballaghmore road, which was the former chief highway between Ossory and Thomond.

No. XIII.
The Captive Piper.

LEGEND OF KNOCKANEY, COUNTY OF LIMERICK.

"Amaz'd and curious,
The mirth and fun grew fast and furious:
The piper loud and louder blew,
The dancers quick and quicker flew;
They reel'd, they set, they cross'd, they cleekit,
Till ilka carline swat and reekit."
—Robert Burns' *Tam o' Shanter*.

IT is related, that the Irish fairies have a peculiar language of their own, and that it is always used by them in the presence of mortals, who have been abducted to their subterranean abodes. This is extremely difficult to learn, but once it has been acquired by persons there detained, they are expelled from the fairy realm, lest they should know any important secrets regarding the mysterious sprites. Even such belief prevailed formerly in Britain. In the twelfth century a curious story is told by Giraldus Cambrensis, in his "Itinirarium Kambriæ," lib. i., cap. viii., about a boy who was carried off by the fairies to a beautiful region of their own in Wales. Among other matters, on escaping from their dominion, he related certain words they used, very conformable to the Greek idiom, and these words closely resembled the British. Thus when the fairies wanted water, they cried out *Yyor ydorum*, rendered in Latin "aquam affer." The learned and somewhat pedantic Archdeacon thence takes occasion to trace a similarity between the Greek word *Ydor*, which signifies "water," and the British word, *Duur*, having a like meaning. How far this linguistic resemblance might be carried we know not, but a further vocabulary has been supplied; for when the Welsh fairies required salt, they said *Halgein ydorum*, Latinised "salem affer," and here again is traced the analogy between *Hal*, the Greek term for "salt," and the British word *Haleyn*, meaning the same thing. After such examples given, Giraldus has a thought, that as the ancestors of the Britons were Trojans, deriving their name from a leader Brutus, who, after the destruction of Troy, abode for some time in Greece; so it is not wonderful to him that many of the old British words, and even the fairy language, may be derived from that classic land. Probably less rational speculations have satisfied the researches of empirical scientists, and fed the superstitious fancies of the multitudes imposed on by them; however, we have only to deal with romance, and not with strict realism, although in our present narrative rather encroaching on the domain of misty historic Irish traditions.

At the close of the second and in the beginning of the third century of the Christian era, flourished the renowned King of Munster, Oilioll Oluim, from whom many distinguished families of the south claim descent. He had married Sadhbh or Sabia, daughter to Conn of the Hundred Battles, monarch of Erin. But, the actions of his life, which brought most disgrace upon Oilioll Oluim were the violation of Aine, the beautiful daughter of Ogamuil, whom he had slain. The death of Aine soon followed, and her grave was made on the remarkable elevation called after her, and now known as Knockaney, which gives name to a townland and parish, in the barony of Small County, and in the County of Limerick. The village of Aney occupies a pleasant site on the Commogue River, and not far removed is the beautiful Lough Gur, irregular in outline, but measuring about four miles in circumference. It contains one island of about sixty acres, or rather a peninsula, connected with the eastern shore by a causeway. This is called Knock-a-dun or the Fortress Hill; and when the Desmonds ruled supreme in this part of the country, two strong and square towers defended the most accessible points of approach on the eastern and southern sides. One of those towers is called the Black Castle. Three or four other islets stud the surface of Lough Gur, which is surrounded by swelling hills, some of which are rocky, while others are covered with rich herbage.

However, the chief objects of interest for the antiquarian visitor, are the Druidical remains on Knock-a-dun, and extending around the lake for several miles. Three singular stone circles are close to the high road leading from Limerick to Cork. From a roofless old church, on the south shore of Lough Gur, may be seen various stone circles and other massive antiquities, while a long serpentine passage between lines of huge stones leads from the lake's margin to a tract of low ground, which is called the Red Bog. Those remains are associated by the country people with the Tuatha De Danaan race, and they are thought still to have relation with the enchantments of those immortal beings, who dwell in subterranean abodes.

Now, a well-known inhabitant of the place, named Donal O'Grady, happened to be returning home from a wedding party in the neighbourhood, at an early hour one fine summer morning. Considered to rank among the best pipers in Munster, his musical skill had been in requisition the whole of the preceding night, and indeed until the day began to dawn, when the merry dancers were obliged to seek their respective homes. At intervals between the dances and songs, which he accompanied with the union pipes, Donal drained an occasional tumbler of punch and partook of other refreshments, which the pressing instances of the host, hostess, and guests rendered it difficult to decline. Accordingly, his spirits were light enough to throw energy and fantasy combined into the thrilling and lively strains of jigs, reels, and hornpipes that followed one another in rapid succession. For his musical performances he was not only rapturously applauded, but also generously rewarded; and, at parting, all wished him a good morning and safe home. There he might have arrived in good time, but feeling somewhat wearied as he passed the enchanted rath of Aine, and sitting down to rest for awhile, he yoked on the pipes, when, to keep his hands and elbows in practice, he struck up a joyous reel.

He had hardly commenced the first bars of "Morieen Ruadh," than looking towards the rath, a door on the embankment suddenly opened. Out rushed a number of liveried pigmy lacqueys, and without more ado, they seized upon Donal O'Grady and his pipes. In the twinkling of an eye, they were whisked within the opening, and bang went the door, while to secure it a bolt was shot into the locker. In mortal fear of what should become of him, Donal was hurried along the passage on the shoulders of the little men. Just at the end, another door flew open, and there a most magnificent sight met his view. A grand hall of vast proportions, and a ceiling of exquisite beauty supported by lofty marble pillars, were lighted by a thousand lamps, which hung over the heads of a fairy throng of men and women, arrayed in the most gorgeous and fantastic costumes. Looking onwards, at the upper part of the hall, and on a throne of state, Donal beheld a lady of exquisite beauty, who wore a gold crown, all in a blaze with diamonds and brilliants, holding a reception for the crowds of tiny creatures who flocked to render her obeisance. All were chattering around, but in a language he could not understand. However, he heard the name of Aine so frequently repeated, that he guessed the Queen on the throne could be no other personage, especially as she was the object of so much respectful greeting.

At last it was Donal's turn to be introduced, and the master of the ceremonies, a dapper little gentleman, appeared, and led him by the hand to the lowest step of the throne. Not willing to be deficient in manners, but also ignorant of the etiquette practised in courts, he had noticed how gracefully the fairy lords and ladies had approached and retired, the men bowing very low, and the women courtesying almost to the ground, then kissing the Queen's right hand, and afterwards backing out with repeated bows and courtesies, until lost behind the groups still advancing. However, fearing he might too awkwardly imitate those court manœuvres, when Donal O'Grady appeared before the throne, taking off his straw hat, with the left hand, and pulling down the front lock of hair on his forehead with the right, he gave a quick jerk with the right knee, bending the left, and in such a fashion as made the fairy courtiers giggle and titter. Donal was not a little annoyed at these indications of what he thought to be bad manners; but, when the Queen graciously held out her hand and smiled benignantly, he also kissed it, and all his rising resentment was quickly appeased, especially as Aine said something in fairy language to the High-Chamberlain, and pointed to the pipes of Donal O'Grady, which during the presentation he had slung over his shoulder.

Soon the Master of Ceremonies waved a white wand, when all the fairy lords and ladies retired to the elegant cushioned seats prepared for them. Making a signal to Donal, he was led to a chair. Then the pipes were removed from his shoulders, and placed on his knee. He understood what was required of him, and observing the Queen giving her hand to some favoured gentleman, while other fairy lords began to select their partners, Donal set the pipes in motion, and finding the couples ranged in two long lines, he supposed they desired to have a sprightly country dance. He began to think what tune he might best select for their gratification. At last, Donal deemed the "Fairy Dance" not inappropriate. The moment he began to play, nothing but glee and merriment passed along the *vis-a-vis* lines of ladies and gentlemen. The Queen and her partner with the foremost couples led off, and soon the mazes of the dance were executed by the various couples in succession, to the evident delight of the performers, and to the great admiration of their musician, as afterwards he narrated this unique experience in his life. Donal observed, that all the fairy gentlemen he saw there, although finely dressed, were little wizened creatures, their faces old-looking, covered with wrinkles, and ugly as sin, while their bodies and limbs were for all the world like those of "Daddy Long Legs," the beetle or cockatrice so well known to the country people. In like manner, the ladies in the matter of charms greatly resembled their lords; all, with the single exception of Queen Aine, who was the greatest beauty Donal's eyes ever beheld. Having danced a variety of jigs and reels, alternating with the country dances, all seemed to be well satisfied. At a signal given, the Queen and all the dancers then filed before Donal O'Grady, with smiles of approval and with graceful salutes. Afterwards they suddenly vanished, and the lights were all extinguished. The imprisoned piper was then left alone in complete darkness, and there abandoned to his own disconsolate reflections.

Willingly would Donal make his escape from his subterranean prison, but on groping about, he could not find that passage, through which he had been carried. Moreover, he knew that even if it were discovered, the bolt and lock had been too fastly secured to admit of outlet through the door by which he had entered. Hours had passed over in this forlorn state. After some time, however, he could observe the fairies flitting through the hall, and jabbering to one another, but he found it was not Irish—which he could understand—that they spoke. At last, all the fairy men seemed to congregate in military array, and mounted on tiny steeds, as if bent on some outdoor expedition. A dim light began to open also on their movements. Donal saw the chief draw out at the head of his cavalcade and approach the door, through which himself had been ushered into that apartment. Then raising his sword, the fairy leader shouted out, "Tatther Rura," and every one of his warriors repeated "Tatther Rura." Immediately the door opened, all rushed out through the passage. The door again closed behind them.

The imprisoned piper had now learned the fairies' password, and when their sounds were lost in the distance, he also cried out, "Tatther Rura." The door at once opened, and the passage was found to be clear to the outer entrance, the cavalcade having disappeared, and bound on their distant expedition. Again, Donal shouted "Tatther Rura," and the door flew open, so that he was enabled to rush out, and gaze once more on the scenes around Knockaney. He deemed it thus fortunate to have learned the meaning of two words of the Tuatha De Danaan or fairy language, and which were of such practical utility to him. Gathering the pipes under his arm, he joyfully hastened homewards. For many a long day, Donal O'Grady was enabled to narrate his extraordinary presentation to Queen Aine and her courtiers, on the frequent recurrence of fairs, christenings, weddings, and country parties, where his admirable chaunter performances were in such general requisition.

No. XIV.

The Peistha Discomfited.

LEGEND OF DRUMSNA, COUNTY OF MONAGHAN.

> "The savage foe escaped, to seek again
> More hospitable shelter from the main;
> The ghastly spectres that were doom'd at last
> To tell as true a tale of dangers past
> As ever the dark annals of the deep
> Disclosed for man to dread or woman weep."
> —Lord George Gordon Noel Byron's *Island*,
> Canto i., sect. ix.

HARDLY any deep lake in Ireland is without the occupancy of an uncouth monster, seldom seen on the surface, but often observed in motion, far down in the depths of the water. Imagination is frequently exercised by the peasantry, to divine its exact form, which is supposed to differ in species from that of any known denizen of the deep; and mystery shrouding its functions, the Peistha is dreaded as a malignant demon, always bent upon mischief, and especially towards the human race. The boatmen cast many a furtive glance downwards, to see that it approach not within stroke of their oars, as they greatly desire to give it a wide berth. Any provoked hostility on their part is apt to procure a dangerous retaliation ; and in his frequented waters, the Peistha is believed to be master of the situation.

At one time St. Molua, who travelled much through Ireland on his mission of founding churches, visited the ancient Drumsneachta, now Drumsna, in the County of Monaghan. In a neighbouring lake, he saw two boys swimming. But, advancing on them, and with a forefront large as a boat of considerable size, appeared the monster of that lake, as if about to devour them. Not wishing to terrify the boys, he shouted to them : "Swim, my boys, with all speed towards me, so that I may reward the one who shall first arrive, and that I may know who will swim the fastest." Both struck out towards him, and soon gained the shore. No sooner had they landed, than Molua reached them his hand. Having landed safely, they looked back towards the lake, and were greatly frightened at seeing the monster, which had almost gained upon them. Immediately the saint raising his staff struck the Peistha with it on the breast, and it gave a terrific roar. Filled with excitement and alarm, one of the boys died on the instant. However, the holy man prayed for him, and afterwards he came to life. But, a malison he pronounced on the Water Sherrie, ordering it to return and to remain under the waters of that lake. Thenceforward it was condemned never to molest man or beast to the Day of Judgment.

No. XV.
The Leinster Tribute.
LEGEND OF TARA, COUNTY OF MEATH.

"When tyrants scourge or demagogues embroil
A land, or when the rabble's headlong rage
Order transforms to anarchy and spoil,
Deep-versed in man the philosophic sage
Prepares with lenient hand their frenzy to assuage.

"'Tis he alone, whose comprehensive mind,
From situation, temper, soil, and clime
Explored, a nation's various powers can bind,
And various orders, in one form sublime
Of polity, that, midst the wrecks of time,
Secure shall lift its head on high, nor fear
Th' assault of foreign or domestic crime,
While public faith and public love sincere,
And industry and law maintain their sway severe."
—James Beattie's *Minstrel*, Book ii.

IT is indeed a shameful story to relate, how the pagan king of Leinster, Eochaidh Aincheann, visited the monarch Tuathal the Legitimate at Tara, A.D. 106, and married his daughter Dairiné, whom he brought to Leinster, and lived with her for some time. Afterwards, he became enamoured of her sister, who remained at Tara; when, full of perfidy, on returning there he immured poor Dairiné in a dungeon, and then spread the report that she was dead. Some time elapsed, when he asked her sister in marriage, and the father having given his consent, the princess was brought to Leinster. However, Dairiné contrived to escape from her prison, and then she appeared in the presence both of her husband and of her sister, to reproach the former with his baseness and atrocity. Having thus seen Dairiné, and owing to the shock, her later espoused sister fell dead on the spot, for she thought Dairiné to have been dead. Such event however was not long deferred. The injured Dairiné pined away, and died of a broken heart. The true state of things soon reached Tuathal, who vowed by all his gods, that he would take signal vengeance on the king of Leinster. For the vices of the dynast, as usual in such cases, his people were destined to suffer; for their whole province was ravaged and burned, when the monarch marched with a large army into Leinster. Nor did he desist until he had utterly subdued their king, who was slain; and afterwards, Tuathal imposed on the people, for ever, that oppressive tax known as the Borumha-Laighean, or "Leinster Tribute," which had to be paid triennially. This led to repeated periodical and sanguinary conflicts between the Leinster kings and people, who sought its remission, and the monarchs of Ireland, who insisted on its enforcement. These quarrels continued from the time of Tuathal to that of Finnachta Fleadhach or the Festive, who reigned over Ireland in the latter half of the seventh century, and who lived contemporaneously with St. Moling of Teach-Moling.

The latter was a holy man, and he had great influence, not alone among the Leinster people, but also with the Irish monarch. The former assembled at a convention with their king Bran, and requested Moling, with some other deputies, to set out for Tara, there to represent the oppressiveness and injury of that tribute to the monarch. This mission they undertook to accomplish; but the sequel shows, that the negotiation was hardly creditable to any of the chief parties concerned. St. Moling was a famous Irish poet, and, knowing that a prelude of panegyric must be acceptable to the festive Finnachta, he composed his celebrated Song of Praise, beginning with the line "Finnachta a húib Neill." However, there was another celebrated— but a very envious—poet named Tollcend in his train, and the latter wished to outshine the bishop in the Royal Court at Tara.

The whole company then set out, and came to the house of Cobthach mac Colman, where a feast was made for them. Meanwhile, the poet's attendants remonstrated with him for holding a subordinate position in the train of the clerics. "Why then," said the poet, "let us leave the clerics, and go on to the house of the king." When they arrived, the "man of song" recited the Hymn of Praise before the king, and said he had composed it himself. When Moling reached the king's fortress on the following day, the king's son had just met his death by an accidental shot in hunting. Finnachta thereupon inquired the cause for the great lamentation that was being made. The saint had to communicate to him the sad news. Filled with anguish, yet with great faith, Finnachta cried out, "Awake the youth, O cleric! and thou shalt have thy reward." "I ask," said Moling, "for my song, and for the awakening of thy son, and for heaven to be obtained by thyself, no other boon than the remission of the *Bórumha* until Lúan," which has for meaning Monday. "It shall be thine," said the king. So Moling bound him by the Trinity and by the Four Gospels, and then he sang the Song of Praise.

As the king had heard it before, he charged Moling with falsely claiming to be the author of a poem, that had been made for him by the poet Tollcend. The saint calmly replied: "If it was he that made it, let him arise and recite his poem." So the poet rose up before him, and, being confused, this is what he said: "Dríbor drábor cerca is cábail," etc. After delivering himself of this unmeaning rubbish, the unfortunate poet ran away like a madman, and drowned himself. When Finnachta saw such a proof of the saint's truth and power, the monarch fell at his feet, besought Moling to awake his son, and promised that he should get whatever he had come to demand. Thereupon St. Moling arose, and placed himself at the head of the youth; he then prayed the Lord fervently, so that for sake of Moling the Almighty restored to life the king's son.

Now in the engagement given, the Irish monarch merely promised to stay the levying of the Leinster tribute for one natural day and night, which St. Moling, by a kind of logic not very intelligible, interpreted to mean *for ever;* for, by a singular use of the ambiguous Irish word *Luan*— which means Monday, as also the Day of Judgment—in his covenant with the monarch, Moling had desired to abolish this exorbitant tribute, not till Monday, as the monarch understood, but till the Day of Judgment, as the saint intended.

However, it would seem, that such equivocation originated in the fanciful brain of the author of the Borumean Laighaen, who displays his own and not St. Moling's morality, in the many strange incidents and dull inventions, with which he embellishes the simple events of history.

Moling then journeyed southwards to Leinster, with his good news regarding the remission of the Bórumha. Now, Moling had promised heaven to Finnachta before he left Tara. But Finnachta conceived, that Moling had deceived him in the term used, and he said to his people: "Go in pursuit of that holy man, who has gone away from me, and say to him that I have given respite for the Bórumha to him only for one day and one night; moreover, methinks the holy man has deceived me, since there is but one day and one night in the whole world." But, when Moling knew that they were coming in pursuit of him, he ran actively and hastily until he reached his own house at Teach-Moling. The people of the king sent from Tara did not come up to him at all, and then had to return, after vainly trying to overtake him. However, the Bórumha was forgiven to Moling from that time until the Day of Judgment. Although Finnachta was sorry for losing his tribute, he was not able to levy it; since it was for the sake of obtaining heaven the king had granted its remission.

At this period, the celebrated St. Adamnán was in Ireland. Contrary to the will of this latter great personage, who wished that the Leinstermen should pay tribute to the race of Tuathal for ever, Moling's sanctity prevailed against the desires of Tuathal and his aristocratic relative Adamnán, Abbot of Iona. It has been asserted, it was owing to the anger of Adamnán at this remission of the Bórumha, that the men of Ireland went in pursuit of St. Moling. He thereupon implored the protection of God and the saints in a celebrated poem, beginning, "A mo chomdiu cumactach," etc., which he composed while running away at full speed.

Notwithstanding Finnachta's promise, the Abbot of Iona, who was a resolute character and somewhat of a courtier, resolved on seeing the monarch, who did not care to be disturbed about that question. Accompanied by a cleric, Adamnán presented himself before the gates of the royal palace at Tara. He then sent the cleric in, to demand an audience from the monarch. When the servant brought this message, the king was displeased—for he was a good-natured soul,—and he cried out: "I wish Adamnán was at Jericho, or even minding his own affairs at Iona; but, as a matter of courtesy and court etiquette, we cannot refuse admittance to his chaplain." Accordingly, the latter was ushered into the royal presence. Finnachta was then engaged playing chess. "Come to converse with Adamnán," said the cleric. "I will not, until this game is finished," said Finnachta. The cleric returned to Adamnán, and told him the answer of Finnachta. "Go thou to him and say to him, that I shall sing fifty psalms during that time, and there is a psalm among that fifty, in which I shall pray the Lord that a son or grandson of his, or a man of his name, may never assume the sovereignty of Erin." The cleric accordingly went and told that threat to Finnachta; however, the king took no notice, but played at his chess till the game was finished. "Come to converse with Adamnán. O Finnachta," said the cleric. "I will not go," said Finnachta, "till this next game is finished." The cleric returned and told this to Adamnán. "Say unto him," replied Adamnán, "that I will sing fifty psalms during that time, and that there is a psalm among that fifty, in which I will ask and beseech the Lord to shorten his life." The cleric told this to Finnachta; still he took no notice of it, but played away at his chess till the game was again finished. "Come to converse with Adamnán," said the cleric. "I will not," said Finnachta, "till the third game is finished." The cleric once more repeated to Adamnán the answer of Finnachta. "Go to him," said Adamnán, greatly incensed, "and tell him that I will sing the third fifty psalms, and there is a psalm in that fifty, in which I will beseech the Lord that he may not obtain the kingdom of heaven." When Finnachta heard this, he suddenly put away the chess-board from him, and he came to Adamnán. The latter said, "What has brought thee to me now, and why didst thou not come at the other messages?" "What induced me to come," said Finnachta, "were those threats which thou didst hold forth to me, viz., that no son or grandson of mine should ever reign, and that no man of my name should ever assume the sovereignty of Erin, and that I should have shortness of life. Still, I deemed these threats to be light; but, when thou didst engage to take heaven from me, I then came suddenly, because I could not endure such a privation." "Is it true," said Adamnán, "that the Bórumha was remitted by thee for a day and a night to Moling?" "It is true," returned Finnachta. "Thou hast been deceived," said Adamnán, "for this is the same as to remit it for ever." Then he went on scolding the monarch, and bitterly he sung in Irish this lay, as translated into English :—

"To-day though they bind the locks of the white-haired, toothless king,
The cows which he forgave to Moling, are due to a wiser head:
If I were Finnachta, and that I were Chief of Teamhair [Tara],
Never would I forgive the tribute. I would not do what he has done.

Of every king who remits not his tribute, long shall the stories remain.
Woe to him, who gave this respite! To the weak it is sorrow.
Thy wisdom has ended and given way to folly."

However, Adamnán concluded this poem by paying a tribute of praise to St. Moling's virtues; and Finnachta made a very humble submission to the Abbot of Iona, by placing his head on the holy man's bosom. This was an act of humility very acceptable to the renowned archimandrite. Wherefore, Adamnán was reconciled to the remission of the Bórumha, and he departed from Tara, blessing its religious monarch.

No. XVI.

Fin-mac-Cool's Stone-throw.

LEGEND OF THE CLOUGH-MOR, COUNTY OF DOWN.

> "Hanc, ut prona jugo lævum incumbebat ad amnen,
> Dexter in adversum nitens concussit, et imis
> Avulsum solvit radicibus; inde repente
> Impulit: impulsu quo maximus insonat æther."
> —P. Virgilii Maronis *Æneidos*,
> Lib. viii., ll. 236 to 239.

> "The leaning head hung threatening o'er the flood,
> And nodded to the left. The hero stood
> Averse, with planted feet, and, from the right,
> Tugged at the solid stone with all his might.
> Thus heaved, the fixed foundations of the rock
> Gave way; heaven echoed at the rattling shock."
> —Dryden's *Virgil's Æneis*.
> Book viii., ll. 311 to 316.

NOT far away from but high over the romantic town of Rosstrevor rises the great hill of Clough-mor, one of the Mourne range of mountains. Upon a projecting cliff, nearly midway up the ascent, is to be seen a huge mass of granite, weighing over thirty tons, as has been estimated. Naturalists and geologists have wasted their speculations in vain, to account for its present isolated position; for, it rests only on a pivot, and it seems ready to roll off at any moment to a lower station. It has been noticed, that it can hardly be a contribution from any of the neighbouring heights, for the greater elevations are at a considerable distance, while a valley of some depth and space intervenes. What forms a mystery for the geologist and natural philosopher, however, is a matter easy of solution to the people who live near.

The renowned giant Fin-mac-Cool—the strongest man then living—had been visited at a time remote by a Scotch giant of great size and strength. A controversy arose between them, as to their relative prowess, when it was resolved that two great fragments of rock, which lay near Carlingford, on the opposite side of the bay, and which were of nearly equal size, should be lifted from their places, and cast over the sea beneath. A large bet was pending on the result. They threw up a halfpenny for the choice of stone, and the Scotch giant won the toss. Of course, he selected that one he deemed to be lighter of the two. Poising it on his right hand and swaying his body, he put forth all his strength; but, he was unable to send the fragment of rock to the opposite shore, and it fell into the sea. Now came Finn's turn. He took up the remaining and larger fragment, and then with great ease, he was not only able to clear the strait, but to land it high and dry on the cliffs beyond, where, as the Clough-mor, it still remains an evidence of his superior strength.

No. XVII.
The Death-Coach.

LEGEND OF TIMOGUE, QUEEN'S COUNTY.

> "Thou thing of mystery, stern and drear,
> Thy secrets who hath told ?—
> The warrior and his sword are there,
> The merchant and his gold.
>
> There lie their myriads in thy pall,
> Secure from steel and storm;
> And he the feaster on them all,
> The canker-worm."
> —Rev. George Croly's *Island of Atlantis.*

THERE can be no question but that historical and traditional stories are strangely woven together, and with many tangles of net-work, in the fireside narratives of our peasantry. These regarding Timogue old church, and the castle which formerly stood near it, are examples of fact and fiction, it should prove difficult at present to unravel. Although of comparatively modern erection and architecturally of a debased style, the church seems to rise on the ruins of an earlier structure; for on the exterior, the grass-covered graves, and rude heading stones, noteless of inscriptions, rise nearly to the sills of the windows, owing to the accumulation of mouldering human remains that have been deposited under earth, so frequently re-opened in the well-known family burial-plots, for centuries long past. Those first entombed there are unrecorded in documents, and not remembered in traditions. All over the cemetery—a popular place for interments—flag-tombs, half hidden in the mould, or head-stones sinking deeper into it each year, are interspersed with the furrows showing where the latest graves had been opened and sodded over, while crowned with a luxurious crop of grass and weeds. Solitude has settled round the site by day; and night adds to it a still deeper gloom.

At some short distance from the declivity, a bright stream, taking its course from the Luggarcurran hills, meanders over its bed, strewn with smoothed rocks, and innumerable pebbles of nearly every variety of shape and hue. Near the high-road stood the former castle, where, it is stated, the

O'Kellys, the Fitzgeralds, and the Byrnes held sway in succession. Numerous are the tales of massacre and usurpation which built up the later inheritance, and of fraud united with cruelty, that rooted out the original possessors, clansmen of the O'Moores. Reprisals were the consequence; nor are the traditions at all inconsistent with a lawless state of society which prevailed but a few centuries back, and which preserves for the present age many romantic episodes of family history.

During the reign of Queen Elizabeth, the Castle of Moret, adjoining the Great Heath of Maryborough, was sacked and burned by the Irish. It was then occupied by Gerald Fitzgerald, married to a daughter of the detested John Bowen, the *Shawn a-Fiecha* of Ballyadams Castle, which still remains in a good state of preservation. His life, and probably that of his wife, was forfeited on this occasion; however this be, the remains of both lie within a vault of the church, as a marble monument, with an inscription and armorial bearings on it, still certifies. The children of Sir Gregory Byrne, an army contractor during the reign of King Charles II., and a person of much celebrity at that time, formed family alliances with the Fitzgeralds of Timogue. The inscriptions on their flagstone tombs within the church, and yet legible, indicate their respective names and relationship. However, no trace of their castle now exists; the proprietorship of their lands has passed to other occupants; the old flour-mill, a later erection, is in ruins on the river bank beside that bridge over which the road leads, and under the arches of which the stream gurgles. But weird stories were told of goblins that haunted that neighbourhood, and especially of melancholy groans that were heard from the churchyard during the still hours of night!

Late in the last century, the trade in wool was very considerable in the midland counties of Ireland, and a revival of home manufactures caused a brisk demand for fleeces, which were brought in packs by the shepherd farmers to certain established fairs for sale. On one of those occasions, a wool-comber and his driver of the cart, on which the well-stuffed wool-packs had been placed, were returning from the fair of Ballynakill, and rather belated, they were approaching the old graveyard of Timogue, which was observed on their right with the high wall surrounding it on the roadside. The night was dark and stormy; the witching hour for goblins stalking abroad had come ; nor was it pleasant to trudge the miry way ; when suddenly, a blaze of fire shot up from the graveyard within the wall, in which a breach seemed to yawn wider each moment, until at length it opened for several yards. Then followed a loud rumbling noise, while a black coach, with a coachman and four headless horses, was observed rolling out towards the road, to the horror of the unprotected travellers. Nevertheless, as the urgency of fear was uppermost, and as flight towards the bridge and their homeward-bound course was instinctive, the driver and his master jumped on the cart, the former raised his whip, and the horse, in like manner seized with terror, bounded forward. Nearer and nearer the unearthly equipage seemed to gain upon them ; louder and louder arose the rereward clattering of hoofs and the rolling of wheels. Petrified with fright, the fugitives ventured to look behind, and they beheld one of the most diabolical countenances it could be possible to imagine looking out of the coach, and with a mouth grinning from ear to ear, as if gloating over the idea of seizing the fugitives.

Agonized beyond endurance at this awful spectacle, the driver and his companion screamed out with all their might; but they had already reached the crowning arch of the bridge, where the water beneath proved to be their safe-guard, and a barrier over which the demon coach could not pass. Suddenly it stopped short ; then turned back ; by degrees, the sounds of horses' feet and rolling wheels grew fainter, as that apparition vanished in the distance. Such was the story as narrated to the writer, now many long years ago.

No. XVIII.

The Blessed Trouts.

LEGEND OF THE THREE WELLS, COUNTY OF WICKLOW.

"And while night, noon, or morning meal no other plenty brings,
No beverage than the water-draught from old spontaneous springs;
They, sure, may deem them holy wells, that yield from day to day,
One blessing which no tyrant hand can taint, or take away."
—John Fraser's *Holy Wells.*

IN a wild and romantic region of Wicklow County, in the parish of Ballykine, and taking its rise from the southern slope of Macreddin Mountain, a bright and lively stream flows into the Aughrim River. Near its source are the Three Wells, from which the townland takes its name; and the peasantry around have numberless stories of fairies, that are frequently seen in troops haunting the hills and valleys along the course of the Sheeanamore rivulet, which unites its waters with the stream already mentioned. The word Sheeanamore signifies the "big fairy hills," as indicating the existence of mounds and raths of considerable size in that place. Moreover, not far apart is the Fairies' Hollow, and we may suppose this to have been one of their haunts, when imagination had freer scope than at present. However, we must leave for others the subjects to be drawn from those local features, and confine our attention to the following topic.

In the Three Wells are to be seen the ubiquitous Blessed Trouts: two in each well, and these are supposed to have lived there a charmed life and from time immemorial. Again the people say, they are destined to remain in those wells until the Day of Judgment. What is most remarkable in their case, the number seen is never greater and never less. To capture or injure those beautiful creatures should be deemed an act of profanation, which the country people would regard with detestation and horror. Nor do we find the Blessed Trout confined to this particular place in Ireland; for wherever there are clear pools of water, from or through which flow purling streams, the peasantry are quite ready to aver, that the immortal fishes are to be found disporting themselves in the water, or sometimes hiding beneath the banks, when mortals approach to look on their gambols. We have not been able to ascertain if this belief has come down to us as formed in Pagan times, when our ancestors held that there were tutelary spirits of the hills and streams, or whether in Christian times the pilgrims who resorted to the holy wells had a veneration for all those sportive fishes that were seen or contained in them. But, the stories told of the Blessed Trout are very numerous, and universally diffused throughout all parts of our island.

No. XIX.

Mistaken Identity.

LEGEND OF SANDYMOUNT, COUNTY OF DUBLIN.

"Omne tulit punctum qui miscuit utile dulci,
Lectorem delectando, pariterque monendo."
—Quintus Horatius Flaccus,
De Arte Poetica, ll. 343, 344,

" Who useful truth with pleasing fancy blends
Delights the reader, and his thought extends
To wisdom's goal, while gained, such objects he defends."
—English Translation.

THE tram-cars and railroad conduct the citizens of Dublin in short time to the sea-side village of Sandymount, and thither many repair on Sundays and Holydays to enjoy a pleasant ramble over the winding and umbrageous roads, skirted with handsome villas, or to have a delightful stroll over the far extending strand, when the tide is full out, to inhale the balmy ozone of the Irish Channel. The odoriferous water and air exhalations of the Liffey, confined by the long South-sea Wall to a northern course of fully three miles from the Point of Ringsend to Poolbeg Lighthouse, there undergoes a process of purification in the briny waves of ocean. Besides the crowd of grown pedestrians, who are able to advance very leisurely for three or four miles after the ebb tide, without soiling the sole of a shoe, and to retreat in like manner before the returning flow ; groups of little children with their nurses are to be seen, exercising their wooden toy shovels, and busily engaged in searching out the numerous tiny mounds of blue sand, certain indications of the cockle bedded beneath, and soon to be unearthed by the least intelligent and smallest of juveniles. A few years back, the fore-shore was lined with bathing boxes, to many of which ponies and donkeys were yoked, and from those boxes the bathers waded far out into any chosen stage of water for a swim or a dabble, as the case might be; while many humble servitors, men and women, earned a comfortable and honest livelihood, owing to attentions and civility always readily afforded to their patrons. In his baby days, the illustrious and inimitable bard of Erin, Tom Moore, was accustomed to take his morning dip in the shallow tide-waves. At that time, a considerable stretch of green fields—now encroached upon by houses—ran between Sandymount and Dublin, and the roads in the suburbs were infested by footpads. One of these had demanded a gentleman's purse, and received in exchange a pistol shot which left him dead on the road-side. Early in the morning, returning from Sandymount to Dublin, as related in his Diary—Tom Moore and his uncle found the dead robber lying beside the road, and he had been shot just under the eye, there being no other mark than the small hole through which the bullet had entered. An old woman who was present, moved to pity, and doubtless admiring the fine features of the dead, cried out, "It was the blessing of God it didn't hit his eye," for she imagined it must have concerned the robber, to present the appearance of a pretty corpse after that untoward accident.

Not alone towards the close of the last century, but far later in the present, Sandymount and Irishtown were gay and stirring villages, especially during the Summer and Autumn season. Crowds of people from the provinces were sure to engage in advance and occupy the various lodging-houses near the strand for the benefit of sea-bathing. The working and middle-class people of Dublin, before the Omnibus and Tram-car service ran, had found a number of the Sandymount outside car-drivers lobbing for fares at College Green, and the "two-penny" drive was a favourite one, when a party of six could be collected at once. If otherwise, the jarvey was sure to wait until his number was completed, and this was not easily obtained on ordinary days of the week, so that the tide was often out before a start would be made. The hot-water baths at Cranfield's establishment were always beset with a number of expectants for a turn on warm days; while their time and patience were often sorely tried, before all the waiters could be accommodated. That building has since gone to ruin, yet not for want of patronage, could the baths have been extended or otherwise suitably provided.

From the foreshore, likewise, the bathing boxes, which had garnished it for centuries, have been removed during the last few years, thus depriving the general public of a healthful and popular resource during the warm days of Summer and Autumn. This is how it happened. The Pembroke Township Commissioners, having procured Parliamentary powers of jurisdiction over the strand, and having in view the construction of Public Baths and a Promenade Pier, resolved on the destruction of the private bathing boxes, and issued a decree for their removal. This very naturally created great indignation and remonstrance among the inhabitants of Irishtown, Ringsend and Sandymount; more especially, among those industrious people, whose prescriptive rights and means of livelihood were thus unjustly sacrificed, and without the slightest compensation having been made or even offered. The former influx of visitors to the sea-side soon ceased; many of the lodging-house keepers, who in former times hardly ever had to complain of having a vacant room, were ofttimes left without the means of paying their own rents, and were only living in hopes of seeing realized the promised improvement, which it was expected must so greatly benefit the immediate neighbourhood and the general public.

The next step taken in that direction was the starting of a Limited Liability Company for the construction of Public Baths and a Promenade Pier at Merrion. For a site, no place could be more eligible or present fairer attractions; all the contingent facilities and surroundings being admirably adapted to erect a Pier and Promenade by gradual extension, and as funds were made available, to carry both for at least three miles over the strand at ebb-tide, while at the return flow, the flooring might rise over the surrounding waves, and enable visitors to stroll for such a length, thus to inhale the refreshing ozone with the salt-sea breeze during the Summer and Autumn seasons. Moreover, on either side of the Promenade and at suitable distances from the entrance gate separate cold water basins could have been constructed, on one side for gentlemen, and on the other for ladies; while still more remote from the shore, open sea-bathing and bathing dresses could be provided for men and women, at respective stations and apart, with all necessary safeguards against accident or impropriety. Thus might the cold water baths be rendered wide of range, free for swimming exercise, and invigorating, owing to the freshness of the sea-water. Where for the accommodation of young children or timid adults the bathing must necessarily be confined to the enclosed basins, the concreted or tiled floors of these baths should be on a level with, or even slightly raised over the strand-surface; and a simple pumping apparatus twice in every twenty-four hours should supply fresh salt-water, while the former used water could be wholly ejected through a sluice, at those intervals when the tide was fully out, and even the floors could be swept clean before admitting a new supply.

Such a general plan should commend itself to ordinary intelligence; but designers and directors are restrained by no special desire of accommodating the funds provided by shareholders to secure useful ends; and accordingly, in the case of erecting those Merrion Baths and the Promenade Pier, want of forethought has been most absurdly manifested in a radically wrong design, and even great expense has been incurred to render that design still more objectionable in the mode of construction. The Promenade, for which a Band Stand has been provided, is completely stunted in length, and then blocked up at the end with an octagonal concreted basin, divided by a wall into separate compartments for males and females, of very limited dimensions for cold water bathing or swimming purposes. Moreover, as if to spoil the freshness of the water more effectually, a large sum of money has been spent in excavating a bank of blue mud, and in forming a deep pool under the surface of the strand, so that the water within the basins becomes in a great measure stagnant and foul, and the sediment which collects at the bottom can only be removed by artificial means and at considerable outlay. In other details, various defects both of plan and execution might be specified. Those enumerated, however, have tended largely to send persons who have had experience of them in other directions, to enjoy the benefit of open sea-bathing.

Moreover, it seems not to have been at all considered, that more than half the community, owing to age or constitutional infirmity, cannot avail of cold water baths, and no effort has been hitherto made to provide hot water baths for their accommodation and use. Under such circumstances as these, little wonder may be expressed, that small revenue has been returned from the Merrion Public Baths and Promenade Pier; nor does it seem probable that condition shall be reversed, unless better management prevail, and measures be taken for a complete remodelling of the original construction, and for supplying the wants of patrons, who have means and inclination to indulge in the luxury of sea-water bathing. However, all this is irrelevant to the subject which prompted us to introduce the following narrative, and give it a place in this collection.

Whether it be legitimate or not, to engraft on the stem of legend an "ower true tale" of Irish life; it may at least be amusing, to record a well authenticated incident, which occurred not many years ago, and which afterwards obtained the ephemeral notoriety of a newspaper paragraph. As a matter of course, it survives in the recollection of many, who were participants in or witnesses to the transaction, and who have often wondered why they had not greater shrewdness of perception, than to be deceived by the evidence of their senses, especially when fairly challenged to submit their judgment to the test of ordinary examination. It occurred, moreover, in the midst of an enlightened community adjoining the city of Dublin, and not in the remote glens or wilds of Connemara or among the mountains of Kerry.

Several years have passed since Mickey Kieran was a well-known and popular resident of Sandymount, where he kept a dairy shop and cows, being in rather comfortable circumstances. Time went by, however, and notwithstanding his industry, fortune proved faithless in bestowing her just awards, and a succession of unfavourable years caused numbers of his cattle to be attacked with disease, which carried them off; and much to the regret of all his neighbours, poor Kieran gradually sank beneath his difficulties, and in his old age, surviving family and relations, he became impoverished to such a degree, that after a vain struggle to maintain himself in the village, no other resource remained than refuge in the South Dublin Union workhouse, since to labour he was unable, and to beg he was ashamed. In his better days, Mickey Kieran was cheerful and good-humoured; indeed regarded by all his acquaintances as a very comical man, and as such, very general sympathy was expressed, but little support tendered, when he had taken the resolution of seeking that shelter from the buffets of adversity. No doubt, some of his former friends and familiars paid him occasional visits ; but after a while, these became less frequent, and having in a great measure severed connection from the world without, in turn his very existence was almost forgotten, even by his distant relatives, who yet remembered him with esteem and affection.

At this time, it so happened, there were two Michael Kierans entered on the Admission Books of the South Dublin Union—distinct in family, local origin and connexions, yet nearly of an age coinciding, and that was one rather advanced in years. It seems more than likely, they were intimates during the times of social intercourse freely allowed there to the aged and infirm.

Some years having elapsed, one of the two Michael Kierans was overtaken by illness, which confined him to the ward, and it resulted finally in his removal thence to the Dead House. It is customary, when family relations are known to survive out of doors, and living at no great distance, to send word of such an occurrence, so that the corpse may be removed by them for wake and interment, not at the expense of the Union. Having a knowledge of Michael Kieran's former connexion with Sandymount, and assuming that his friends there should naturally desire to learn the particulars of his death ; an official messenger was hastily despatched thither, and when the news was duly announced, it was resolved, as a mark of respect and sympathy, that a coffin should be procured, and arrangements made for a private interment in the family plot of ground registered in the Cemetery at Glasnevin. Accordingly the undertaker discharged his commission by going to the Dead House, and taking dimensions for the coffin that had been ordered. When the remains had been cased therein, a small cortege of friends attended and brought them to Sandymount, where the lid of the coffin was raised, and the corpse was duly laid out for a wake, with the view further to prepare a public funeral.

On such occasions, it is customary for the friends and acquaintances of the deceased to assemble and manifest by their presence and condolences with each other, their remembrance and respect. All were seated in silence or subdued conversation in the death-chamber, and as a matter of course, having their looks directed towards the corpse, their recollections were carried back over score of years, and to the time when Mickey Kieran was alive and well in the village of Sandymount. At length, among others, when he could spare an hour from duty, the Tramcar driver Michael MacManus entered, and approaching the bedside, he gazed with some surprise on the features of the dead. Then instituting a more rigorous examination, a feeling of incredulity began to arise in his mind. After a little deliberation, yet with a somewhat embarrassed air, at length he cried out to others who were present: "Why, bless me, but yees are waking the wrong man, for as shure as I'm livin', this is not Mickey Kieran's corpse!" Now, indeed, the people assembled came nearer to the dead body, and eagerly scanned the features; still as many years elapsed since they had seen him alive, none could clearly recollect any distinctive peculiarity of countenance, that might lead them to entertain a negative doubt, especially as they had official warrant for the identity of the deceased with the living subject. At last it was agreed, that death oftentimes strangely alters the features, and aged indications undoubtedly corresponded with the appearance of the corpse there lying before them. No further serious questions were raised, and attended by a goodly number of his former friends and acquaintances to the family place of interment, the last rites were discharged towards the remains of Michael Kieran in Glasnevin.

Little more was thought about those occurrences for another year, when it chanced that a poor old resident of Sandymount, named Barney Quinn, was obliged to take up his quarters as an inmate in the South Dublin Union workhouse. Being duly entered on the Admission Book, and having donned the gray uniform provided, no sooner had the new-comer crossed the yard, than he started with affright. Suddenly his old acquaintance Mickey Kieran of Sandymount appeared and advanced to meet him with a familiar smile of recognition. Recalling all the circumstances of the former wake and interment at which he had assisted, poor Barney Quinn fancied he saw the ghost of his old acquaintance and friend, while in his distress, and shuddering at the idea of grasping the proffered hand, he stammered out in amazement: "Why, Mickey Kieran, I thought we buried you this time twelve months in Glasnevin, and all your friends in Sandymount thought the same, and now to see you livin' again and to the fore!" He then related what had happened at the time, to the no small wonder of his friend, who then understood the reason why he had not received a single visit from any one of the Sandymount people, during the whole of the previous twelvemonths. The cordiality and friendship of former days were resumed, and reminiscences of the past formed the topic of many a conversation between them, so long as they remained fellow inmates of the South Dublin Bastile, as its poor occupants are pleased ironically to designate that large building.

Soon, however, these incidents were made known, and news reached Sandymount, that its former resident Mickey Kieran was still in the land of the living. Then the sagacity and opinion of Michael MacManus were recognized and approved, although formerly rejected and contemned; while the scorners who attended the wake and funeral of a man unknown did not care to have it stated, they had been victims of an illusion. Even the ridicule attaching to them, and an unwillingness to revive any recollection of their error, caused them to neglect poor Michael Kieran, who did not long survive the attendance of his friends at the funeral of his namesake. Moreover, it must be related, that when his own death actually took place, his remains were not decreed the usual mortuary tokens of respect in his native village, but were brought, according to the ordinary custom of pauper burial, from the workhouse to the grave.

No. XX.

The Druid's Betrayal.

LEGEND OF THE RIVER BANN, COUNTY OF LONDONDERRY.

> " 'Twas vain: the loud waves lashed the shore,
> Return or aid preventing,
> The waters wild went o'er his child,
> And he was left lamenting."
> —Thomas Campbell's *Lord Ullin's Daughter.*

DURING the old Pagan times in Ireland, and about three hundred years before the Christian era, flourished the monarch Conall Collomrach, according to the calculation of the chronologists. Like most of the kings who preceded him, little is known of his exploits, but that his reign was brief, and his end a violent one, are recorded by the annalists. Tradition asserts, however, that he had a lovely daughter, named Tuag, and who was only an infant at the time of his death. The fame of her beauty, and the fact that she was an unprotected orphan, reached the ears of the celebrated Conaire Mor, who had the reputation of being one of the most just, brave and compassionate of men. His long reign was glorious and prosperous for a period of seventy years. To get possession of the child, he sought the aid of a Druid, named Fer-Fi, son of Eogabail, and belonging to the Tuatha De Danaan race. This magician lived in a fort, situated on the banks of the Upper Bann, which comes streaming down in many branches from the Mourne Mountains, and uniting the various contingents near Rathfriland, in the County Down, the torrent becomes considerable onwards to Banbridge and Portadown, whence taking a northerly course, it enters the south-western extremity of Lough Neagh.

That Druid was a most skilled performer on the harp, and he could modulate its strings to produce any tones of melody, from the heroic to the lively and soul-inspiriting ; from the most solemn to the most soothing and plaintive strains. Magical influences were supposed attaching to the songs he composed, and to which the lyre formed an accompaniment. Wherefore, that harpist was famed through the length and breadth of Ireland ; and roving minstrel as he was, the halls of Emania received him as an honoured guest, while every petty prince and chief vied with each other to invite him on the first available occasion to their respective forts. Such an adroit messenger obtained ready access to the habitation of the infant Tuag's fosterer ; and admiring her great beauty, at such a tender age, the minstrel composed a song in her praise, and suiting it to the softest and sweetest lullaby, he threw the fosterer, his wife, children and the baby princess, into a profound sleep. This was the opportunity he desired, and gently lifting the infant from her cradle, he wrapped her in a warm covering. Then, carrying the harp on his back, he set out on the road for Conaire Mor's royal residence, at Emania, and soon presented the little princess to the generous monarch, who immediately became her guardian and protector.

The king was generous in bestowing a large reward on the Druid, and looking on the infantile expression of features, he dearly loved the child. Placing her under the guardianship of female attendants, he gave the retinue instructions that none of the princes or chiefs of his court should have access to her, until she attained an age, when the tympanist Fer-Fi should return and take charge of her musical and literary education. Every day the monarch saw her, and rejoiced to find her grow in grace and beauty, until she reached the tenth year, when Fer-Fi came to court according to agreement. He brought her on departing to his own home, where every convenience and comfort had been provided for the young princess. Each year he promised a visit to Emania, so that while entertaining the court with his songs and harp, he might furnish a report also, on her progress and accomplishments.

To great beauty of person, the Princess Tuag united great powers of mind and an exquisite taste for music, so that by degrees her reputation spread all over Ireland; but, no prince or chief dare visit or make proposals of marriage to her in disregard of the monarch's strict injunctions to the Druid. However, a notorious magician, named Manahan MacLir, ruled as king over the Isle of Man, and he felt so desirous to obtain possession of the maiden, that he practised all manner of intrigue and incantations to succeed in his design. At length, he sent a female messenger to his brother Druid, and having a commission to bribe Fer-Fi with a large sum of money, the latter was not proof to such a temptation, and accordingly he promised to meet Manahan MacLir with his sea-fleet, at the mouth of the River Bann. He agreed likewise, to deliver up the beautiful young princess to him, and in a manner unknown to the monarch of Ireland.

Often had the royal maiden rambled along the banks of the pleasant Bann. She admired the scenery and rushing waters of its many streams through ravines and dells, where the oak forests grew thickly along its course; but always she was accompanied by the guardian, who was now about to betray his trust. Confiding as she lived with him, that project was easily accomplished, especially as he could bring magic arts to his aid. On an evening selected for the purpose, he had a canoe hollowed out from the trunk of a gigantic tree, and it was moored on the river bank. Taking his harp as usual, the Druid ran his fingers over the strings, and began by playing the slow lullaby for the young princess, until her eyes closed in a mesmeric sleep. Then lifting the innocent maiden in his arms, and carrying her to the boat, he placed her in a recumbent position in the stern, and unfastened the cord which bound the gunwale to a tree on the river-bank. The canoe, with an occasional paddle of the oars, glided rapidly along with the current, until Fer-Fi and the sleeping princess came to the expansive opening of Lough Neagh.

There the Druid set up a mast, and having fixed it firmly in the socket, he spread a sail, and careered over the surface of the lake, until he came to the northern extremity, whence issued its volume of water into the Lower Bann. This fine river they now entered, and glided swiftly on the current through the territory of Dalriada, broad valleys on either side and thickly wooded. At last, the boat reached the embouchure which united it with the ocean. The fleet of Manahan MacLir was not then in sight, and this circumstance greatly embarrassed Fer-Fi. The estuary bore the name of Inber n-Glas, at that time. There the Druid lifted the sleeping beauty, and laid her gently on the strand, while a sigh of repentance escaped his lips and tears fell from his eyes. The princess seemed as in a trance. But, fearing the wrath of King Conaire, the magician turned away to seek a sea-worthy vessel, which might serve to convey himself and his charge to the Isle of Man. There he hoped for safety, and even persuaded himself, that the princess should enjoy peace and happiness, as queen consort to the renowned sea-rover, Manahan MacLir.

This expectation however was soon dispelled; for, during his absence, a great wave came rolling from the northern ocean, and swept over the strand on which Tuag lay. The lovely maiden never awoke again, and when the tide rolled back, she was a corpse. Her base betrayer, in trying to effect his escape from the bounds of Erinn, was overtaken by a tempest, and perished in the depths of the ocean. When those tidings came to the knowledge of the monarch and people of Ireland, all bemoaned the fate of the unfortunate and deeply-injured princess. Thenceforward, the embouchure of the River Bann changed its former name: and, to commemorate the sorrowful issue, it was called Tuag Inbir, by succeeding generations.

No. XXI.

The Gobban Saer's Ingenuity.

LEGEND OF ST. MULLINS, COUNTY OF CARLOW.

"Men called him Gobban Saer, and many a tale
Yet lingers in the bye-ways of the land,
Of how he cleft the rock, and down the vale
Led the bright river, child-like, in his hand:
Or how on giant ships he spread great sail,
And many marvels else by him first plann'd."

—Thomas Darcy M'Gee's *The Gobban Saer.*

MANY traditions of the Gobban Saer are still told in the locality of St. Mullins; one of these relates how, being the cleverest builder in Ireland, he arrived once footsore and weary at the Church of St. Mullins, which was then building. He always took a great interest in the erection of churches, and when not engaged as the architect himself, the Gobban had a turn for visiting places, where he knew work of the kind to be progressing, so that he might aid or give useful hints to the builders. He usually travelled in his working dress, which was ragged and torn; so that from his outward appearance, no one could suspect he was an architect of the greatest genius. When he reached St. Mullins, a number of mechanics and labourers were busy under a foreman's direction, and they were then engaged in putting on the church-roof. He sat down on a stone that was near, and gazed intently on their labours.

The workmen who were engaged there noticed the stranger, and scoffed at his poor appearance, as he was looking at their work. At last, they gave vent to rather uncomplimentary observations, and the accomplished Gobban had to bear patiently such remarks as these, although he began with the common salutation of "God bless the work, boys!"

"Musha where did you shtroll from to-day, for an idle thramp?" cried out a man that was on the roof.

"That's none of your business to know," returned the Gobban Saer.

"Do you want a job, my good fellow, or can you do a hand's turn, at all?" inquired another labourer.

"That you'll find out in good time," replied the Gobban to his impertinent questioner.

"Did you ever learn any thrade?" asked the foreman.

"May be I did, and may be I didn't," said the Gobban, "and you may want my help before long."

"And what thrade were you brought up to, my good man?" inquired the foreman.

"I know a great many," returned the Gobban.

"Then I suppose you are a Jack-of-All Thrades, and good at none," said the foreman.

"Are ye a mason?" cried one of the craft, who was engaged dressing a quoin-stone for building the vestry.

"I am, and a master-mason at that," replied the Gobban.

"And may be ye are a carpenter, too," cried another, who was sawing planks for the construction of the church doors.

"Yes, and a first-class one," answered the Gobban.

"I suppose you can do smith-work also," cried out a man that was working at the anvil to forge iron bolts for the doors.

"I am, and a lock-smith, and a gold-smith, moreover," returned the Gobban to the last questioner.

"Do you belong to any regular Thrade Society, at all," inquired the foreman, "or can you show your card of membership?"

"That I do not, and cannot," said the Gobban, "but while I am eating a bit of oaten cake, and resting myself here, I'll just be at hand to let you know what I can do."

At that moment, the man on the unfinished roof was laying the rafters, and he desired to shape a plug or wedge to secure one of these to a beam ; but after repeated efforts with an adze, he found it would not fit the hole for which it had been intended, and at last, he told the foreman of his failure. As being such a very clever fellow, the foreman then asked Gobban was he able to chop it out in a shape to fill the space. Asking to see what place the plug was required for, Gobban was pointed out a hole high up in one of the timbers of the roof. "Give me a hatchet," said he, "and I'll fashion the plug here, in less than a jiffey." The foreman then reached an axe to the Gobban Saer. Spreading his handkerchief on a stone at hand, "to save the edge of the hatchet," he soon chopped out the plug. Then tossing it up into the hole, he secured it there, by throwing up the hatchet after it, and the instrument fell on the plug, which entered the right spot, where it fitted exactly the opening.

"Can any of yees do the like of that?" cried the stranger, as he gazed in triumph around the circle of workmen present.

"Begorra," shouted all, "that bangs Banagher, and you're a regular genius!"

"Didn't I tell yees," says he, "that yees 'ud want my help, and I don't think yees 'ill sneer at me any longer." He had then rested sufficiently, and having finished the last morsel of his oaten cake, he put on his hat, took his blackthorn stick in his hand, and proceeded on his journey.

He had not told them his name, nor was it necessary; for the workmen all knew, that no man in Ireland could attempt the feat he accomplished other than the Gobban Saer.

No. XXII.

The Peistha of Saint's Island.

LEGEND OF LOUGH DERG, COUNTY OF DONEGAL.

"Yet there
He lives not long; but respiration needs
At proper intervals. * * * *
* * * * * That spear has pierc'd
His neck; the crimson waves confess the wound,
Fix'd is the bearded lance, unwelcome guest,
Where'er he flies."
—William Somerville's *Chase*, Book iv.

"Para que con esta acabe
La historia, que nos refiere
Dionisio, el gran Cartusiano,
Con Enrique Saltarense,
Cesario, Mateo Rodulfo,
Dominicano Esturbaquense,
Membrosio, Marco Marulo,
David Roto, y el prudente
Primado de toda Hibernia,
Belarmino, Beda, Serpi,
Fray Dimas, Jacob S'olino,
Mensinghano, y finalmente
La piedad y la opinion
Cristiana, que lo defiende."
—Don Pedro Calderon de la Barca's *Comedias.*
El Purgatorio de San Patricio, Aut. iii., Sce. iv.

"For with this is now concluded
The historic legend told us
By Dionysius the great Carthusian,
With Henricus Salteriensis,
Cæsarius Heisterbachensis,
Matthew Paris and Ranulphus,
Monbrisius, Marolicus Siculus,
David Rothe, and the judicious
Primate over all Hibernia,
Bellarmino, Beda, Serpi,
Friar Dymas, Jacob Solin,
Messingham, and in conclusion
The belief and pious feeling
Which have everywhere maintained it."
—Denis Florence MacCarthy's English Translation of the
Dramas of Calderon, vol. ii.
The Purgatory of Saint Patrick, Act iii., Scene iv.

IN no other part of Ireland can wilder or grander scenery be found, than over the surface and around the sea-coast of the County of Donegal. Given a few weeks of fine Summer weather, and the hire of an outside jaunting car—which can be procured at any of the towns or villages along the route—and the tourist may reach with personal convenience all the points of greatest interest; while the road-side inns will afford sufficiently comfortable if not luxurious accommodation. A pleasant travelling companion will relieve the feeling of solitariness, which the loneliness of that region should otherwise be likely to create. Considering its mountainous characteristics, the chief public roads are planned with much engineering judgment, and have as few steep ascents or descents as the nature of the place can admit. Deep valleys and glens are to be seen in the recesses of the mountains, and clear beautiful streams winding through them. The lover of nature, in her most charming aspects, can indulge his reveries, as fancy and the occasion may excite. He must certainly find scenic effects and objects of curiosity to awaken interest and admiration, at every stage of his journey.

Happily, too, very excellent Guide Books have been written to conduct the intelligent traveller through every district of this County; to describe its varied scenery, to name its celebrities, and to illustrate its local history. Among these treatises may be specially mentioned " The Donegal Highlands," by the Most Rev. James MacDevitt, D.D., Bishop of Raphoe; " Inis-owen and Tirconnell: Notes, Antiquarian and Topographical," by William James Doherty. First Series, 1891; and still greatly enlarged, " Inis-owen and Tirconnell. Being some Account of Antiquities and Writers of the County of Donegal," by William James Doherty. Second Series, 1895. Besides these most interesting and valuable works may be mentioned the late Monsignor Stephens' "Illustrated Handbook of the Scenery and Antiquities of South-Western Donegal;" Rev. Cæsar Otway's "Sketches in Donegal;" Hugh Allingham's "Ballyshannon: its History and Antiquities;" Michael Harkin's " Inis-Owen;" Lord George Hill's " Facts from Gweedore," and " Hints to Donegal Tourists;" " Memoir of the City and North-Western Liberties of Derry, Parish of Templemore;" and Thomas Colin MacGinley's " Cliff Scenery of South-Western Donegal." Such special works must furnish lore sufficient for the historical and topographical student; his own turn for observation and investigation ought store his memory with recollections of a picturesque and delightful tour.

One of the most interesting localities of Donegal is the gloomy and lonely Lough Derg, which is approached from Ballyshannon by road through the village of Pettigo, from which it is about three miles distant. It covers an area of over two thousand acres, and it contains a few very small islets, the chief of which are Station Island—noted for its Pilgrimages from the 1st of June to the 15th of August—Saint's Island, and Inishgosk. The waters expand in their solitude amid a wide and wild waste of highland moors: while the prospect around is closed in by distant ranges of heath-covered hills, without any considerable elevation or distinctiveness of form. From this Lough proceeds the River Derg, which takes a north-easterly course of sixteen or seventeen miles to the Moyle, and at a point about two miles below Newtown-Stewart, in the County of Tyrone. The natural features and Christian history of this place are fully described in the second and greatly enlarged edition of Very Rev. Daniel O'Connor's illustrated book, "Lough Derg and its Pilgrimages," in which are collected the traditions and romantic narratives, which in former times spread the fame of this locality throughout these islands, and over distant countries on the Continent of Europe. The celebrated Spanish poet Don Pedro Calderon de la Barca has composed a well-known sacred drama, *El Purgatorio de San Patricio*, and it has been elegantly rendered into English metre, corresponding with the original, by our accomplished Irish poet, Denis Florence MacCarthy. The assonances and spirit of the original have been admirably preserved in every line of the translation.

In the summer season, the Pilgrim's Boat is in constant requisition safely to ferry over from the mainland all who desire to visit Station Island, through motives of devotion or curiosity, and thousands of people land there; but still beyond in the Lough lies Saints' Island, now less frequented than formerly, although its celebrity is of earlier date, and reaches back to the sixth century, when St. Dabheoc lived on it as a recluse, and is said to have founded there a monastic establishment. During the Middle Ages, the Canons Regular of Saint Augustine had a religious house on Saints' Island; from which they were expelled in the beginning of King James I.'s reign, A.D. 1603. The ruins of that priory are now scarcely traceable. However with Saints' Island is associated a curious legend, of which the following is an outline.

In the old Pagan times a Peistha, or water serpent, of immense girth and of still greater trail, was believed to haunt the celebrated Lough Derg, in the northern parts of Ireland. Sometimes his horrid head and open jaws were seen above the surface, as if drawing in the upper air. More frequently the fishermen saw him gliding slowly through the depths. When St. Patrick landed at Saints' Island, that large water serpent was known to have tenanted the waters of Lough Derg. He had caused the destruction of many dwelling on the banks. But the saint could not tolerate the presence of such a monster, and accordingly, with a stroke of his staff the Peistha was destroyed. Afterwards, the waters of the Lough began to assume a reddish tinge, so freely did the monster bleed. To the present day has that colour continued, hence the name given to it—the Red Lake. The skeleton remained on Station Island to the beginning of the present century, as the old people living around the shores are ready to asseverate; and many of them have conversed with persons who alleged they saw the last remaining portions of that serpent's body mouldering into dust.

No. XXIII.

The Witch Transformed.

LEGEND OF CULLENAGH, QUEEN'S COUNTY.

"My heart is dull within my breast, mine eyes are full of tears,
My memory is wandering back to long departed years—
To those bright days, long, long ago,
When nought I knew of sordid cares, of worldly woe,
But roved, a gay, light-hearted boy, the wood of Caillino."
—Mrs. Ellen Fitz-Simon's (*née* O'Connell),
Song of the Irish Emigrant in North America.

"There dwelt a dread Enchantress in a nook
Obscure; old helpmate she to him had been,
Lending her aid in many a secret sin;
And there for counsel now his way he took."
—Robert Southey's *Curse of Kehama*, Sect. xi.
The Enchantress, 2.

THE days and nights of the old rustic Shanachie and his stories by the cottage fire-side are now numbered among the customs and traditions of by-gone times; but we well remember the delight it afforded ourselves as juveniles, to have seen and heard such a historiographer, and to have learned much curious lore from his narratives to those audiences so frequently assembled in the evenings, as additions to his domestic circle. The lapse of years has driven the name of that chronicler from our recollection, although having vividly impressed on our memory the scenes presented on such occasions. These were unfolded in the chief apartment of a small farmer's thatched dwelling, entered through an open door, with a half-door usually closed, to exclude the sow and her litter of *boniveens* in the bawn from the interior. Much less imposing than a Cathedral vaulted roof, yet was the apex of the pointed gables and ridge-pole of the cabin highly pitched, the rafters were rude and wide apart, connected with cross braces and stout spans of deal to support the dark heather scraw-roof, which served as a ceiling beneath the superincumbent thick outer covering of straw. The mud-walls were plastered on the inside, while both within and without, they were periodically refreshed with a coating of whitewash, and everything was kept scrupulously clean about the aged couple's household. A great ornament of the interior was the kitchen dresser, with rows of plates, dishes and mugs of Chinese design and gaudy colours displayed, and again these were flanked by a pan and gridiron, with bright tin porringers, hanging from pegs driven into the walls. A kitchen table and a settle were on either side. The latter served its double purpose, "a bed by night, a couch for seats by day,"—we much correct the absurd reading in Oliver Goldsmith's text—a few deal chairs and a few four-legged elm-stools, with the cosy bench in the ingle-nook, and facing the hearth within the partition, accommodated the group of uninvited neighbours and friends, that dropped in during the gloaming of evening to pay visits in a homely way. A cheerful welcome always awaited them from the kindly old master and matron of the home-stead; they were invariably provided with seats; conversation soon became general, and it was often prolonged to late hours in the night before the company separated.

Never did Dryden preside with a greater sense of importance in Will's Coffee House, when the wits and worthies of London flocked thither to enjoy the conversation of "glorious John," than did their Shanachie over the rustics of Cullenagh, who came far and near to learn wisdom from the lips of their venerable and sociable host. When gossip and banter, song and repartee had passed good-humouredly around, it was generally the veteran's turn to pour forth the stores of his varied experience, reflections, and learning, for the information and delight of the men and women, boys and girls assembled. Among these latter, the writer was privileged to take his place, and to learn his first lesson of American history; for the Shanachie's uncle Mick had served, we were told, as a full private under General Burgoyne, and had been necessitated to live upon horse-flesh for some days, before the surrender of his chief at Saratoga to General Gates and the Yankees. The subsequent career of that warrior we have now quite forgotten.

It need scarcely be added, that the master of the cottage was a man of great natural intelligence, and greatly respected by his neighbours and acquaintances. He was a keen politician, moreover, and although not a subscriber for any newspaper of the period—the stamp and paper duty was then prohibitive from allowing such regular and wide circulation as at present in the people's homes—still was a journal of rather old date occasionally procured and read out for the assembled guests, followed by comments and discussions on the stirring events of the time. From the curate of the parish—with whom the Shanachie was an especial favourite—the paper of his choice was generally obtained, after Father Perkinson of Ballyroan had pored over it, and satisfied his own thirst for information, and perhaps had lent it previously to other villagers. About that time, likewise, two rival newspapers, *The Leinster Express* and *The Leinster Independent*, had been started in Maryborough, chiefly for county and provincial circulation, and containing news of political, local and agricultural interest for their respective patrons. A kindly disposed gentleman, named Cooney, proprietor of a large cotton-mill and an extensive employer of many young boys and girls in the neighbourhood, was a subscriber to the former, then issued weekly, and he invariably lent it to the Shanachie, for his own and the delectation of his fire-side club.

Above and before all other topics for discussion, the political state of the country at that time was matter which afforded exciting subjects for comment, and frequently for divided opinion, among the rustic patriots; for all were sincere in their love of country, but in speculation on her future, none could with certainty forecast what measures were likely to be devised or adopted, in order to ameliorate her condition. Party feeling then ran high, and the newspapers were acrimonious and personal in their attacks; while the Queen's County was especially in a disturbed state, owing to the factions of Whitefeet and Blackfeet, and the existence of Orange Lodges—all secret organizations—that gave great unrest to the more sensible and well disposed portion of the population. The Tithe-war was at its most acute stage, and Daniel O'Connell had unfurled the flag of Repeal of the Legislative Union between England and Ireland. The latter great national leader and orator was then in the zenith of his fame and power; he was the people's idol, and by none was he more enthusiastically admired than by our Shanachie, who read his speeches aloud for the attentive listeners around him, and afterwards expounded what he believed to be the various political intentions and motions of the celebrated Agitator. To give the reader an idea of the rustic lecturer's opinions and mode of expressing them, on one occasion of the sort, we heard him declare in a tone of energy and earnestness: "This O'Connell is such a great man, you see, that he is impelled by foreign powers, you see, and if they don't grant his requests for Ireland, you see, he'll knock them from East to West, you see, and Patt Lalor of Tinakill, and Dr. Jacob of Maryborough, and John Dunne of Ballynakill, and Richard Ledbetter and Burrowes Kelly of Stradbally, you see, will stand to him shoulder to shoulder, you see, to put in Peter Gale for the Queen's County, and turn out the Tory Sir Charles Coote, you see, to brain the bloody Tithes, you see." This habitual interpolation was often introduced to impress his audience the more effectively; and seldom, indeed, was a dissenting objection raised to any conclusion the master of the house arrived at, for on the whole, he was regarded as a thoroughly well informed and knowledgable man.

What greatly interested that select gathering in the cottage was their host's reading "The Tales and Legends of the Queen's County Peasantry," contributed by John Keegan, a national schoolmaster and a man of genius as a poet and romancist. Those contributions were well worthy insertion in the best Magazines of that day, and were admired by readers of literary taste and judgment; but they were especially relished by the peasants, familiar with the scenes and customs depicted, with the *patois* of their class he introduced, and sometimes with the topics and characters of their native county. They were most eagerly read for their fun, their fancy, style and descriptive power; while at once, those stories established the reputation and circulation of *The Leinster Express*. Had they issued in any other country than our own, such accessions to a truly national literature should not have remained unculled from the columns of a country newspaper, and they must have found their preservation in book-form, to amuse and instruct succeeding generations. Sixty years have elapsed since they appeared, and still are they hidden away in the earlier volumes and files of a paper, which only gave them an ephemeral and a restricted celebrity. At the time to which we allude, the fame of John Keegan as a story-teller was widely diffused among the people, and his name was a household word throughout the Queen's County. Subsequently, he wrote tales of Irish Life and poetry of exquisite pathos for the *Dublin University Magazine*, *Dolman's Magazine*, and other high-class periodicals; but, when his reputation as a writer had been fairly established, while engaged at his humble and useful calling, he died in 1849, having only completed his fortieth year. What is not generally known must here be recorded: he was a most amiable and lovable character; a man strictly moral and religious; devoted to the duties of his profession, and greatly respected by his family relations and acquaintances. The afternoon of Sundays he usually spent in the rural chapel of Clough—about three miles from Abbeyleix—and then he taught catechism to the children of the parishioners. Some few years have passed over since the late Rev. Denis Murphy, S.J.—so great a lover and promoter of Irish and national literature—made a pilgrimage with the writer to that place, where lived the niece of John Keegan; but we were informed by her, that she was too young at the time of his death to have any personal recollection of her uncle, and that nearly all their surviving relations were then living in the United States of America. She possessed none of his letters or manuscripts, nor could she say if any had been preserved. One prized document, in his elegant handwriting, and framed, contains the Rules of the Christian Confraternity. It is hung against the wall within the chapel of Clough, and probably in the adjoining graveyard the remains of John Keegan were deposited.

No more sincere admirer had that *litteratteur* of *The*

Leinster Express than the Cullenagh Shanachie; but whether any personal acquaintance or correspondence existed between them or not is a problem that cannot be solved by the writer. However, in those days, the themes for narrative were not confined to any particular locality; each peasant could relate his own tale of wonder, and tradition had left him in possession of many coming down from his grandsires, and still well remembered. But, in every townland or parish a specially accomplished *raconteur* was pre-eminent; and for miles around his modest dwelling, none was to be found better versed in such lore than our venerable sage.

One of the Shanachie's stories we still recollect—yet only in general outline—was the following. We were informed the time reached back over a hundred years, and when that picturesque and triple range, the Black, Middle and White Mountains of Cullenagh were covered with a thick growth of primeval timber, the forest was infested with wild black cats, which were known to be malicious, and were dreaded by the country-people, as if they were demons. In a deep gorge, through which a small rapid stream descends in a succession of tiny waterfalls between the Black and Middle Mountains, there lived all alone an old hag, who practised charms, and healed various diseases and affections, by gathering herbs and simples. She gave it to be understood, that these were mixed with the blood of a black cat, which she caught occasionally, and then sacrificed, with some incantations calculated to effect a cure. How she lived there was a mystery to many, and few of the Cullenagh people cared to cultivate the acquaintance of that sorceress, whose reputation for magic, nevertheless, was widely extended. From distant places, people were known to visit her, and having been guided through the by-ways which led to her shieling, they returned with philtres and ointments and drugs to be applied as she directed. A fee was exacted and cheerfully paid in each case. A natural enmity sprang up between herself and the wild cats, so that whenever she ventured abroad, these animals beset her way in troops, and grinned vengefully and screamed loudly on her approach. The hag carried a stout blackthorn stick, which she was able to wield with vigour, and if any came too near its stroke, they were sure to pay the forfeit with their lives. The resentment of the survivors resembled that of the peasant's wild justice of revenge, and it was treasured up for an opportunity of wreaking dire vengeance on the oppressor of their breed and race.

The fine castellated mansion of the Cullenagh Barringtons then arose on the northern slope of the Black Mountain, and there at the present day, its ruined and roofless walls are still to be seen. It was sheltered towards the rear by the spreading forests, then a great covert for game, while an extensive view opened in front over pasture and corn fields, and this was closed in the distance by the circling range of Fossey and Timahoe Mountains. There the celebrated Sir Jonah Barrington spent much of his youthful life in the last century with his aged grandfather, whose peculiarities are so humorously described in his Personal Memoirs. At all times, the Barringtons were addicted to hunting and field sports. They kept packs of harriers, while pointers and setters and greyhounds accompanied their rambles over the fields and through the woods. Frequently their fowling pieces rang through the latter, and being excellent shots, after a day's sport, they returned home, their game-bags usually filled with woodcock, grouse and pheasants.

Now they had a wood-ranger, called Watt, who had charge of preserving the game, and of rambling among the brakes, to warn poachers against tresspass on the hares and rabbits, that preyed in numbers on their tenants' growing corn. Watt was a frolicksome and foolhardy character, never brought up to any other occupation, and who preferred entirely the wood-man's independent and rather solitary life, to any regular course of manual industry. He often passed through that glen, where the old hag's cabin stood, and in his rounds sometimes stopped awhile to make observations; for, in common with all living on the estate, he was curious to glean some definite knowledge of her habits and mode of living. Sometimes she opened the door very cautiously, to learn who was coming, and then to bid him the time of day; but all the professions of friendship and blandishments he used could not induce her to invite him into her cabin.

It so happened, nevertheless, that while on his range one day, with greyhound and gun, and peering through the woods, a hare suddenly appeared across his path-way, and from all sides he heard a growling of wild cats, as if approaching towards himself. He soon found, however, that the object of their pursuit was the poor frightened hare, and in whatever quarter she turned, one or other of the cats seemed to head her off, as the circle narrowed around her. At last, after several doublings, she turned towards Watt, and making one desperate spring, the hare jumped full on to his breast, and she clung to him with paws extended on his shoulders, her heart violently palpitating with fear. At first he was startled, but moved to compassion for the poor animal's terror, he resolved to save her. The dog by his side was even impatient to pounce on the poor creature; yet was he restrained by the looks and motions of his master. Still the growlers around him appeared to be increasing in number, while the trees seemed to be alive with the wild cats, and their shrill screams were piercing to the ear. Meanwhile, to the astonishment of her protector, the hare cried out in a plaintive voice: "For your life, Watt, for your life, Watt, don't let them near me!" Terrified out of his wits, at the idea of holding a bewitched creature in his arms, the wood-ranger lost all presence of mind, and at once vigorously wrenched the hare from his embrace, and threw her far away from him. Immediately the dog gave chase, and she bounded up the glen towards the old hag's cabin with the speed of lightning, the greyhound gaining on her at every stretch, but frequently balked of his prey, by her occasioned doublings. At last she reached the cabin, the window of which lay open, while the woods around echoed the vengeful screams of the wild cats. However, just as the terrified hare had jumped on to the window-sill, the greyhound was so close on her trail, that with open jaws he seized her hindmost leg, and his sharp teeth severed it completely from the body. Having thus narrowly escaped capture, the hare reached the interior, when the window casement suddenly closed down and excluded her pursuer.

Following up the chase with the keen interest of a sportsman, Watt was soon on the scene, and he heard piteous wailings from within the hag's cabin. Raising the latch, he entered, and found only the occupant of his acquaintance in a bed, but with the stump of her amputated limb extended from the covering, and blood streaming from it in great profusion. He now well knew, that she was a sorceress, who had assumed the form of a hare for some unaccountable purpose he could not divine; and therefore he thought it best to get away with all haste from the cottage, unheeding her screams and entreaties to remain and bandage her limb, as otherwise she must bleed to

F

death. In the flurry of the moment, he left the door open, and calling away the greyhound, both followed the bridle-road down the wooded glen. No sooner had the hag been left alone, than the troop of wild cats entered the cabin, and finding its former occupant maimed and helpless, they fell upon her, scratched and gnawed her to that degree, that she perished miserably. Only her mangled remains were found the next day, when such a ghastly discovery was made.

Every vestige of the cabin tenanted by the sorceress has long since disappeared; even the grand forest trees have been cut down, with the exception of a stripe of wood-land, which winds down the rugged glen, on either side of the gurgling stream, that separates the over-topping Slieve Dubh from the Middle Mountain of lesser elevation. In our school-boy days, it was a famous haunt for thrushes and blackbirds; while their melodious throats sent warbling thrills to betoken Summer's approach in the leafy screens, and other feathered minstrels were emulous to rival in vocal efforts those more admired songsters of the grove. We know not if the Shanachie's cosy tenement is yet in possession of any member of his family, for long since he has been gathered to the graves of his kindred. The sports and rambles of childhood soon pass away to engage us in more serious and responsible pursuits; seldom do we revisit the scenes of infancy, when duty calls to a distant sphere of labour. While a brief interval sometimes affords time and leisure to renew an acquaintance with well remembered localities, how seldom do we find all our former playmates and companions of olden times there living. Then do unwelcome regrets overshadow the remembrances of by-gone days, and we feel how swiftly the annual revolutions have passed, and are passing, with a train of reflections sobered and subdued, while gazing on the varied beauties of places so lovingly associated with the friends and resorts of our early youth.

No. XXIV.

The Fool's Fantasies.

LEGEND OF CLOONFUSH, COUNTY OF GALWAY.

> "The charm dissolves apace;
> And as the morning steals upon the night,
> Melting the darkness, so their rising senses
> Begin to chase the ignorant fumes that mantle
> Their clearer reason."
> —William Shakespeare's *Tempest*, Act v., scene i.

AT whatever point of the compass a traveller from the other three provinces of Ireland arrives in Connaught, he is introduced to a stretch of country flat and monotonous, singularly devoid of swelling hills and winding valleys, even where the sluggish rivers and rivulets pour their waters into the "spacious Shenan spreading like a sea," to use the descriptive words of the poet Spenser. Though scanty yet sweet herbage crowns the pastures of light soil, the limestone is to be seen cropping up in ledges of grey and dreary rock, with moor and morass frequently extending their desolate-looking wastes, hardly relieved by a sheltering wood-land, or even by a luxurious hedge-row. Bare walls cross the fields in various directions, and so loosely built, that the stones seem poised lightly on each other, with openings between that give partial views of the sheep-walks beyond their bounds.

In the midst of such a landscape, and on a slight elevation, the old archiepiscopal city of Tuam rises around its market-square and market-house, where its best edifices are grouped; while near these are the imposing tower and cruciform structure of the Roman Catholic Cathedral and the College of St. Jarlath. The former Protestant Cathedral has ceased to be an archiepiscopal one, since the Church Reform Act, when the separate dioceses of Killala and Achonry were annexed to the See of Tuam. There is still a small and well-built church, standing on the site of a former very ancient one, and near it in the surrounding graveyard are some remnants of antiquity, especially the famed and intricately-carved Cross of Tuam. From the central area of the town, five chief streets radiate in various directions, and terminate in rows of wretched thatched cabins as they emerge on the open roads. At present, the town of Tuam has a poverty-stricken appearance; although of late years some building improvements have been effected.

When the old mail-coaches were running, the population larger, and the market-place more crowded with the products of an agricultural country surrounding it, on the occasion of fairs and markets, the streets presented a bustling and business-like appearance. Moreover, the characters and customs of an older generation were more primitive and peculiar, before the railway of later introduction effected its economic and social changes. In those former times, a strange and wild-looking scarecrow figure, known as Crazy Paudeen, was ever to be seen skipping about during the day, and where he rested at night, few of the townspeople seemed to know or care. Now the particular costume he affected was a high conical and peaked huntsman's cap, of faded velvet, and a stained loosely-fitting body-coat of scarlet cloth, much the worse for wear, with nether habiliments of tarnished buckskin. However, his legs and feet were bare, which circumstance gave great freedom to his movements. He also bore in his hand a huntsman's whip, with a long leathern thong and lash, which he had learned to wield and crack with great dexterity. This exercise seemed to afford him a special delight. All those properties mentioned were gifts bestowed on him by the Galway Blazers; for Paudeen never missed a single one of their fox-hunting meetings, and although a pedestrian, he was so alert and sound-chested, that he was able to keep in view, and to halloo with the hounds from their starting of Reynard to the finish of the chase, no matter how quick the pace or how long continued. Nay more: his enthusiasm was unbounded, when the field of sportsmen was fairly under way, and as each of these in succession topped and cleared the fences on their course, a snap of his fingers and a triumphant shout announced his admiration of the feat.

When not engaged in the exciting sport of the chase, Paudeen was usually to be seen lounging about the hotel stables in town. He had a most affectionate regard for horses, and helped the ostlers there to groom and feed them, while waiting the arrival of the Dublin Mail Coach on its way to Castlebar. It was always a mystery to him, why the two large hind wheels could never overtake the two foremost small ones; and when the horses were put to, and the driver set the coach in motion, it aroused his indignation to find, that the big lazy fellows could never gain an inch on the active little wheels in advance of them. From the town and for miles along the road to Castlebar, Paudeen would run from one hind wheel to the other, cracking his whip menacingly, and in reproachful words trying to rouse them to better effort, while these antics afforded the greatest amusement to the passengers and spectators. When tired with such vain endeavours, he turned back to town ; but, it was only to have his anger again incited, by the gibes and nicknames of young urchins escaped from school, and who thought themselves nimble enough to scamper round corners and through lanes from Paudeen's vengeance. This was immediately manifested by taking up any stones he found on the street, and hurling them with all his force against the juvenile offenders. Such outbursts of passion were dreaded by the more respectable inhabitants of the town ; since if the stones missed their intended aim, they frequently flew crashing through shop and parlour windows ; nor could any person hope to obtain damages for losses sustained from the irresponsible individual who had unthinkingly caused them.

Another of Paudeen's freaks was to issue out on clear moonlight nights, and when seeing his own shadow behind or before him to mutter some threat, which he hoped would make it move off, and then finding it to disregard his warning, he struck out into a boxing attitude, which the shadow imitated. His fury was then greatly inflamed, and he struck the dark impression on the road with his knuckles might and main until these bled profusely. Again, he was often seen by the neighbours wandering alone, and talking incoherently to some imaginary persons in the air, while gesticulating violently and with apparent passion. When soothed and spoken to, these fits passed away; but the flights of his imagination were still unchecked. Some extravagant story he would also relate, about adventures in which he had been engaged, and with beings belonging to an invisible world. The country people believe, that innocent or demented creatures like Paudeen have some close relations with the fairies, and therefore he was always treated with compassion and respect, not unmingled with fear, on account of his capricious temper ; but, at whatever farmer's or cottier's house he called, a kindly welcome with bed and board was cordially given, so long as he chose to stay. To one so restless and roaming in disposition, this was seldom more than for a day or night.

About two miles southwards from Tuam, there is an ancient burial-place in the townland of Cloonfush, and the fragment of a ruined church called Teampul Jarlaithe yet remains in it. The spot is lonely and exposed, while interments there are now only those of unbaptised infants. Yet the people have a tradition, that St. Jarlath built his first monastery and established a school at Cloonfush, before he removed for final settlement to Tuam. Thither Paudeen was accustomed to resort, and he was often found there sitting on a rude head-stone, and generally talking to himself. One evening, late in autumn, he strolled out to Cloonfush, and having had much racing during that day, he felt greatly fatigued. Stretching himself under the fragment of the old church, he continued there during the whole of that night.

A comfortable farm-stead in the neighbourhood was tenanted by the Widow Mullally, and her grown-up sons and daughters. As the mistress of the house and her family were always very kind to Paudeen, whenever he rambled that way; so he often made their house a halting-place, and with the inmates he was unusually vivacious and communicative. As the Mullallys were early risers, and as the cold night air had served greatly to stimulate the crazy one's appetite, he had wit enough to know where he should find a good breakfast; and accordingly, he hastened to the open door, which he entered with the usual country salutation, "God save all here." "Musha God save you kindly," returned the good-natured widow, "and yer welcome, Paudeen, bud fhwat brought ye out so early in the mornin'?" "Trot an' Mrs. Mullally, alanna, I slep' all night in de ould churchyard, an' I didn't get much of a supper yistherday evenin' afore I left Tuam, so dat I'm cruel hungry now for a bit of breakwust." "An' that ye'll have with a heart and a half, and in less nor a jiffy," returned the hospitable widow, as she vigorously stirred a pot of stirabout boiling on the fire, told her daughter Mary to spread the table, lay on the noggins of milk, and prepare the big dish for the seething oatmeal, then quite cooked and ready for family consumption.

All sat down to the wholesome and comfortable meal, to which Paudeen especially did ample justice, and afterwards, when placed in the ingle-nook beside a fine blazing turf fire, Mrs. Mullally, in her own agreeable manner opened the conversation: "Whethen, Paudeen avic, what induced ye to sleep out in the cowld churchyard last night, when ye knew we'd be only too glad to give ye supper and a bed here, and a hearty welcome to boot?" "Bedad an' I'll tell ye dat, ma'am," replied Paudeen, who was always delighted to gratify his kind hostess. "I knew dere was an ould villayn about de place, an' planin' mischief for yees all here, an' I intinded to watch for him, an' give him de lent and bret of de whip across de showlders." "And who was he, Paudeen, dear?" insinuatingly inquired the Widow Mullally. "Faix an' dat I didn't know, ma'am, bud shure enough I found him out, de vagabone, an' med him pay for his villayney. Now, jist listen, an' I'll tell ye the whole shtory."

Accordingly Mrs. Mullally and her children, not a little amused and interested, drew their chairs in a semicircle round the fire, in an attitude of attention to the expected narrative; for they noticed Paudeen's eyes dilate and his features lighting up with the usual excited expression, when he had any important information to convey. His tone of voice gradually raised and his tongue increased in volubility, while his imagination and feelings glowed as he proceeded; for his indignation could not be restrained, when he recounted the evil doings of the miscreant he had so lately encountered.

"Fhwy din as I was stretched on de ground near de ould church wall, who turns de corner on me bud a big ugly joynt of a fella, and he looked very impedint at me, and axed what brought me dere. I toult him it was none of his business to know, an' dat he wasn't to be saucy to me, big a fellah as he was. I den took up de whip and med a slash at him acrass de shins, and to keep him out of de way. Thin he got afeard of me, and looked up in de shky for help. He saw a big black cloud dere like a horse, and he called id down, and thin threw his leg over its back, an' catched its mane. Up dey both flew among de shtars, an' as dey raced along, I saw de joynt pullin' de shtars out o' deir places an' puttin' dem one by one into his pockets. 'Shtop dat work,' siz I, 'you bloody tief; is it wantin' to take all de shtars from de shky ye are, and hide dem away in yer coat-pocket?' 'It's not shtars dey are,' siz he, 'bud only silver; dey big ones are half-crowns, dey middle-size ones are shillins', an' dey little ones sixpences.'"

"And fwhat did ye say to that, Paudeen?" interjected the

widow, winking good-humouredly at the other members of her family.

"Tare an' agers, ma'am, fwhat did I say, bud call him a bloody liar, an' I towlt him to lave de shtars in deir places.' 'Dey don't belong to any body,' siz he, 'an' I'll gether dim all up an' keep dim myself.'

"Din I shouted louder at him nor afore, an' axed him what right he had to dim, an' dat fwhen he'd come down may be I wouldn't impty his pockets and horsewhip him for his tieven.' Bud he only laughed at me, an' kept on at his work, until he picked up every shtar as he wint along, an' fwhen his pockets were full, he ran off on his horse through de shky at de rate of a hunt, an' id was so dark thin, I lost sight of his thracks, an' de teivin' pickpocket med his escape. Now Mrs. Mullally, alanna, if ye go out of doors, ye'll see he didn't lave a single shtar in de shky dat he didn't take away wid him.'"

"He was a great rogue, no doubt, Paudeen," replied the widow, "bud I wouldn't mind him any more, if I was you, and let him go about his business, my boy."

"Yerra, ma'am, dat ud be only to rob and shtale from all de neighbours. No, no, Mrs. Mullally, I'll just shtart for town, an' inform de polis, about his doin's an' sind dim out to ketch him and put him in jail," and jumping up instantly, Paudeen rushed out of the house, and on to the high road, without further leave-taking. According to the bent of his prevailing fantasy, and in a mood of great elation, putting the left shoulder forward, and raising a smart trot, he kept plying the whip vigorously with his right hand, and muttering threats of vengeance against the giant of the previous night. While thus preparing to speed the ends of justice against the transgressor, by lodging information with the chief constable in Tuam, on his arrival there the depositions were taken with an assumed gravity, which assured him, that the culprit of his imagination should soon become a prisoner, and be brought to trial before judge and jury.

No. XXV.
Tipperary Tactics.

LEGENDS OF UPPER AND LOWER ORMOND, COUNTY OF TIPPERARY.

> " Within that land was many a malcontent,
> Who cursed the tyranny to which he bent;
> That soil full many a wringing despot saw,
> Who worked his wantonness in form of law.
> Long war without and frequent broil within
> Had made a path for blood and giant sin."
> —Lord George Gordon Noel Byron's *Lara*,
> Canto ii., sect. viii.

> " You're free to share his scanty meal,
> His plighted word he'll never vary—
> In vain they tried with go'd and steel
> To shake the Faith of Tipperary!"
> —Thomas Davis' *National Ballads and Songs*.
> Part. i, Tipperary.

AMONG the most fertile of Irish Counties that of Tipperary claims a foremost place, and although no special historical or statistical account of it has yet been written, still it had been the theatre of remarkable events from a period most remote, even to our own days. There ruled the Kings of Desmond or South Munster, in their regal fortalice of Cashel, proudly rising on its insulated limestone Rock. It was also the seat of a bishop, in early Christian ages, while in mediæval times, it had been elevated to metropolitan distinction. Flourishing towns have grown up in various districts, and roads kept in excellent condition connect them; the different parishes abound in agricultural and pastoral resources; the River Suir and its tributaries flow amid rich and smiling valleys, through all its length; the crested mountains and hills are many and of beautiful outline; while taken altogether, few Counties in Ireland present more or greater attractions.

In Cromwellian times the lands of Tipperary changed owners to a large extent, and the original proprietors were obliged to surrender their possessions to a new class of colonists. The parliamentary soldiers, who had served in Ireland, obtained Land-debentures, which entitled them to possess portions of the confiscated estates in lieu of pay which was in arrear. Many of them remained as settlers in that county; others sold their portions to a different class of adventurers, who became residents and occupied the lands. The history of these transactions is well set forth in John P. Prendergast's admirable work, "The Cromwellian Settlement of Ireland;" and, for the fullest particulars of such transactions, the reader is referred to it, as giving the truest account regarding the confiscations and colonization, which took place in and after the middle of the seventeenth century. It is evident, from what is recorded, and also from what remains of their former mansions, that many of those settlers were men of energy and enterprise, who expended largely in buildings and land-improvement. By degrees, the native peasantry were permitted to become tenants, and to erect houses of their own, but with such restrictions of tenure and political independence as created animosities between the races, and which grew into disorders and crimes, promoted by an intolerant ascendancy class. These circumstances gave rise to secret and illegal confederacies among the peasantry, who thus endeavoured to redress their grievances, and to remove those exactions, for which law and its administration provided no remedy.

The Baronies of Upper and Lower Ormond occupy position in the north-western part of the County, closed in towards the north and west by the River Shannon, and the wide-spreading waters of Lough Derg; while to the south and east, the remarkable outlines of the Devil's Bit Mountains form the general boundary. A whimsical story prevails among the peasantry, that travelling once through that region and feeling very hungry, his satanic majesty took away a great portion of the mountain in his teeth, leaving behind him that singular-looking gap,—such an object of curiosity to all travellers; but, finding the Bit indigestible, he dropped it at a considerable distance to the south, where it afterwards formed the celebrated Rock of Cashel. Whatever degree of credit may attach to such a story, it is certain, that rich fields and comfortable dwellings are to be seen throughout the Baronies of Upper and Lower Ormond; the stately castellated mansions of the planters—mostly built during the reign of Charles II.—often rise to the view, but long since they have been deserted and are in a ruined condition. Modern villa-residences are numerous, and sheltered within well-stocked demesnes or lawns, handsomely ornamented with trees of fine growth. These houses are usually tenanted by the resident proprietor or gentleman-farmer, who gives employment to the cottier peasant and his family; while the farmers manage their several holdings with skill and industry. To such economical and thrifty habits, however, there are some exceptions, which must always be the case, as the dispositions of men are so differently directed. Moreover, it must be stated, that several of the Tipperary gentry and landlords have been kind and indulgent to their tenantry and dependents, so as to merit respect and affection from them; while the reciprocal relations existing between both classes were established by fair dealing and good feeling, which differences of creed or politics never disturbed.

Within our own generation, the social life of Tipperary was peculiar, and influenced much by the conditions of land-holding, which set all chance of improvement at defiance. As in all other parts of Ireland, the owners of real estate never considered it their duty to expend money on the building of houses suitable for holdings, to fence or preserve boundaries of fields, at their own expense, or to effect any arrangement, that might add sightliness and permanent value to their lands; as a matter of course, and with few exceptions, the tenants were allowed to occupy the thatched dwellings erected by their predecessors on the farm, or put up by themselves, and in which every plan dictated by taste and comfort must be set at nought and sacrificed to cheapness and emergency, while their fields were only half-cultivated and left nearly in their natural state, for want of means to deepen or fertilize the soil. Fox hunting, racing and field sports were the chief occupations of the resident gentry; while the owners of large estates lived abroad, scarcely ever visiting those places, from which their rents had been drawn, and with little knowledge of the persons or habits of their tenants.

Many of the gentry or their progenitors had lived in a style too extravagant for their incomes; heavy mortgages were on their estates; the rents which were fairly moderate under former leases, on their expiration, were arbitrarily raised; as grand jurors and magistrates they had absolute power to regulate the statute laws, so as to suit their inclinations or convenience; to question their authority or its exercise was deemed an insolence and a practice not to be tolerated. Constant communications were interchanged between themselves and the authorities at Dublin Castle;

the informations of abandoned and perjured informers were forwarded just as these were inclined to trade on the fears and prejudices of their patrons, while the public money was furnished in return and secretly distributed, to keep such wretches in pay. The rents were rigorously exacted, the law of distress or eviction being invoked, in too many instances, to intensify the bitterness, which existed between the owners and cultivators of the soil, and often at times when unexpected difficulties arose to prevent the exact fulfilment of a contract.

Under such conditions the tenants had no motive nor heart for highly cultivating their farms or improving their dwellings and out-offices. Nay more : it was their interest and policy to appear poorly clothed, to hoard their money in an unproductive manner as provision or marriage portions for sons or daughters, while their dietary though plain was abundant and nutritious, but rarely consisting of animal food. The hovels of agricultural labourers were wretched in the extreme, and their lives were eked out in a miserable state of unrest and anxiety, without any reasonable hope of bettering their condition. Oftentimes seasons proved unfavourable, and crops failed—sometimes in succession ; unforeseen calamities frequently rendered it difficult to meet the gale-day ; nevertheless, agents, bailiffs and rent-warners were exacting, and evictions followed to such an extent as to excite evil passions and to disturb social relations. Agrarian outrages and murders were frequently the result, and in those times, Tipperary had acquired an evil repute from prejudiced persons, who had not cared closely to examine the origin and condition of existing affairs.

The first great check given to the ascendancy party in Tipperary was when the Melbourne administration came into power, and appointed Lord Mulgrave Irish Viceroy, with Lord Morpeth, Chief Secretary, and Thomas Drummond, Under Secretary for Ireland. The latter was a Scotchman, but long resident in the country and thoroughly conversant with the dependent condition of the people, as also with the power and proclivities of their oppressors. Between both classes, he was resolved to keep the balance of justice and protection even ; yet, such a course of proceeding was bitterly resented and violently impeached by the landlords and the magistrates, who called for police, for coercive measures, and powers to prosecute domiciliary searches, urging constant exaggerated representations of outrage and intimidation, which were completely at variance with official information received by the government. However, it was well known, that those clamours proceeded from factions and party motives, to preserve their own irresponsible privileges, to resist any measures for the abolition of Tithes, or to prevent the introduction of a Poor Law, which should oblige the levying of a rate for support of the poor on land-owners. The restraints imposed on Orangeism —then declared to be illegal—was bitterly resented ; while charges were made, that the General Association of O'Connell was allowed to send his pacificators in every direction, where crime required to be repressed, and to carry on an agitation openly and constitutionally for the redress of existing grievances.

At a meeting of Tipperary magistrates held in Cashel, April 7th, 1838, on the occasion of Mr. Austin Cooper's murder, a representation was made to His Excellency Earl Mulgrave, that neither life nor property was safe in that part of the country, and that juries were intimidated at trials of the incriminated from returning just verdicts. An inquiry was instituted to ascertain what evidence could be adduced to establish the truth of such charges ; and in a celebrated letter, written by Thomas Drummond to the Earl of Donoughmore, Lord Lieutenant of the County, and dated Dublin Castle, 22nd May 1838, the statements made were entirely disproved, while returns of the police showed that crime had decreased, although the number of ejectments in 1837 was not less than double the number of these in 1833. However, the sorest reflection on the memorialists was that contained in the celebrated axiom then introduced ; " Property has its duties as well as its rights ; to the neglect of those duties in times past is mainly to be ascribed that diseased state of society in which such crimes take their rise ; and it is not in the enactment or enforcement of statutes of extraordinary severity, but chiefly in the better and more faithful performance of those duties, and the more enlightened and humane exercise of those rights, that a permanent remedy for such disorders is to be sought." The reflections contained in this letter were such, that the Lord Lieutenant and magistrates of Tipperary studiously suppressed it, until afterwards brought to light in the Committee moved for by Lord Roden in the House of Lords, and appointed to inquire into the nature and causes of Irish disturbances.

With a gentleman, who lived in this part of Tipperary, we were intimate; and on one of our visits to his residence, we remained some days, so as to take short excursions or walks through that neighbourhood, with which he was quite familiar. Mr. R—— was very popular, and although renting the house and farm where he lived, he had lately come into possession of a handsome property, purchased in the Encumbered Estates' Court, and which was then tenanted by some dozen or more of comfortable farmers. These he was in the habit of constantly visiting, in their houses and in the fields, aiding them with his sage advice, and through his shrewd observations giving them many useful hints regarding the proper management and cultivation of land, as also in the rearing of cattle and stock. We were pleased to observe the cordial relations existing between himself and the tenants, who seemed willing enough to adopt any suggestions he made, and which they knew to have been prompted by good sense and a desire for their interests and welfare.

Before he had become a landed proprietor, Mr. R—— was agent for a lady, the owner of a considerable estate, which adjoined his own, and of which his homestead and farm formed a portion. During the most disturbed times in Tipperary, he was obliged to manage that property, so as to secure the rents and to receive them in a bulk sum or by instalments for its owner, to keep up good relations between herself and the tenants, and still more, to direct the operations on his own large farm, which, as a principle of policy, he held at a high rent. He related many anecdotes of an exceedingly interesting character, which served to furnish an idea regarding the life-conditions of which he had experience, and which proved sufficiently how difficult and troublesome these were in many instances. Nevertheless, he had ready resources of thought to cope with them.

By way of illustrating the subject of conversation, he led the writer to a farmer's house on the road-side, and near an old ruinous mansion, that formerly belonged to the celebrated Sir Toby Butler, in the beginning of the last century. The farmer, an elderly man, was busily engaged at that time in getting his stacks of grain erected in the haggard, and no sooner did he see Mr. R—— approach, than he hastened down from the stack, and with demonstrations of cordial welcome, he came to meet us. A hearty shake of the hand was given to each visitor, and we were invited to enter the house. There we were pressed very earnestly to take some refreshment, and we chose glasses of delicious fresh milk for a beverage, although strongly recommended by our host in the first instance, to have something still stronger from a black bottle which he placed on the table. Friendly inquiries and conversation ensued, and when information was given and obtained, on subjects of personal and common interest, we took leave of our good-natured host, and expressed our sense of his kindly hospitality.

As we walked along, Mr. R—— gave me the following account regarding the personal relations between our entertainer and himself. In the troubled times, he was one of those tenants who fell into arrear, and while negligent and unthrifty in the business of farming, he was rather too social on the occasions of attending fairs and markets—often returning home in a state of excitement and intoxication. Such habits grew upon him rather than decreased. Like most persons so addicted, he was hardly aware, that he indulged to any great degree; although his friends, and among them Mr. R——, often advised him to avoid drinking companions, to keep much at home, and to devote more of his time to industry and economy. All this advice seemed to produce no change in his mode of life, and by degrees he fell into arrear when the rent became due, and still always held out promises and the hope that it should be paid at a more convenient time. He was warned of the consequences, should he not redeem those promises, and in the most friendly manner; yet still deeper did he sink into debt, with all who might trust him, and the less was presented any prospect of clearing off his arrears. At last, he was informed by Mr. R—— that a process of ejectment from his holding must be taken out against him, as no effort had been made to fulfil his obligations to that lady, upon whose estate he lived. Notice was accordingly served, but still no sign of settlement was forthcoming.

One morning, Mr. R—— received a letter, badly spelled, and through the Post Office. It warned him personally not to imitate the example of other tyrannical agents in Tipperary, as otherwise he would be visited or attacked by "the boys," when he least expected it, and that vengeance would be taken on him, for turning a poor man out from his house and home. As an illustration to this threat, the sketch of a coffin was rudely traced at the bottom, and the document was signed "Terry Alt." Now it did not require the shrewdness of Mr. R—— to divine the quarter whence the missive came, or to infer from its wording the identity of its writer. Accordingly, taking the letter with him, Mr. R—— visited the home of the tenant in arrear, who exhibited signs of visible embarrassment when he appeared, yet thinking to conceal it by an air of affected indifference. However, his visitor began to address him in a good-humoured manner, and in such terms as these. "Paddy," for so he was called, "I always thought you were my good friend, and that you had more sense than to write the foolish letter, I got from you this morning. Didn't you know, I had only to place it in the hands of the police, to bring you into trouble; but, as I completely disregard whatever is stated in a letter to which the writer is afraid or ashamed to add his name, and as I well knew from the phrases it contained, that you had written it under the influence of drink, I now come to put it into your own hands, to do whatever you please with it. However, you must know, that I cannot give you any favour, but what the most honest and industrious tenants on the estate deserve; and moreover, my duty to the lady who owns it demands, that if you are to hold the farm, the rent must be paid, especially as you well know, that for much better land than I cultivate, you are not charged per acre half what I very willingly and punctually pay her. Now, like a good fellow, as I know you to be, let me advise you to mend your habits of life, to take the Temperance pledge, and to mind the business of your farm for the future. If you do this, as I require you, I shall still give you some further time for the payment of your rent arrears, which I will take from you in convenient instalments, and help you in every way to be as independent and comfortable as are the other honest and industrious tenants, who all pay whenever the gale falls due. Now, as you have done a foolish act, of which you should feel thoroughly ashamed, none shall be the wiser of what has passed between you and me, in this instance; here is your wretched letter, and keep or show it to others, just as you think best." During the whole of this discourse, the incriminated man coloured deeply, for he was agitated with contending emotions. Then taking the letter he tore it into small pieces, which he scattered to the winds, as he replied: "Mr. R—— you're the gintleman I always knew you to be, and I'll folly your advice, and pay you every penny of the rent I owe. Only let nobody know I was such a blasted scoundrel as to write that letther, and all on account of that damned dhrink, and the devil a dhrop more of it I'll ever take, for it's the ruination of us all." As he spoke these words, his eyes filled with tears, and he pressed Mr. R——'s hand in token of gratitude when he was about to leave.

That gentleman assured me, our friend thenceforth became a different manner of man, in the latter part of his life. He fulfilled the promise made to take Father Mathew's pledge of Total Abstinence from the curate of his parish ; he became most regular in the discharge of his Christian duties ; he acquired habits of industry and thrift ; while in due course, and with some indulgence granted, he wiped out all arrears of rent due, and never omitted to pay half-yearly his current account. He was then in comfortable circumstances, and greatly esteemed by all his neighbours. Parting with his agency lessened not the interest Mr. R—— took in that farmer's concerns, but none were conversant with that accident, which was the turning point in his conversion ; for the writer was assured, it had been kept between them as a profound secret, and only then revealed, because it was not likely to cause any prejudice to the character or honour of either party. Both have passed from life many years back ; but a record of that incident illustrates a peculiar phase of Irish social customs, and serves to prove, that a thoughtful act done or a kind word seasonably spoken to the rudest peasant, may reach the soul and conscience of one, whose evil habits of living had been considered too deep-rooted and inveterate for reformation.

The writer was brought with some friends about the same time to the residence of a gentleman in that neighbourhood, and then an absentee from a property offered for sale. The house stood within a handsome demesne, and Mr. R—— was intimate with the owner in former days. We knocked at the front entrance, and after a little delay, a window opened on the upper story. A woman who was the sole occupant having reconnoitred the besieging force, and seeing there were ladies of the party, came down to admit us within the mansion. Mr. R—— spoke to her in a friendly manner, inquired about her name—for the accent assured us she was an English woman—her length of residence in Ireland, and the name of her husband, then engaged on some out-door business—for work seemed to be altogether suspended around that beautiful place. Then

G

having inquired about her master, and thus ingratiated himself into favour with the domestic, we were shown through the deserted apartments. Last of all, we lingered for a time in the drawingroom and diningroom, on the ground-floor, where Mr. R—— had formerly passed many a social evening with the owner of the mansion. He then amused the house-keeper, as he did ourselves, by going over to the window-shutters, which were elegantly pannelled and decorated in front, but when opened from their recesses, one by one, they displayed a heavy mass of iron-sheathing behind, which was certainly quite capable of repelling any bullet of lesser size and momentum than a cannon-shot. The same defensive armour guarded all the windows around the lower story, while the doors were secured by massive chains and bolts within their several lockers.

Having had a little badinage with the English woman, whose imagination must have been considerably wrought upon by her surroundings, and whose Saxon prejudices were deep-rooted against the Celtic population—probably from some of the wild tales she had heard of Tipperary life—she very freely confessed to us, that she was heartily tired of Ireland, and that she wished greatly her return to England. Mr. R—— tried in vain to assure her, that if she cared to cultivate the acquaintance of the farmers and peasants in the neighbourhood, she would find them both friendly and hospitable—all the more as she was a stranger to their country and its usages. He took leave of her by giving his name and address, with an invitation to her husband and herself to visit Mr. and Mrs. R——, —who were of our party—at their own house, and where they should have a warm welcome. The woman expressed herself thankful for this kindness, and promised so soon as she conveniently could to avail of the invitation.

On our way homewards, we learned that the owner of that estate had a constant fear of being attacked by night, in that lonely mansion; and in the troubled times, it was garrisoned by a police force sent from Dublin Castle for his protection. In such contingency, while the lower story of his house had been prepared for defence, in the manner related, he designed to fire from the upper windows on any number of the Terry Alts, who might assemble to attack him. His morbid apprehensions were not realized, however, but he lived in a state of terror from some warnings he had received, and which for aught could be known were sent to him by magisterial spies and pensioned informers of the lowest character.

Since that time, the conditions of land-tenure have been ameliorated, but they are still far from having reached that degree of perfection to which they might be brought, by just and wise remedial measures of legislation. Several of the former tenants-at-will have become purchasers, and the proprietors of their former rented farms; the value of land-rental has been determined by arbitration or judicial decision, for a term of years, between landlords and occupiers. However artificial, anomalous and imperfect such a practice may be, expediency required it, in the case of their actual relations; yet, until indefeasible titles to land are ascertained by judicial investigation, confirmed by decree and registration, with a system of free sale and ready transfer, while through State-aided purchase, by loans rendered remunerative to government and occupying purchasers, no radical reform of Irish land tenure can well be effected.

A most objectionable practice still prevails in our land courts, when properties are brought into them for sale by their owners, or when necessity calls for the foreclosure of mortgages, in such a manner. In all these cases, if only to uphold the value of land, sale to the highest *bona fide* bidder should be made absolute and without reserve. Moreover, a standing rule of court should be, to sell such properties, and in separate occupied lots, where they are situated, and where their value can best be ascertained by intending purchasers, at or before the date of sale. There the actual tenant can afford to outbid all competitors in price, since he receives a government loan for the purchase, which he will not fail to redeem, with principal and interest. To pretend that a property does not realize its full selling value under such conditions is only to deceive bidders, uselessly invited to a pretended public sale, and to institute *mock auctions*. The result of withdrawing an estate or any of its lots from absolute sale, because the expectations of an owner, or a mortgagee, or mortgageor, be not realized, tends only to diminish still more the value of such land held over; since if unencumbered or mortgaged, law expenses must necessarily be incurred, lawyers and agents must be paid, and still have their own private interest in the withdrawal and continuous mismanagement of a deteriorating property until it is finally parted with, by a succeeding sale in the public court, or by private purchase, and at a less remunerative price than could have been realized in the first instance. However, it should prove an almost endless task to comment on the many anomalies and defects of land legislation and land tenure, that still require to be remedied, both in the interests of landlords and tenants; nor at present do we find any serious effort made to remove the artificial and legal difficulties that remain, and which have served to disturb and distract our existing unsocial relations. Yet, it is not only a possible, but quite a practical, business, and a duty still to be accomplished, before harmony can be wholly restored, and land-tenure assimilated to the more rational, simple, and perfect conditions, that regulate it in nearly all the civilized nations and states of the Eastern and Western Hemisphere. The most conservative countries for social peace and order are those, where absolute proprietors are most numerous; and, in them also must be the fewest absentees, who spend the resources of a country beyond its proper bounds, thus largely contributing to its impoverishment and distress.

No. XXVI.

The Battle of the Cats.

LEGEND OF IRISHTOWN, COUNTY OF DUBLIN.

> " The dreadful toils of raging Mars I write,
> The springs of contest, and the fields of fight;
> . . . .
> Not louder tumults shook Olympus' tow'rs,
> When earth-born giants dar'd immortal pow'rs.
> These equal acts an equal glory claim,
> And thus the Muse records the tale of fame.
> . . . .
> All dreaded these, and dreadful o'er the rest,
> The potent warriors of the tabby vest."
> —Thomas Parnell; *Battle of the Frogs and Mice*, Book i.

IN the mediæval times, when the Palesmen were pent within their walled cities and towns throughout Ireland, and when their gates were jealously closed at night against the Irish enemy; yet were to be found groups of shielings and huts in the immediate vicinity, tenanted by a colony of native craftsmen, sutlers and labourers, who ministered to the wants of those burghers engaged in trades or manufactures. Such villages, as distinguished from houses within the walls and inhabited by the English or Anglo-Irish civilians, were generally known in the aggregate by the designation of Irishtown. As no municipal laws or even proprietorial direction restrained such denizens, so were their cabins and lanes usually detached and scattered about in the most varied forms, and at every imaginable diversity of angle, covering waste spaces, and with hardly any gardens attached. Traces of the original artless grouping may be detected in many existing survivals; and as suburbs are only the parasites of cities and towns, those offshoots hardly ever keep proportionate pace with the relative improvements of the latter. Especially was it so in Ireland, where social conditions were strained and antagonistic; race and prejudice conflicting, mutual jealousy and mistrust predominating.

Such an Irishtown as we have described has long existed, without the municipal boundaries of Dublin, yet retaining its name on the sea-shore, and near the harbour entrance. For some centuries past, a primitive thatched chapel stood on the site of Mearns' buildings, known as St. Mary's Terrace, and this served as a place of worship for the Roman Catholic inhabitants of the surrounding districts. Even was it resorted to by many of the Dublin people, when no public church was allowed to be erected within the city. During the reign of Queen Anne, the present Protestant Church was erected; and, at that time, the River Dodder did not join the River Liffey, but rather formed a *delta*, before it reached Irishtown, while one of its branches ran out upon the strand a little to the north, and the other emptied into the sea immediately behind the present Star of the Sea Catholic Church. Irishtown was then an island, but connected by a bridge with the city. Towards the close of last century, the Dodder was diverted by a sharp bend to form the Grand Canal Basin, and since then, it has made its exit directly north to the River Liffey.

There are those living, who recollect the small mound-like appearance presented on that site, where the Star of the Sea Church now stands. Both that piece of ground and Leahy Terrace, on the opposite side of the lately-formed road to the strand, were a field, usually cultivated and planted with potatoes, by the former proprietor of Cranfield's Baths. These have since disappeared. That site also formed an embankment of the Dodder, at one of its branches, and the sub-soil is curiously composed of coarse boulder-gravel, layers of fine sea-sand, with quantities of cockle and other shell-fish relics abounding. That spot was then termed Scald Hill. Near it, on the strand, was Waxes' Dargle; because it is said the impecunious shoemakers, who could not afford to take an outside jaunting-car to the romantic glen near Bray, were able to avail of the twopenny jarvey drive from Dublin to Irishtown, on Easter and Whit Monday, there to dance the merry jig or reel, with their wives, daughters or sweethearts, as the case might be. Of course the local connection with the Wicklow Dargle was only nominal, and the scenery remotely fanciful.

Somewhat removed, and a little above the Dodder cut, was Haig's Brewery, occupying the present site of the Lansdowne-road Station on the Dublin, Wicklow and Wexford Railway. There is still a deep trench on the river-side, with indications of arches now closed up under the elevated railway embankment. These show where the stored waters above made their course for escape to the running waters below, while the mashing process went on within the Brewery. Such topographical sketches may be necessary to give the reader at a distance some general idea of the ground over which we are to travel. Besides, most judicious historians are accustomed to describe the general features of a battle-field before relating the incidents of an encounter. As the scenes have since changed very considerably, and as a remarkable contest has to be recorded in the present legend, with an introduction of the narrator —happily a living authority in the neighbourhood—so may all the particulars be still verified by the curious investigator of folk-lore traditions.

One of the best, most honest-minded and most industrious of men is John Kearns of Irishtown, and while engaged with his well-cared horse in drawing sand for some building improvements at the Star of the Sea Church, he put the following query to the superintendent: "Did you iver hear the name of this place forty years ago?" The uninformed person replied, that he did not. "Thin it wint by the name of Scald Hill, afore Dean O'Connell the Parish Priest got the site from the Hon. Sydney Herbert, and thin he built the Star. And I'll tell you besides a stranger thing nor that; for it was here the great Battle of the Cats took place, now a long time ago, and whin Father Corrigan was curate in the Parish, afore it was divided into three, Donnybrook, Haddingdon-road and Irishtown."

This was an item of information never before conveyed to the superintendent and his men; so John Kearns was eagerly pressed to tell the story, and all present listened with great attention while he proceeded.

"Well thin, one fine summer evenin' towards dusk, when Father Corrigan was comin' home from a sick call to Irishtown along Simonscourt-road—it was a lonely place thin and few houses along the way—he obsarved an exthrordinary number of cats movin' along, and mewin' as if they were grumblin' to one another, and he wondhered where they all kem from, bud he saw they were on the way ahead. Whin he came to Scald Hill, he found it all covered widh other cats, and many were still comin' from different quarthers. There they all set up a thremindous howlin' and screechin'. He thought it mighty quare intirely, but he was tired, and wint home to bed. No sooner was he there, than the noise kep' on at such a rate, that niver a wink he could sleep until afther midnight. Thin the ruction seemed to be over, and he fell asleep, and didn't waken until mornin'.

"Shure enough, ivery one of the Irishtown people hard the racket as well as Father Corrigan; bud early next day, word kem to him that the whole of Scald Hill was covered with the dead bodies of cats. They had a great battle over night, and kilt one another in hapes, nor was any of thim known to lave that place alive. Well, so great was the number, that it took six of Haig's Brewery carts to remove and bury them durin' the day; and the like of that battle was niver known afore nor since, for the cats kem from all parts of Ireland."

That was a wonderful story, indeed, but one of the hearers inquired how John Kearns was able to prove that the cats came from all parts of Ireland. "I'll tell you the rason," he replied, "one of thim was found wid a brass collar around its nick, and that had the name of a Galway lady graved on it, so you may be shure whin that was the case, others must have come from places quite as far away."

Whether the inference warranted the conclusion or not may be questioned; but to have placed upon record such a narrative, relating to the earlier part of the present century and surviving to its close, must add one more to the quaint old popular traditions, now fast fading from the recollections and grasp of curious or interested folk-lorists.

No. XXVII.

Humours and Humorists.

LEGENDS OF BALLYROAN, QUEEN'S COUNTY.

"Yet he was kind ; or if severe in aught,
The love he bore to learning was in fault ;
. . . .
While words of learned length, and thundering sound,
Amazed the gazing rustics ranged around ;
And still they gazed, and still the wonder grew,
That one small head could carry all he knew.
But past is all his fame: the very spot,
Where many a time he triumphed, is forgot."
—Oliver Goldsmith's *Deserted Village*.

On the former mail-coach road between Dublin and Cork is situated the village of Ballyroan, giving name also to a parish, having an area of 9,682 acres, in the barony of Cullinagh, Queen's County. That it is an ancient town, formerly under the jurisdiction of the O'Mores, chieftains of Leix, can scarcely be questioned ; for a very remarkable high conical and artificial moat is still to be seen in the immediate vicinity, probably sustaining some sort of fortification on its summit in former times. A winding path-way affords gradual ascent from below, and trees have been planted along its sides. The earliest known Map of Leix we possess is that to be found in the Cottonian collection of the British Museum, supposed to have been made about 1563, in the reign of Queen Elizabeth. That it is misleading, both in topographical admeasurements and local denominations, must be admitted. Even a copy of that Map, with the names more clearly and correctly written, and now preserved in Trinity College Library, Dublin, labours under similar defects. Although Ballyroan is doubtless to be found marked by some one or other of the castellated figures, near to Coulinogh Mountain ; yet, under the blundering designations supplied by the Saxon draftsman, it is quite impossible to define there with accuracy its exact position. However, after the subjugation of Leix, and when the Hetheringtons became possessors of Ballyroan, it began to grow into a considerable town; and, in 1686, Alderman Preston of Dublin founded there a Protestant Grammar School, endowed with lands in Cappaloughlan, which he bequeathed for its support, and assigned to trustees for its maintenance. In like manner, he founded a Protestant school at Navan, allowing £35, Irish money, as salary for the schoolmaster. Altogether 1,737 acres of land were granted to carry out the bequest of that testator.

The principal of the school at Ballyroan was a graduate of Trinity College, Dublin, whose salary we may suppose to have varied at times, according to the revenue drawn from the estate, not always judiciously managed by the trustees. From Alderman Preston's foundation, the school was to be aided with £52, Irish money, *per annum*. A suit respecting his endowment was commenced in 1734, and for seventy-four years afterwards, the law costs amounted to £3,000. In the Irish Parliament, abuses connected with that endowment were fully set forth before the Committee of Inquiry into abused charities in the House of Lords of 1764; as also before the Education Commissioners of 1791, and before the Royal Commissioners of 1807-12. In consequence of those abuses, a special clause was introduced into the Act of 1813, 53 George III., chap. 107, sect. 14, vesting the estate in the Commissioners of Education established under that statute.

Small and remote as it was, still Ballyroan had its celebrities in days now past, and we have only to open the pages of Sir Jonah Barrington's amusing "Personal Sketches and Recollections of his Own Times" to learn the facetious baronet's relations with its parish. The Rev. Mr. Barrett was rector there during the last century, and he was father to the celebrated and eccentric Rev. Dr. John Barrett, Vice-provost of Dublin University. On the occasion of a trial for libel in the King's Bench, happening to be counsel for Theophilus Swift defendant, Sir Jonah was engaged in the cross-examination of Dr. Barrett for more than an hour, without gaining a single point in law or logic from the learned witness he endeavoured to circumvent. At length, he thought to try cajolery and conciliation with the Vice-provost, by stating that his father had christened him Sir Jonah. "Oh! indeed," retorted Dr. Barrett, " I did not know you were a Christian." This unexpected repartee raised such a laugh among his brother barristers, and in the court, that Sir Jonah could not further proceed with his cross-examination, and his client was sentenced to twelve months' imprisonment in the gaol of Newgate.

In the year 1833, the law-suit connected with Ballyroan School concluded, having lasted for nearly 100 years; and in 1834, the writer of this notice—then a boy of thirteen—was first introduced to the principal Arthur Hutchins, an M.A. of Trinity College, Dublin, and examined by him for entrance to a Greek and Latin class. Having already received an elementary English and classical education, under a far more competent instructor, in his native town; the juvenile scholar was allowed to continue his Greek Testament and Lucian, with Virgil and Sallust as Latin authors, by a gracious permission of the head-master, as he then took care to remark. At that time, a Mr. Henderson was usher, conducting the English department in writing and arithmetic. About once a week, the Protestant curate of the parish attended to give catechetical instruction to the boys of his congregation.

At the period to which we allude, the large house in which Mr. Hutchins and his family lived was retired somewhat from the main street of the village; while on one side of it was an old-fashioned and dilapidated building, which as we conceive might have been erected about a century previous,—the original casements of doors and windows having been removed. The masonry had even crumbled away from the openings. It seemed to have been the former foundation school-house, but then, the lower door and window spaces were built up with rough masonry, in front, while the interior was choked with mortar and slates, *debris* from the fallen roof. At the rear, all the doors and windows had been built on a level with the wall, and smoothly cemented, to serve for a ball-court, near which was the boys' play-ground. The modern school-house was a presentable and comfortable two-storied house, having many rooms above and below, while its extension towards the rear was considerable. The building was then centrally placed in the town of Ballyroan. About twenty boys were boarders in that house; while an equal number of day-boys frequented the school, from the town and neighbourhood.

The master was quite an original and eccentric character, yet notwithstanding all his peculiarities, popular with his pupils and the townspeople, to whom he was a familiar and respected personage. He was advanced in years, and the father of grown sons and daughters, who lived with him. Their mother superintended the household affairs very judiciously, and was assisted in the work by some female servants. Mr. Hutchins was rather a tall man, of lithesome shape, and having a good set of features, in which seriousness and vivacity were at once blended. His motions were restless, both within and without the house, and when walking abroad his thumbs were placed in the armlets of his vest, while the tips of his fingers were continually tatooing his breast on either side. In dress he was a stylish gentleman of the olden time, wearing a long-skirted black broad-cloth frock-coat with lappels, a waistcoat and pantaloons to match, a black silk stock, with shirt collars protruding on either side of his cheeks. His shapely silk hat was worn with a jaunty air, and his boots were highly polished; but probably the most noticeable appendage of his dress was a cambric frill, snowy white, and elegantly crimped, which escaped in full display from the upper part of the vest. Altogether, he was a figure to attract very particular notice, and he had a self-satisfied air of superiority, when he appeared among his pupils or the villagers.

As became his profession, although well versed in the Greek and Latin authors, Mr. Hutchins was a pedant, fond of interlarding his vernacular conversation with classical phrases and quotations, which to him were quite in use. Whenever he desired to asseverate very strongly, or to express surprise at any statement, his usual exclamation was "By Hercules!" Hence it was the *soubriquet* by which he was called among the pupils and townspeople, but not in his own hearing; since he was too aristocratic and solemn looking, not to repel familiarity or disrespect. His manner was formal and condescendingly courteous to the humblest person who touched a hat to him in the street, or who approached, either to seek a favour, or to transact any ordinary business.

The school opened each morning about ten o'clock, and closed at three in the afternoon. The pupils for the most part were well grown lads, and many of them young men who aspired to the Catholic priesthood. Although excellent English and Classical Schools had been set up under competent instructors, in the more considerable Irish towns; yet, Catholic Colleges were then few, and only confined to some dioceses, nor had the National System of Lord Stanley made much progress to meet public requirements, or to arrest the higher educational enterprise of individual teachers. In our school of Ballyroan, a general laxity of discipline was allowed; except during the class-hours for individuals of the higher and lower grades, the other boys were mostly absent and amusing themselves in the playground, or in the fields adjoining the town, instead of preparing their coming lessons; frequently the principal was absent from the room in some other part of the house, or as often happened, sauntering about the street and gossipping with some person, as might be seen from the windows, and then all the wild spirits of the boys were in commotion to create as much confusion as possible, with all that love of mischief-making, so congenial to youths uncontrolled by the exercise of authority. Although a good classical scholar himself, still had Mr. Arthur Hutchins a defective manner for imparting instruction to tyros, being addicted to grandiloquent speech, and indulging in dissertations which his pupils could hardly comprehend, without those practical explanations suited to their age and intellectual capacity.

Withal such pomposity and high bearing, there was an undefinable simplicity of character in the man, and while he was approached with deference and respect, a latent sense of his amiable complacency and credulity caused many a practical joke to be played at his expense. Two or three small fields adjoining Ballyroan had been held by Mr. Hutchins; and these were in part under crops, and in part pasture for cows. One of his special foibles was to study farming, as if it had been a science of much importance to his establishment, and during the school-hours he wished to seek advice from boys accustomed to agricultural pursuits, even at a time which should be devoted to class and teaching. Opinions were thus elicited of a very complex and even contradictory description; while discussions were prolonged, owing to the freedom of debate invited, and to the number of pupils, who desired to spend the hours in a more agreeable round of relaxation than could be obtained from the prosecution of classical exercises. Thus many lessons were cut short, if not postponed to the day following, and the mental strain of a studious evening for the morrow was saved to the urchins for boyish sports and capricious idleness.

The boarders were all Protestants, with a single exception, and that boy had been very thoughtlessly placed by his parents or guardians under influences, not calculated to ground or direct him in Catholic doctrines and observances. Nearly all the other day-scholars were the sons of Catholic parents or friends living in the town or neighbourhood. Among the latter was the writer, who trudged each morning a distance of two miles from an old grand-uncle's house, Mr. John Lalor of Pass, and back again each evening, bearing a satchel rather heavily laden with books. In those days, it did not occur to publishers that the classics might be issued in any other form than in a complete collection of an author's works, usually enlarged with an editor's annotations; so that to carry a Delphin Virgil, M'Caul's Horace, and a Valpy's Homer, with accessories of an Eton Latin Grammar and a student's Latin Dictionary or Greek Lexicon, besides other books, was rather much of a burden for young arms and shoulders. At present, the texts read by school-boys are cheaper, issued in smaller compass, and more to serve the practical work of special study. Moreover, in districts remote from Dublin—then a great centre for the publication of school classics and mostly edited by Trinity College men—it was difficult to procure the books in use, except at high prices—even when second-hand works—and through the book-pedlars, who travelled with cart-loads of a varied assortment through the provincial towns and villages. Many of our school-books were borrowed from friends that had used them, and not for the first time, as they had an antiquated imprint and a soiled appearance, while the texts or margins were interlined by comments, glosses, and *memoranda* of scholars belonging to a former generation. Through frequent use or want of care, the covers were worn or patched in most instances, and no uniform set of an author studied was ever to be seen in the hands of our class-mates. Our master's books were of a similar description, well thumbed and interlined, as we had frequent opportunities for observing, while he was engaged in hearing our lessons.

Some of the day scholars, more fully grown and knowing than the writer, joined him on the road to Ballyroan, and were always his companions on the way homewards, until they dropped off one by one at their several houses. For some time after my first acquaintance and arrival, they had a standing joke at my expense. A merry farmer's wife on the road-side used to accost us with some cheery remark; but taking advantage of unsuspecting innocence, and observing the load of books which the little fellow carried over his shoulder, she inquired in a seemingly serious manner if she might be permitted to place a dozen of eggs in my satchel, "like a good boy," and bring them to a huxter living in Ballyroan. The request was an exceedingly distressing one, at the time, as under the embarrassment of contending thoughts and emotions, it afflicted me to be disobliging towards a person so agreeable to myself and companions, while ashamed to be considered by them an egg-deliverer, and to one unknown to me, not to speak of the difficulty of preserving such a number unbroken, and my books from the danger of being besmeared with the contents. However, having passively assented to the proposal, but in no very cheerful humour, the eggs were collected, and the mouth of the satchel opened to the great amusement of all present; when to my great relief, the jovial housewife said she thought better of the project, and that she should send them in a basket by some one else who passed that way. For a long time afterwards, a cause for deep concern lest such a proposal might be renewed was excited, and my roguish comrades played on my fears very frequently, by calling out the farmer's wife, to ask if she had any more eggs for the shop in Ballyroan. At length it began to dawn on my comprehension, from the nods and winks interchanged, that all was intended merely as a hoax on a being so credulous and foolish as myself.

In those days, also, a teacher of far humbler pretensions than Mr. Hutchins kept a small boys' and girls' school, in one of the cabins which were placed at the entrance to Ballyroan, and those were taught the rudiments of spelling, reading, writing and arithmetic. The master's name was Charley Duffy, and besides these elementary branches, being a very correct man, he taught the little creatures under his charge polite behaviour towards all well dressed persons met by them in the village or on the road; so that, bareheaded and barefooted, for the most part, the boys made a low bow in passing with a pull of their front locks, as a mark of obeisance, while the girls gave a stiff jerk downwards, by way of curtsey. And as Ballyroan lay on the high road from Dublin to Cork, so Peter Purcell's mail-coach passed it twice daily, morning and evening, usually filled with well dressed passengers, inside and outside. These ladies and gentlemen were especially the objects of greatest respect and consideration, while the young urchins felt greatly delighted when their awkward salutes were politely returned.

The town of Ballyroan had a motley population, and in some of the thatched cabins that garnished its outlets were varlets, that led rather idle lives, doing job works occasionally, but for the most part living on their wits, or stealing from their more industrious neighbours. Poor Mr. Hutchins knew from experience, that after reaping his croft of wheat or oats, it was necessary to have a day and night watchman to guard it from the raiders. One Johnny Whelan had been engaged for that purpose; but notwithstanding, it was reported to the owner, that the latter was often lured away by some village "divarsion," which caused him to neglect his night vigils, and that in consequence, many of the wheaten stooks had been carried off. Before his kitchen-maids, Mr. Hutchins had declared by Hercules, that his determination was to go out that very night and see if the guardian to whom he paid regular wages had been at his post. Now it so happened, that Johnny was a suitor for the hand of one among those girls, and he was duly informed by her of the master's purpose. Johnny Whelan took measures accordingly, and armed with a toughly knotted blackthorn stick, he contrived to keep himself concealed behind a high ditch well covered with brambles. When midnight was approaching, Mr. Hutchins sallied forth to inspect the field, where the stooks of corn were ranged in rows, but no sign of a watchman could be discovered. By way of test, he advanced stealthily to one of the stooks, and inserting his shoulders beneath the sheaves began to bear it away; but almost immediately afterwards, Johnny Whelan was on his track, and soon his vociferous shout was heard, with a hard thwack of the blackthorn on the moving stook. "You bloody vagabone! is that the way you come to steal the honest gintleman's corn? But I'll beat your brains out, you scamp of perdition, before ye lave the field. Take that"—whack—"and that" —whack—"and that"—whack. For a time, the blows rained incessantly on the pyramid of wheat; while from underneath his frail armour of straw, a voice ejaculated in frighted and piteous tones: "Johnny, Johnny Whelan, it's

I, Arthur Hutchins, it's I, Arthur Hutchins; stop, stop, for God's sake!" Still more vigorously fell the strokes of the blackthorn, and still more menacingly rose the voice: "I'll tache ye, my good fellow, to keep betther hours nor this, and brake every bone in yer body, afore I give you up to the polis!" Having well thrashed the sheaves of wheat, and staggered the bearer, whom he affected not to know; at last, Johnny Whelan allowed him to protrude the head from its covering, and there by the misty light stood Mr. Hutchins fully revealed. "Oh, Sir," cried Johnny, "I beg a thousand pardons, but I never suspected that you could have come here to steal away your own sheaves!" The employer felt humiliated beyond measure, when he was enabled to fully extricate himself; yet, as he could not find the watchman neglectful of his trust, he in turn was obliged to beg the servant's pardon, for entertaining unworthy suspicions of his fidelity. Mr. Hutchins reasoned as a philosopher and logician. With aching arms and shoulders, he returned home, leaving Johnny Whelan to continue his vigil on the field, and triumphant in that worthy's own estimation. Thenceforward, he rose in the master's confidence, and on all occasions he was highly praised for his honest and faithful discharge of duties entrusted to him. The story got abroad, however, and to all others in the town of Ballyroan, Whelan was regarded as "a lad"—the expression intimating, that he was ever ready to indulge in a practical joke, and that no great reliance could be placed on his earnestness or sincerity.

Another anecdote of a nearly similar character must here be related. Those same fields were more a source of annoyance than of profit to Mr. Arthur Hutchins. Among the wild boys of Ballyroan was a tinker, who rambled in a wide circuit from the village with an ass and cart filled with tinware, as also with implements and materials to mend pots, kettles and pans at the farmers' houses. When at home, the ass was brought out to graze on the road-side, wherever the grass appeared growing plentifully in the ditches or under the hedge-rows; but occasionally, the wily owner, who was on the look out, opened a gate and introduced the poor animal to more luxuriant pasturage, or mayhap watched his opportunity to take an armful of hay or oats from the field to regale him. Now Mr. Hutchins' field was convenient as any other to turn the donkey loose in, and so frequent were the trespasses reported, that after repeated warnings and without any satisfactory result, the principal of our school, taking one of his sons along with him, sallied forth and surprised the ass, *flagrante delicto*. He expressed a firm resolution to have the offending animal put into pound—the gaol then destined for the detention of all such delinquents. Accordingly, the donkey was driven out of the field by the master and his well grown son, while the former, in his usual pompous manner, and with his thumbs in the armlets of his vest, nodded his head very ominously. Full of wrath against the vagrant owner and his beast, Mr. Hutchins exclaimed: "By Hercules, my good ass, you have fallen into severe hands!" However, the tinker was on the alert. Jumping over the road-side fence and flourishing a stout *kippeen*, he faced the principal and his attendant in a threatening manner, crying out, "No, but by Hercules, you have fallen into severe hands, Mr. Hutchins, if you put the poor creathur into pound. It would be the manest action of your life, Sir, bekase she took a little mouthful of grass from your field, whin she saw the gate open. The creathur meanin' no harm in life, would have come out of her own accord in a few minutes, and now to deprive a poor man of his baste and his manes of livin' would make you the laughin' stock of the whole town and neighbourhood. So you had better think well of it, and let her alone!" As he spoke in angry tones, and thus pleaded for the poor innocent donkey, the son's resentment was sufficiently manifested; but never distinguished for personal bravery, Mr. Hutchins began to tremble violently, affrighted at the menacing aspect of that tinker, who played alternately on his fears and his reason. He hastily capitulated, and surrendered the ass to the importunate and impudent rascal to whom it belonged. Returning to town, abashed in the presence of his plucky son, who was ready for a rude encounter, Mr. Hutchins never afterwards attempted to restrain the ass, although a continuous trespasser, lest he might again arouse the resentment of its wicked owner.

One of the singular characters that still survived in Ballyroan was Jemmy Doxey, already celebrated as having figured in Sir Jonah Barrington's original pages. It must be remarked, that in some later editions the anecdote has been omitted. On a certain occasion, when the Queen's County gentry were engaged in the chase of Reynard, one of the number got a fall from his horse, and was so stunned thereby, that he lay senseless and motionless for a considerable time. Among the sons of Hubert was a doctor from Mountrath, who in the general confusion dismounted with other members of the hunt, whose sympathies and assistance were excited on behalf of their prostrate companion. The doctor approached, and having felt his pulse and otherwise hastily examined the gentleman's body, shook his head with emotion, and at once professionally pronounced him dead. In turn, however, Jemmy Doxey approached, and felt the pulse. Turning to the crowd of hunters around, he declared there was still life in the prostrate form, and by way of proof—drawing a flask of brandy which he uncorked from his side pocket—applied it in the first instance to the gentleman's nose. This had such an effect, that his eyes opened to the delight of all present,—the doctor alone excepted; and a second application to the patient's mouth, into which some of the liquor was poured, proved so effective, that his consciousness gradually returned. Soon was he enabled to rise and thank his benefactor for the timely service rendered. The result of all was, that the gentleman, thus quite restored and to the great delight of his friends. the doctor was discredited before most of his influential patrons present, and especially when the story became generally known; while Jemmy Doxey's fame spread abroad, distinguished alike by his forethought and skill in the application of a remedy, equally gratifying to the taste and conducive to the restoration of a fellow-creature *in extremis*.

This humorist lived with his son Hector Doxey of Ballyroan, and he had a grandson, a day scholar in our school, which circumstance furnished a pretext for frequent visits to us, during the hour set apart for luncheon and recreation. He was evidently fond of the boys' society, and having no settled occupation, as a gentleman at large he amused us exceedingly with his antics and funny stories, as also with a number of hunting and comic songs, which were current in his prime of life; nor were these all of the most delicate sentiment, as sung by the sporting gentry of his early days. The townspeople used to designate him "a divartin' vagabond," and of course such a character always enjoyed a great measure of popularity. Whenever he appeared in the ball-court, all play was suspended, and a group of the boys was immediately formed around the old man, whose powers of mimicry and grimace were really surprising, while these were sure to elicit shouts of laughter and approbation from his youthful auditors.

Among the denizens of Ballyroan then living, and commemorated by Sir Jonah Barrington, was Moll Harding, a woman possessing in a remarkable degree a fund of genuine humour and a readiness of repartee, not sufficiently illustrated in the single anecdote related of her by that rollicking writer. As frequently seen and heard by ourselves, although much advanced beyond middle life at the time, she presented a full and portly figure, a florid and clear complexion, with masculine bearing and gestures, features characteristic of resolution and self-assertion, eyes sparkling with intelligence and expressive of shrewdness, her whole countenance and manner indicating business capacity, and a long experience through life with people of all grades in the social ladder. During earlier years and while her husband lived, she managed the public hostelry of Ballyroan, at which the mail-coach from Dublin to Cork there changed horses, and with which a considerable car and posting establishment was then connected. Besides, Mr. and Mrs. Harding held a large farm adjoining the town. Both were in very comfortable circumstances, before and after retiring from the hotel business. At that period of active life, Dame Quickley herself evinced not greater aptitude, in the management of her hostelry, and in humouring the varied characters she was obliged to entertain, than did the hostess of Ballyroan with the motley gang that served within her inn, or without in the stables. Indeed, Sir John Falstaff should have met his match better in the wordy contest, had he to deal with Mistress Harding, rather than with the landlady of the Eastcheap tavern. One resolute word spoken by the termagant was quite enough to awe the maid-servants and to enforce ready obedience; while the ostlers were quick as lightning in getting horses ready and harnessed for a journey, nor were the field-labourers allowed one moment of idleness, for all were quite aware that she would stand no nonsense, as their wages were justly and punctually paid.

The hostess was an especial favourite with the Queen's County gentry, and especially with the sporting characters who patronised her establishment. They delighted in her sallies of wit and humour, and whenever choosing to challenge either to a contest, they invariably received tit-for-tat in exchange. As such friendly familiarities invited return, in compliment to their rank and influence, no reply was given, but what was sure to evoke enjoyment and peals of hearty laughter. Far different was it when pretentious and low-bred persons attempted to assume airs unbecoming their position, or when they fell into awkward mistakes and escapades in the conduct of their affairs. Then, indeed, ludicrous and sarcastic enough were the winged words of caustic application in reproof and condemnation, that fell from the lips of Mistress Harding. By the townspeople those sayings were well remembered, and by our school-fellows repeated with special zest; but, how lively were the sallies of wit or how racy the humour, we cannot here record, as the occasions and persons to whom they had reference are at present well nigh forgotten.

A talented and handsome young priest of the diocese, as likewise an accomplished classical scholar, was a son of Mrs. Harding, and having been a pupil of Mr. Hutchins, whenever he came on a family visit to Ballyroan, he was sure to see his former teacher and the boys during school-hours—thus keeping up a standing intimacy, and renewing old or forming new acquaintances. He was complimented, likewise, in being asked to teach one or other of our classes, which task he readily undertook and executed with distinguished ability. We all desired much to have the benefit of his instructions. Moreover, the Rev. Nicholas Harding had other qualifications, which rendered him not less popular among the school-boys; for we knew him to be fond of athletic sports, and able to beat the best of our ball-players in the alley during hours of recreation. But, what we enjoyed of all other performances was to see him mounted on a magnificent hunter, which he constantly rode, and brought out for exercise into the fields, at the rere of Mr. Hutchins' garden. Having thence a commanding view, we witnessed the grace and agility with which his hunter and himself took the leaps and cleared the fences, until both were sufficiently heated with the exertion. In after life, we knew the Rev. Nicholas Harding socially, as a most agreeable and well informed gentleman; but he lived not to middle age, for his health became impaired, and he fell into a premature decline. When last we met him, the appearances of approaching dissolution had far advanced; he was breathing with difficulty, and on inquiring about his state, he replied sadly with the classical phrase, "hæret lateri lethalis arundo." He did not long survive.

One of our teacher's illustrations regarding the manner in which our classic studies were to proceed was peculiar. He would first place the Latin Grammar on the table, clap it with his open palm, then lay the Latin Dictionary over that corner-stone; afterwards, he piled in succession Swain's Sentences, Hoole's Terminations, Cordery's Colloquies, Cæsar's Commentaries, Ovid's Metamorphoses, Sallust, Virgil, Livy, Horace, and lastly Tacitus, which latter author usually crowned the serial edifice. This enumeration formed the school *curriculum*, and when the structure was completed, an energetic stroke was bestowed on the upper *stratum*. It is doubtful if the pupils derived much practical instruction from the object-lesson. But, on a certain occasion, when the master had furnished as he conceived a sufficient exposition of his system, and had left the school-room for a moment ; a tall and active boy, lithe and agile as a grey hound, placing both his hands on the table, to the great amusement of his comrades, vaulted completely over Mr. Hutchins' classic pyramid.

In those days, political feeling ran high between Tories and Liberals, while polemical controversies between Catholics and Protestants were also rife ; and as a matter of course, in our school were exciting debates and discussions among the boys, on the men and measures there occupying public attention. While O'Connell and Repeal of the Union were subjects for the approval of one party, they were as vigorously denounced by the other ; since both were equally earnest and vociferous in their pronouncements, while their views clouded with family and school-boy prejudices were tempered with heat and passion, as also with occasional offensive expressions. As an exemplification of a mixed system of training, the results did not lead to kindly or conciliatory feeling, nor tend to promote private or personal friendship in after life. Indeed, by a sort of mutual aversion then contracted by the Catholic and Protestant boys at school, they did not afterwards when grown to manhood seek to renew and cultivate the acquaintance then formed. Our master—to his credit be it spoken—was not a promoter of those boyish disputes, which even took place without his knowledge ; and to the last, he preserved the esteem and respect of all his pupils.

The Endowed Schools Commission of 1858 reported

most unfavourably regarding both the schools, founded by Alderman Preston, viz., Navan and Ballyroan, and censured the Commissioners of Education for their neglect of the benevolent and material interests involved. The latter school had not been inspected by them for ten years previously. Relating to Ballyroan school, the annual value of premises was then estimated at £23 17s. 5d., the master of which had £92 6s. 2d. a-year, and a house worth £12, with an assistant having £55 7s. 8d. a-year, and a cottage worth £5, or a total income of £164 13s. 10d. It was then reported as being in a disgraceful condition, attended by only two day pupils, out of three on the roll, and it stated, moreover, that their education was very much neglected.

In subsequent years, that former building we have already described was deserted, when the school was removed to a mansion outside of Ballyroan, and known as Rockbrook. There a Rev. Mr. Lyons conducted it for some years; and of late, under more favourable auspices, the testamentary conditions being changed by Act of Parliament, that endowment of Alderman Preston has been re-modelled, and the establishment itself transferred to the more prosperous and populous town of Abbeyleix. Every trace of the Ballyroan endowed school has been effaced, but, on its former site, a Police Barrack and a Dispensary have been erected, all other features of the town remaining little changed since the days of its classical celebrity. However, more than a generation has elapsed since the events occurred, as we have here related them; and few of those actors on the stage of life now survive, as we have known them in earlier times. Moreover, to seize the passing features as they were presented, in point of fact and fancy, may instruct or amuse our readers, who desire to learn some particulars of manners and customs as they then transpired, while only faint traces now remain partially to revive their recollection and note their record.

No. XXVIII.

The Witch's Fate.

LEGEND OF ANTRIM, COUNTY OF ANTRIM.

> "In each human heart terror survives
> The ruin it has gorged: the loftiest fear
> All that they would disdain to think were true:
> Hypocrisy and custom make their minds
> The fanes of many a worship, now outworn.
> They dare not devise good for man's estate,
> And yet they know not that they do not dare.
> The good want power, but to weep barren tears.
> The powerful goodness want: worse need for them.
> The wise want love; and those who love want wisdom;
> And all best things are thus confused to ill.
> Many are strong and rich, and would be just,
> But live among their suffering fellow-men
> As if none felt: they know not what they do."
> —Percy Bysshe Shelley's *Prometheus Unbound*, Act. i.

As popularly understood by the term, witchcraft seems to have been generally known and exercised in Ireland, only after the Anglo-Norman Invasion. The earliest accounts we find of witchery and enchantment are those given by the Franciscan friar John Clyn, who lived in the convent of that Order in Kilkenny, and who relates at the year 1324, in his Annals of Ireland, that a certain Dame Alicia Kyteler had been accused of divers sorceries and heresies before the spiritual court of Richard Ledred, formerly a Franciscan friar of London, and then Bishop of Ossory. At this trial were present John Darcy, Justiciary of Ireland, the Prior of Kilmainham, Chancellor and Treasurer, as also Arnald le Poer, the Seneschal of Kilkenny. This happened on Monday, July 2nd, which was the Feast day of the Martyrs Processus and Martinian. Dame Alicia was found guilty and condemned to death, according to the precedents drawn from other countries; since the chronicler takes care to state, that none had been known to suffer such penalty in Ireland previously, on the score of heresy. However, during the same year, and on the day succeeding All Souls' festival, one Petronilla of Meath was accused of being a follower of Dame Alicia Kyteler, and an accomplice in her crimes of heresy, witchcraft, and immolation of victims to demons. She was likewise found guilty and condemned to be burned to death. Nevertheless, Bishop Ledred was denounced for his unjust proceedings, and afterwards he was accused of heresy by his Metropolitan, Alexander Bicknor, Archbishop of Dublin.

Under the Mosaic law, witches and wizards on account of their evil practices were condemned to death. (Exodus xxii. 18.) By this it would seem, that those practising pagan superstitions and magic arts, or using charms and invocations in use among the heathen nations, were so designated. They are often referred to in the Sacred Scriptures. Christian writers from an early period have affirmed, that the gods of the ancients were evil spirits, who had led the world away from worship of the true God. Hence was derived an opinion, that the spirit of evil had a direct agency in human affairs, and that compacts were often formed between the devil and wicked or designing persons, considered to have been witches or sorcerers. Throughout the Middle Ages, in nearly all European countries, the most severe laws were enacted against them, until in the fifteenth century proceedings to stop the prevalence of witchcraft assumed their excessively hideous form. Fear and hatred of such practices combined to enact the most repressive and cruel punishments, with death by burning; while through mere suspicion, and hardly with any process of just trial, thousands of innocent persons were accused and condemned to the flames. In England, the Duchess of Gloucester was charged with using sorcery to waste and destroy King Henry VI. Jewel, the Protestant Bishop of Salisbury, preaching before Queen Elizabeth, stated, that his own eyes had seen most evident and manifest marks of wicked enchantments and witchery, while he warned her in these terms: "It may please your grace to understand that witches and sorcerers within these last few years are marvelously increased within your grace's realm. Your grace's subjects pine away, even unto the death, their colour fadeth, their flesh rotteth, their speech is benumbed, their senses are bereft. I pray God, they never practice further than upon the subject." One might readily suppose that such occurrences should be common enough, and without the intervention of supernatural phenomena.

During the following reign, the sapient King James I. wrote his curious and remarkable book on "Demonology," which furnishes sufficient proof of the hold such opinions had on even the most highly educated of his period. The successive statutes of Henry VI., of Henry VII. in 1541, of Elizabeth in 1562, and of James I. in 1603, were not repealed in these realms until 1736. The number of those put to a fearful death in England, and for sorcery alone, has been estimated at about 30,000 ! Sir Walter Scott has written a most interesting work intituled, " Letters on Demonology and Witchcraft," in which he reveals the extent and cases of credulity in his own country. He informs us, that the last victim who perished in Scotland was an insane old woman in 1722. She had such little idea of her situation as to rejoice at the sight of the fire which was destined to consume her. We believe the case which follows may be regarded as the latest execution on the charge of witchcraft, and which stains the criminal annals of our own Island.

A pamphlet printed in 1699 and intituled, " The Bewitching of a Child in Ireland," contains the very curious account regarding a young lady of good family, who lived in the town of Antrim. She was inferior to none in the place for beauty and education. She was remarkable, also, for her charitable disposition and kindness to the poor, so that she became a universal favourite; and it was supposed, that no person could have any feeling but that of respect and affection towards her.

Nevertheless, when she was about nineteen years of age, and on the 9th of May, 1698, a beggar-woman came to the door of her parents, and requesting an alms or something in the way of refreshment, the compassionate young lady gave her bread and beer. She had then no idea, that the wretch whom she had thus relieved was a witch, as it transpired from what followed. The woman, whose motives were unknown, presented her with a leaf of sorrel, and she was induced to eat it; but no sooner had she done so, than an intolerable pain tortured her stomach and bowels. She trembled violently all over, and became convulsive. In fine, she swooned away, and lay as one dead. Doctors were at hand, but all their remedies were used to no purpose. The lady still continued in the most dreadful paroxysm, and having learned the particulars of that interview, which caused her excessive agony, it was concluded she had been bewitched. This opinion was more than confirmed, when the patient first began to roll herself about, and then vomit needles, pins, hairs, feathers, bottoms of thread, pieces of glass, window-nails, eggs, fish-shells, nails drawn out of a cart or coach-wheel, as also an iron knife, more than a span in length.

The minister of her parish was sent for, and scarcely had his hand been placed upon her, than she was turned by a demon into the most frightful shapes. All these occurrences caused the greatest alarm in her family circle and among her friends. Soon it was noticed, that when the witch, who still roamed at large, came near or even looked towards the house in which the young lady lived; although it were two hundred paces distant, still all the most violent torments were renewed, and her immediate death was apprehended. However, when the witch was removed to a greater distance, those paroxysms ceased.

All the foregoing circumstances combined, or as furnished by common report, were sufficient to cause an information to be lodged against the wretched accused woman, who was apprehended, and brought before a judge and jury. Having examined various witnesses, they condemned her to be strangled and burnt, according to the criminal law then in force. Before strangling her, she was desired to undo the incantation, and thus relieve the victim from her sufferings; but the witch declared she could not, because others had likewise practised enchantments against her. At the same time, the condemned sorceress confessed to many spells of a similar character, and of which she had been guilty.

Having paid the penalty of her crime, real or supposed, the trial and its result became a matter of notoriety; and few there were, at that time, who questioned the justice or propriety of those proceedings. Moreover, it is recorded, that about the middle of September following, the young lady had been carried to a gentleman's house, where many other things happened, and scarcely credible, were it not that several ministers of reputation for veracity and the gentleman in question attested their occurrence. Although the laws now in force no longer recognise witchcraft and sorcery, as punishable by any criminal process; still have the traditions of former times taken hold on the imagination of ignorant and superstitious persons, nor have the practices of spells and charms been altogether disused, to counteract their supposed evil influences, or to invoke their direct agencies.

No. XXIX.

The Confederate Peddlers.

LEGEND OF DINGLE, COUNTY OF KERRY.

"Yes, sir, puffing is of various sorts; the principal are, the puff direct, the puff preliminary, the puff collateral, the puff collusive, and the puff oblique, or puff by implication. * * * * * O lud, yes, sir! the number of those who undergo the fatigue of judging for themselves is very small indeed. * * * * Now, sir, the puff collateral is much used as an appendage to advertisements. * * * But the puff collusive is the newest of any; for it acts in the disguise of determined hostility."—Richard Brinsley Sheridan, *The Critics, or a Tragedy Rehearsed*, Act i., Scene i.

NESTLING under a chain of lofty mountains protecting it from the north, and nearly at the extreme end of a promontory jutting out into the Atlantic, is built the town of Dingle, in the barony of Corkaguiney, County of Kerry. It stands at the head of Dingle Harbour. On a fine summer day, no view can be imagined more charming and extensive from its site, than that extending over the Bay, the waves chasing one another in flashes of rolling sun-light to the southern highlands of Iveragh, and the towering peaks of Carraun Toul closing the scene towards the far-famed Lakes of Killarney. The town, formerly known as Dingle-i-Couch had a flourishing linen manufactory, towards the close of the last century; while some finely built shops and antique looking mansions still exhibit traces of departed prosperity, but in their present squalid appearance and crumbling to decay, those houses are tenanted only by the poorest classes.

The changes of time bring with them modifications of customs and methods, while in few other cases are the peculiarities of social life more marked than in the pictures now presented at Irish fairs and markets and those which were to be seen in the beginning of the present century. The facilities of locomotion have dispersed merchandise and orders for goods to other centres of trade and commerce; they have removed agricultural products, horses, cattle, sheep, pigs and fowl to metropolitan markets, in a great measure; and, as a consequence, only a limited and for the most part local traffic at present exists in the towns and on the fair-greens, that were formerly crowded, when the country was more populous, and when mechanical and industrial pursuits were more restricted to their neighbouring places for supply and demand. Irish fairs and markets now present a comparatively deserted appearance, nor can we at all recognise in them that animation and bustle, which prevailed over half a century ago, and to which period our story has a special relation.

The fairs held at Dingle were usually well attended by the country gentry, farmers and dealers for miles around; while considerable local trade was transacted by the different retailers and vendors of wares and goods in greatest demand among the peasantry of that district. On the eve of such an assemblage, the converging roads were filled with drovers and cattle, country men and women in cars or on foot, every individual having some personal interest or speculation in mind, and all destined to return with more or less of gratification or disappointment. Horses and their riders were advancing at a rapid pace. Country carts, loaded with various commodities, or covered with quilts over straw on which were seated the farmers' wives and daughters, trailed along in rapid succession, and driven by the farmers themselves or by their sons. Even the humbler peasants were conveyed in their asses' cars from distances remote, and as during night the journey had been commenced, when day was about to break, all were approaching the town. The scene was one presenting animation and bustle of no ordinary occurrence; while business and pleasure combined to vary the monotony of country life, as the fair or market of the nearest town or village had an important bearing on the periodical fortunes or failures of the people at large.

Among the hurrying groups were to be noticed three travelling caravans with coved tops of some height covered with canvas to protect the draperies contained beneath, while the respective drivers were comfortably clad in overcoats, suited for their journeyings around the different towns and villages of Ireland. They were not in file, however, but kept at respectful distances along the road from Tralee, until night closed in, when selecting a suitable spot for encampment on the road-side, the three wagonettes were well screened from the observation of all way-farers.

Those who have frequented an Irish fair can well understand how busy and varied are the motley throngs to the sight, and how ineuphonious their sounds to the ear, arising from a mingled concourse of bipeds and quadrupeds, in constantly changing positions, and in a very discordant concert of voices and tones. The morning is usually ushered in with the lowing of cows, the neighing of horses, the bleating of sheep, the grunting of pigs, and the shouts of their care-takers, driving them through various groups or trying to preserve them from scattering in different directions. Then commence the animated and noisy asseverations of cattle or stocks buyers and sellers, until the sales are effected, and the luck-penny deposited. Booths are erected in the market place, and under their temporary covering, various cheap articles are arranged to attract the attention of purchasers, old and young. Every device of handicraft is displayed, and in the most public places, to gather customers, and to persuade the interested spectators that articles were cheaply exchangeable for ready money. Thus, the vendor of crockery and delft was holding up his glazed pans and plates, or striking them with his knuckles to prove they had a true ring of durability; the country carpenter had a display of plain deal tables and chairs for adults, or three-legged stools for children's use; bacon-sellers, butchers and bakers had their several stalls around which were numerous buyers; the cobbler was busy mending and making brogues or shoes; the tinker had his fire lighted with the soldering-iron red hot, while re-vamping leaky pots, kettles and tinpans; the cutler was bent over his revolving wheel, while sparks flew from knives, scissors and razors he was engaged in grinding; in short, every branch of rude manual industry was exhibited, either perfected or in course of actual operation. Mountebanks upon the street were performing ground and lofty tumbling, or necromancers showing feats of legerdemain in the midst of admiring circles; while the show-box, with its limited company of actors and musicians, had its crowds of frequenters to enjoy the spectacles within, at the small charge of a penny to the pit and two pence to the gallery reserved seats.

The juveniles had interests and speculations of their own on each recurring fair-day, and were sure to levy their recognised tribute of a *fairing* from all their relatives and friends who had business to transact in town. The pence soon accumulated to sixpences and shillings, thus forming a small fund, which was sure to be spent in various ways before the evening came to a close. For their peculiar tastes and desires stalls were likewise provided, set out with an array of toys and other fancy articles, not reaching to a much higher figure than the penny or twopences, which were at the ready disposal of the youthful purchasers. These felt gratified beyond measure to carry home with them the speaking parrot, the wax-doll, and the tin-trumpet, all of which acquisitions were carefully and jealously preserved, until the air of novelty wore gradually away, and other possessions came in turn to be more greatly prized. The fruit-stalls were usually crowded with a number of children, who kept the apple or orange vendor employed in exchanging her ripe fruit for the pence that were offered. Not far removed was the seller of sugar-sticks and of "rale India rock," who loudly proclaimed to the multitude, that it must cure the colic, and drive the wind out of the stomach; while he had peppermint lozenges, that were warranted to heal sore-throats, coughs and colds. Another itinerant doctor had what he declared to be "straight-going pills," and "sure to dhrive the inimy out of the garrison and make him surrendher at discretion." A rival medicine man had for sale boluses and bottles containing some sort of coloured liquid, which were described as most efficacious and agreeable to the taste; while in Stentorian tones, he cried out in praise of the specific, "It 'ill neither gripe ye, nor purge ye, but it 'll sarch ye gintly, like a fine tooth comb!" At suitable stations along the streets were cars propped up under the shafts, and supporting a frame-work of rods covered with a brown home-spun quilt, and under this shelter were to be seen piles of soft cakes, gingerbread and sweet biscuits. The custodian was usually a middle aged woman of respectable appearance, arrayed in a homely dress and head gear, seated in front of her store, whilst at intervals in a clear tone and shrilly voice she announced: "Every eight a ha'penny, and every sixteen a penny. Every tup-pence worth here going for a penny! Come on, my darling boys and girls: good value here for yer money!" Moreover, the ballad-singers, men and women, were exercising their vocal powers, and moving at a slow pace up and down the streets, followed by those who were captivated by the favourite and well known old airs, while anxious to procure the words of the new songs contained in the several ballads. These were grotesquely illustrated on top with a wretched wood-cut, and printed by some "prentice han'," in a job office of the town—the spelling and irregularities of type having a ludicrous and almost unintelligible appearance for the eye even of a practised reader. Sometimes the ballads were sung by a man and woman in a unison of discordant voices, and they were sold at the small charge of one half-penny each. Altogether, a Babel of sounds filled the air, and as the day advanced, still greater became the crowds flocking to the fair, and more curious were the incidents revealed.

Early on the scene, however, and standing on the platform in front of his wagonette—drawn up in the market-place—was one of the roving individuals already mentioned, attired in a bright red fez cap, in his shirt sleeves and plaited frontlet of dazzling whiteness, the cuffs displaying handsome pearl studs, in a vest of saffron-colour, elegantly embroidered, and in a lavender-coloured pantaloons, strapped down over highly polished dandy-boots. Altogether a good-looking young man, and of intelligent animated features, his dress was worn for the sake of effect, and it harmonized well with his years and active athletic figure. On temporary shelves within the caravan, and with some of the most showy ribbons, silks, satins and gauzes ranged on the outside, in the style of a gipsy's travelling wagon, a varied assortment of dress articles was exposed to view. These within the caravan were neatly folded in their proper compartments. Soon the strange merchant began to ring a bell, the sound of which immediately collected a crowd of men, women and children around him. Having drawn a sufficiently large and appreciative audience, the bell ceased, and in a merry mood with suitable gestures, with the peculiarly Yankee pronunciation and nasal twang, he commenced an oration, frequently interrupted by the laughter and applause of his hearers.

"Good people of Dingle and the west of Kerry generally, you were to be pitied by all honest folk, that know the way you are treated in your dealings with the shop-keepers of this town and neighbourhood. Their profits are outrageous, I guess, charging you double prices for all the articles of clothing and dress you bought from them; and no mistake they were able to live in grand style themselves and families, when ye had no other friends to take ye out of their clutches —the extortioners; for of course, you couldn't travel all the way to Dublin to get bargains and value for your hardly-earned money. Well, this day puts an end to that state of affairs. Hearing of your case, I travelled all the way from the United States of America, the land of freedom and happy homes for so many of your exiled country people, and lately I heard of the wreck of a French merchant vessel that was stranded on the coast of Waterford, with a cargo of the most beautiful and fashionable fabrics, and I hastened there to see the captain and ship-agent, to bargain with them for the articles I am now going to expose for sale. I tell you it was fortunate for me to secure such prizes and at a most reduced rate, as under those circumstances the goods were almost a dead loss to the owners. They are all warranted sound and first-class, for the use and wear of any lady or gentleman that wants to try their chance, and such another opportunity will never again take place in the town of Dingle. I intend to sell them for less than half their value, and to bring home with me the blessings of all the fine young men and bonny lasses of the town, and of all the respectable farmers and their handsome wives and daughters in the neighbourhood. I want to see every man, woman and child of you well dressed, and as I calculate, at prices next to nothing. Not to waste time, I'll begin at once on the just and ready principle of the Dutch auction: Falling the price from high to low, sale to the first bidder, and cash down."

Having finished this exordium, the vendor drew from one of the shelves a remnant of printed calico with showy chintz pattern, and quickly unfolding it, he sent several yards floating over the heads of the multitude, and with such dexterity, that it bounded from left to right and in front, each matron and maiden in the crowd straining to catch hold and detain the piece for a hurried inspection. Without loss of time, the salesman, assuming a complaisant and courteous manner, addressed the parties evidently most desirous to secure his goods at a bargain : " Yes, madam, no less than fourteen yards in that beautiful print ; full dress for a lady, and most becoming style for a Sunday or Holyday ; yes, miss, examine it and judge for yourself, it would look charming with your lovely features and figure. Quick now, I must throw it over to another elegant girl, who wants to admire it ; but I have much business to finish today, and I can't wait any longer. It is the way we work in Yankee-land. So here begins the sale. I suppose if I'd say thirty shillings for the dress, you'd all think it too dear —well no—I'll set it up at a pound, and down we go— nineteen shillings—eighteen shillings—seventeen shillings —sixteen shillings—fifteen shillings—fourteen shillings—

thirteen shillings—twelve shillings—eleven shillings—ten shillings—who bids?—great bargain, ladies!—well, nine shillings, eight and sixpence—eight shillings, seven and sixpence!" "Seven and sixpence bid for it," returned a mincing voice near the platform. "Sold!" cried the merchant, "and to a girl of real taste and judgment. Cash, miss, down, and thanks; may be you won't shine in that dress, when your mantua maker puts it out of hands!"

Another ring of the bell, and out came an imitation cashmere shawl, with its bright and intricate pattern looking very gay and brilliant. "Come now, ladies, who bids? who bids first for this valuable shawl? Worth two pounds, ladies! Well, I'll not set it up at that price; nor at the half of that; nor at the half of that again. I'll say nine shillings—eight shillings—seven shillings—six shillings—five and sixpence—five shillings—four and sixpence—come now a dead bargain—four shillings, ladies!" "Four shillings," echoed a voice, and a farmer's wife searched her capacious pockets for the money. "All right, ma'am," and the witty Cheap John lost no time with his hearty and pleasant congratulations on her new acquisition, while he was engaged unfolding a piece of lawn, which like a banner sporting in the breeze floated over the individuals present. "A grand remnant of the finest Belfast linen!" shouted the well-dressed Peddler, "Now comes the gentlemen's turn, married men or bachelors—all the same—like the women" —a knowing wink—"we're vain of our good looks— Heaven help us!—but it's the stylish shirt collar and sleeves that marks the difference between the master and the boor. The Dingle linen is good enough for every-day wear among the country labourers, but the respectable farmer likes to show off to advantage at fair or market, wedding or christening, before his own wife or the wives of others. The smart young bachelor—and there are many of them about me—won't be outdone in style by the married man, because he has to chose a girl for his wife, who'd cry shame upon him if he were like a gawk to meet her at dance or pattern. Unless he catch her eye and captivate her good opinion with a shirt of fine Belfast linen, he has no chance of her hand, and he'll rank among the unmarried sleeveens and slovens all the dear days of his life. Hints enough for the wise; now, gentlemen, we begin the auction for the Belfast linen!" The bell again rings. "Fifteen shillings for this beautiful piece of cambric—fourteen shillings—thirteen

I

shillings—twelve shillings!" The auctioneer's watchful eye, closely scanning the people around him, noticed a farmer and his wife speaking in undertones and handling the linen whenever it came within reach. "You're right, ma'am, you're right; if your good man lets it go lower, he'll lose the chance. Eleven shillings,"—a pause—"ten shillings!" "Ten shillings," responded the farmer, and immediately produced payment.

Amid banter and cajolery of this sort, swiftly proceeded sales with the crowd, that was momently increasing, as the Peddler's stock began to change hands and disappear, until the shelves were emptied completely, and the various articles found new owners. However, as the horse was put to the light wagon, and as its owner turned the way by which he had entered, another vehicle similarly appointed came into view. The driver, holding the reins with one hand, applied a trumpet to his mouth with the other. He blew a blast so loud and shrill, that it reverberated to the very ends of the town.

When the drivers passed each other, scowling looks of apparent envy and ill-feeling were exchanged, while these were interpreted by the crowd to mean jealousy and rivalry in business; but curiosity was the more excited to witness the result, as the new comer drew his wagonette up in the market place, and proceeded to expose his merchandise for sale. Still more varied seemed the assortment, and the more anxious became the people to contrast the articles and prices with those of previous purchases. The day was still young, but approaching noon, and as the new Cheap John was expeditious in arranging his booth, a vast multitude soon collected around the van. He blew the trumpet by way of commanding attention, and then assuming a discomposed and indignant air and attitude, attractively attired as in the former case, and in his shirt sleeves, with folded arms he commenced an oration in these words:—

"My guid folks o' the town o' Dingle an' the kintra aroun', I wad hae wissd to hae raught ye earlier i' the dawin; forbye had I kenn'd a glib-gabbit o' a fella gaed here afore mysel, I'd hae maked mair haste amang ye. He sklented aiblins an' wus unco wrang to tittle anent the Waterford shipwrack, I rede ye. I warran' the shopkeepers o' Dingle sell their gear to ye at twa prices; but I trow their troggin are guid, trig, an' winsome eneugh for thae wha hae siller to sneck. Vera weel, they are naething like fresh an' brent-new gudes. Ye may sware, the loon, wha lea'ed the toun just noo gave ye nae fairins ere his gawn, but maistly charged ye ower muckle for ony thing he sell't ye, wi' his raiblin' gab. The folk here tauld me a wee bit, what-reck, on comin' i' the toun, that he bleth'red anent a shipwrack on the coast o' Waterford, an' that he bad low for the roons an' orra-duddies he gar't ye to buy. Hech friens, the ginglin' skyte wi' his vap'rin sud be i' the Tolbooth an' prosecutet for his tricksies an' imposturs on simple folk. It's unco hard for honest dealers to mak a livin' in business wi' sae mony rogues abread! Weel ma friens, I hae a sicker an' trowthfu' story to tell ye, anent thae gudes I brought frae Belfast, whar there was a great fier i' one o' the bonniest warehooses o' the North, an' I claught monie o' the best troggins feckly weel grippet awa, an' they gaed to me at a laigh niffer, by the marchant, wha owned them; for he wiss'd to big his hoose anaw and stock it wi' new gear. Sae it was bonnie luck for us a' to gang an' forgather i' the toun o' Dingle, whar the folk hae sae muckle gumption, an' the gudeman and guidwife, the lads an' lassies, hae sic a kennen themsel o' swappin' an' wairin' siller for caller an' unskaith'd gudes. I'll sell ye first-rate articles at the lowest possible prices. That's the hale trowth, genties, an' there is naething like fair dealin' atween mon an' mon."

The front covering of the van was then removed, and after a blast on the trumpet, the salesman unfolded a number of silk handkerchiefs and other dry-goods. Whereupon, he resumed the work of selling on the principle of the Dutch auction. There was an affectation of candour and sincerity about this travelling merchant, contrasting greatly with the volatile and lively quips and cranks of his predecessor, that quite recommended him to the country people. Having fully gained their confidence, the sales proceeded to the mutual satisfaction of the vendor and his customers. While the former Peddler was pronounced to be nothing better than a humbug and a dishonest knave, the serious merchant at once became popular, and by common acclaim he was deemed to be a fair trader and a gentleman. Before many hours were passed, he had sold at sufficiently good prices nearly all those articles which he had brought in the wagonette. In turn, folding up the frame-work, putting the horse harnessed to his vehicle, and taking his place on the driver's seat, the crowd was then about to disperse.

Just at that moment, another stranger made his appearance. He was differently costumed from the previous visitors, and wore a dress-suit of grey tweed, with a green neck-tie and a broad-brimmed white straw hat. He too was seated on a box in front of a wagonette, set out and furnished with wearables of various kinds. The incomer and the outgoer nodded distantly and coldly to each other, not seeming to recognise or acknowledge any former cordial acquaintanceship. Moreover, the new actor on the stage of life drove his horse with an air of triumph to the market-place. There, having chosen his position, the coverings of his goods-van were soon removed, and everything necessary was done to prepare for his special share of the performance.

In the first instance, a drum was suspended by its band from his neck, when a boy procured for the occasion jumping up on the platform beside the travelling merchant produced a fife from his breast pocket, and applying it to his lips, the lively and well known air of "Garryowen" was struck up, the drum sticks being skilfully used to effect a resonant accompaniment, which greatly delighted the crowd, beginning to assemble again from all quarters. The business affairs of cattle-dealing had then been well nigh transacted; while the comfortable farmers and the humbler peasants had disposed of their stock and had money in their purses, to invest in other articles necessary for use and ornament. The afternoon was advanced, and the various attractions of the fair had ceased to be novelties; while the bargains between buyers and sellers were closed with the usual treat, in one or other of the most frequented public-houses of Dingle. As a consequence, no little elevation of spirit and good feeling prevailed, although it was questionable if the judgment was generally steady and well balanced among the speculators who flocked to hear the inspiriting sounds of the fife and drum. The music soon ceased, however, and the instruments having been laid aside, the stranger Peddler took his stand in front of his opened wagonette, when in a vein of humour, and in a dialect more "racy of the soil" than his earlier competitors employed, began in a speech to court popular favour with different arguments, and addressed still more to the feelings or prejudices of the audience he had collected.

"My fellow-counthrymin and counthrywimin, and honest people o' Dingle, I'm sarry to find I wash late for the openin' o' your fair to-day, an' that as I'm informed two cheeky fellows got here afore me to impose on yees the stuffs they sowld, and cheated yees widh their ways and manes of carryin' on buisness. The first of thim that kem here was a cute Yankee, as yees knew by his accent, and the people of his counthry are able to bate all creation in sharp dealin', especially widh the soft innocent Irish, that ar'n't up to their thricks and notions. About goods in gineral, they'd persuade yees that black is white, and take every advantage of poor craythures, that don't know the differ of a good from a bad article. Musha and shure enough, they buy in the chapest market, and make their profit by imposin' on all their cushtomers, and in spinin' long yarns to desave those that are promised bargains. The first chap towld yees, that his stock was bought from a captain whose vessel was wracked on the coast of Watherford, and may be it was so; but take my word for it, the articles of dhress he sowld yees were damaged by the saltwather, and war good for nothin' whin they were bought, and they're worse nor ever now that he has got your money for takin' thim off his hands. Before yees wear thim two months, they'd be in rags, and all the needles and threads yees 'ud use couldn't keep thim together any longer to presint a dacent appearance.

"The second fella that kem here was from the black North, and bad as the Yankee was for cuteness and desate, the Ulsther vagabone would distance him in sharpness of thrade practishes. Augh! it's I that knows well what a set of shkin-flints the Ulsthermen are; and above all, their Peddlers that thravel through the other provinces of Ireland have no object in view, but to make as much money as they can out o' yees, and give the worst article that can be found to yees in exchange. He towld yees that his goods were bought from a Belfast merchant at a low figure, bekase his premisses was burned down, and he wanted to build new ones and shtart in bus'niss agin. Yees may be sure the goods were singed or scorched by the fire, or else why wouldn't the marchant of Belfast keep them for his new shop. It bates the world to think how such arrant chates can make sinsible people b'lieve their lyin' stories, and spind their money on the worthless and gim-crack articles they set up for sale.

"Agin yees had the shcemein' Dutch auction brought into play, only to prevint yees from havin' time to examine the showy rags that were offered for sale, and to take yees by surprise when biddin' for them. Augh! shure it's always the case, a fool and his money soon parted. Yees 'ill find that many 'ill be sorry enough afore this day month, that they bought any thing from the flash Yankee or from the canny Ulsther Peddler at the fair of Dingle. Oh! the murdherin' thieves, to throw dust in the eyes of honest and industhrious people, that earn their money hard enough, and that want to lay it out for the advantage of thimselves and families.

"Now I'm one of your own counthrymin, that wants to promote the sale of honest Irish goods, and the prosperity of home manufacthers; and in throth, go where yees will, all the world over, yees 'ill find nothin' betther nor more substantial for serviceable wear, nor betther value for yer money, bekase I wouldn't have my name and repetation for rale articles of worth and bargains run down among yees, whin I visit the fair of Dingle, as I hope to do agin, afore many years pass over. I take the tower of Ireland, through all the big towns, day afther day, and month afther month, and everywhere I go, I give satisfaction to the people, bekase I only bring useful and valuable goods in my van, and save their pockets too, whin they dale widh me, and not widh the shopkeepers, or worse still, widh the vagabonds that thravel the counthry widh showy and damaged articles, like those fellows here afore me sowld yees. They'll soon lose their colours and look shabby enough afore they are long worn. Augh, no, my friends, the stuffs that I brings yees for sale are the rale Cork corduroys and tweeds, the Kilkenny blue cloths, the County Meath gray frizes, and the Galway black frizes, the Mountrath tammies, the Mountmellick calicoes, plain and printed, the twilled and well dyed stuffs, the Rathdrum blankets, the Drogheda sheetings, the Waxford checks and linsey woolsies, the County Monaghan linen shirtings, and the Belfast fine linen for cuffs and collars; in fact, every article sowld guaranteed sound and good, and all med in Ireland, so that while dhrivin' an honest thrade both buyer and seller 'ill be afther keepin' money in the counthry, and helpin' hus all to live in comfort and proshperity. I saw there was an open for such a thrade, and the people wanted good value. I wished to spread Irish manufacthered goods through the length and breadth of the Imerald Isle, and it's the thrue way of showin' one's pathrotism, whin one has'nt a mint of money to carry out great improvements in town and counthry.

"We can't all be mimbers of parliament, my good friends, like Daniel O'Connell—God bless him!—and those that have crassed the say widh him, to sthruggle for the Repale of the Union, and the rights of Ireland, to give hus the management of our own affairs, and to promote our national welfare; but until the day of indepindince comes, we must all take his advice, which was that given by Dane Swift over a hundred years ago, to incourage our own manufactherers that remain, and to thry and revive the industhries of the last century, now fast decayin' undher the competition of worthless English and foreign articles, and chates that circulate thim everywhere over the counthry. When the Tithes are abolished, the lands in the ownership of the tinants and full scope for their industhry, nor charged with rack-rints by an idle, gambling, horse-racing, extravagant and absentee set of landlords; whin the taxes and duties levied on the people are well laid out and to their advantage, on public improvements, by capable and thrust-worthy managers, directed by a home government that cares for the consarns and welfare of the counthry; whin there is an ind of jobbery and partisan officialism, and aiqual rights for all, Catheelic and Prodestan; thin we may expect pace and happiness in the land, and as our grand poet Tom Moore says, she must become

'great, glorious and free,
First flower of the earth and first jim of the say.'"

Here a loud and general cheer burst forth from the multitude present, and having thus wrought on their patriotic feelings, the travelling merchant came to his peroration.

"But, my friends, we must now lave politics aside, and turn to thrade, where I'm not goin' to have Dutch auctions or other foreign thricks to chate yees; but I'll show yees the goods, handle them yerselves, judge of their soundness and value; I'll tell yees the number of yards in each piece put up for sale, and I'll venture to say, you'll find thim chaper than any goods ever offered for sale in the town of Dingle."

Having delivered the foregoing oration with a volubility of utterance—the result of open-air speeches practised on many former occasions—and with an energy of voice and gesticulation which fairly arrested the attention of the large audience then assembled around his van, the travelling merchant produced his wearables in succession—this time chiefly catering for the wants of the men, as the women had most generally completed their purchases of finery in the forenoon. The auction now commenced and concluded in the old well known style of ascending bids, and these were rapidly given, with occasional interjected remarks of the auctioneer, to speed the sales. Pithy and humorous observations were at command of the salesman, and were freely used to keep the bidders in a merry mood, and to stimulate the general desire of obtaining great bargains. One by one the pieces set up for competition were knocked down to the highest bidder, and the cash for each was immediately produced ; so that, at the approach of evening, the van was nearly emptied of its contents. Then the owner re-arranged his tarpauling over its roof, to take leave of his customers. These waited for the last moment of exposure, to chance the possession of some article which the merchant declared he was anxious to part with, and at a loss to himself, so as to sell off the remainder of his stock, and to procure new goods for the next sale.

When the shades of night had set in, the three travelling merchants of that day's adventures were to be found in friendly companionship, with their vans drawn up in a sheltered and secluded spot, not far from the public road leading to Tralee. It was only there, and when they might escape public observation in their selected bivouac, that a watch fire could be kindled and kept aglow with the roots and briars abounding in the place. With such fuel and a few cookery utensils, a supper, consisting of rashers and eggs fried in a pan, with potatoes simmering in a pot, was hastily and skilfully prepared, while the kettle was full of boiling-water to make tea and to mix tumblers of punch as the finale of the evening's entertainment. Their busy work at the fair left them little leisure to take more than a slight luncheon, and so long as money was coming in, they could not afford to lose time for any more substantial refreshment. However, as their trade transactions in Dingle had been eminently successful and satisfactory, their meal was all the more relished ; and as the magical enlivenment of the whiskey-punch produced its natural exhilaration, so were their spirits elevated, while long and loud was the laughter provoked in mutually relating the amusing incidents of their several sales and anecdotes of the credulous customers taken in by their persuasions, when leaving the fair with fancied bargains.

The travelling merchants were three Munster brothers, who had been adventurers in early life, and who had sought different places and methods in pursuit of gain. The first in the fair, had emigrated to the United States, and having acquired there some knowledge of sharp dealing and the country accent had returned to his native land well practised in the mysteries of a peddling business, which he followed for some time in the backwoods. The second brother had left his home in the south for Scotland when very young, and afterwards he returned to Ireland, where he lived for a time in the northern province. While in Ulster, he was engaged at a Belfast retail establishment. There he had learned the art of dealing with shrewd buyers and sellers of shop goods. As a matter of course, he had gradually exchanged his native soft pronunciation for the hard Scotch and Doric dialect there prevalent.

These practised and intelligent retailers of dry goods and articles for men's and women's wear had a third brother, who remained at home in their native province of Munster. Having resolved on a clever scheme to start and conduct a family joint-stock company, he was trained to act his part in the concern. They had so planned it, that each one should seem a rival to the other, when acting on the theatre and in the scenes of their respective performances. Moreover, their customers in towns and villages through which they passed were not allowed to suspect any collusion between the confederates, who were to have all the appearance of competing independently for public favour and patronage. Hence it happened, that the third brother, who could not disguise his native accent in any part of Ireland, was able to represent his partners as a Yankee and Ulsterman respectively, when he came to close the afternoon sales. The scenes and procedure were often reversed, as the circumstances of place and policy varied; but the actors were always the same, to whatever town or district they travelled, while their circuits were extended even to the most remote extremities of England and Scotland.

There can be no doubt, our adventurers had better studied the propensities of human beings, and the great extent to which their gullibility may be carried, than did the philosopher Locke, who maintained the very questionable theory, that words are the signs of our ideas, and that they tend to convey our meaning between man and man. Such indeed ought be their use and purport, if strict integrity and honesty of intention generally prevailed; but indirectness of speech and hypocrisy are so frequently the ruling propensities of society, in all grades, that a character, who figured conspicuously in public affairs and in many shadowy transactions of a secret nature, is said to have regarded words, as framed to conceal our thoughts, and mainly to be employed for that end. From the highest concerns of State to the petty schemes that regulate the ordinary actions of life, men are constantly engaged in playing at cross purposes, calculated to deceive their fellow-men, and to divert attention from real motives and objects. It is especially the study of pettifogging diplomacy and statecraft, unwisely to indulge over-vaulting ambition, and to exercise what is only low cunning, in seeking personal ends or political aggrandizement—sure to be followed by the recoil of diminished honour and the sacrifice of true national interests. To succeed in such efforts, misleading schemes and unscrupulous agents must be employed or countenanced, so that responsibilities may be shifted from the principals; especially when failure becomes the penalty, and detection of fraud may be apprehended, with the fear of disgrace and exposure resulting.

Of late, we have had some pregnant instances, showing the want of wisdom, and even the deplorable perversity of moral feelings, with which our men of State disregard or interpret international relations. When it becomes a question of dealing with a small and defenceless territory, threats of force are employed to gain advantages over a people that demand only justice; but when a powerful nation blocks the way, caution and evasion must be observed, in every movement that might be fraught with dangerous consequences. When Venezuela had long sought in vain for the exact definition of a boundary line between herself and British Guiana, Lord Salisbury, the English Premier and Secretary of State, had arrogantly interfered to press his claim for a large accession of territory beyond the disputed line, in apparent ignorance of the Monroe Doctrine, and its bearing on the case; but, he was rather disconcerted, when assured by the United States' government, that it had an interest and a voice in the matter, which must form the subject for an impartial arbitration. Nothing is more hurtful to a responsible minister's pride than to find himself surprised in a false and discomfited position; while expedients must be devised for a safe retreat, unless prepared to preserve his contention, and at a risk which boded rather serious consequences.

Nearly concurrent with the foregoing incidents was the attempt to overturn the independent Transvaal Republic of South Africa. In 1840, a number of Dutch farmers, dissatisfied with the administration of Government at the Cape, left that Colony, and established themselves in Natal. There the British Government interfered, and annexed that settlement. Rather than submit to such usurpation, the majority of Boers again removed from under the English rule, and crossing the Drakensbergen and the Vaal Rivers, established in that territory the South African Republic, acknowledged in 1854 by the English Government as a free and an independent State. The people had many troubles with the Kaffir hordes around them. On pretence of befriending the natives, in 1877 the English Government again interfered, and annexed that country. Meantime, the Boers had increased in numbers, and were determined not to be driven out of their country again; so that after three years of preparation, war broke out on the 16th of December, 1880. Wherever the Boers and English met, although numerically stronger, the latter were decidedly beaten. After the battle of Amajuba, the retrocession of their country by treaty in 1881, and under British suzerainty, was followed by peace. This was modified in 1884, by the British Resident's removal, England reserving to herself the privilege of controlling the foreign relations of the Transvaal, except as regarded the Orange Free State. When the Republic had been formed, S. J. P. Paul Krüger was proclaimed President, and in April 1893, he was re-elected to that office.

Soon after its independence had been established, the southern portion of the Transvaal was discovered to abound in gold and other valuable mineral products, which soon attracted to it a motley and greedy multitude of adventurers —mostly British—from the neighbouring English Colonies. At the very beginning of such inroads, the Dutch Government regarded their movements and objects with suspicion. As their numbers rapidly increased, it was found that agitators were at work to obtain privileges, which were intended ultimately to subvert the Republic, and to re-annex it, with its inhabitants, to the British Crown. Internal and external plots were organised for that purpose. Having arranged a plan of invasion, towards the close of 1895, Dr. Jameson with a number of military officers and other English officials attempted a hostile inroad, which was effectively checked by the Boers. The survivors of that sharp engagement were made prisoners. The failure of such a disgraceful attempt was a subject of great disappointment, both in England, and in her African colonies, while it disconcerted the policy of the Home Cabinet, supposed to have had no knowledge of what was concerted, and nevertheless what was most likely to take place, as generally expected in that remote part of the world.

The Secretary of State for the Colonies, Mr. Joseph Chamberlain, pleaded ignorance of the fillibustering raid, and affected virtuous indignation on account of it being undertaken, by so many of his subaltern officials. However, a new subject of unpleasantness arose for the Ministry, when, after being subjected to a short imprisonment, the raiders were turned over to them for trial according to English law by President Krüger and his Cabinet. When those miscreants arrived in England, the public press and many of the people applauded them for what was called "pluck," regarding them as heroes; and when the German Emperor very significantly conveyed his congratulations to President Krüger on the discomfiture of their enterprise, a cry of rage went forth—not lessened, indeed, when by another complication the Ministry learned, that the United States Government had set up their own independent tribunal, solely to arbitrate after due examination on the pending case of the disputed boundary between Venezuela and the colony of British Guiana. The most ridiculous part of the farce was then played by the responsible advisers of her Majesty the Queen. The newspaper press was set on to spread the rumour, that new taxes should be levied on the nation, as extraordinary preparations were making or to be made in the dock-yards, for increasing the number of war-vessels, and for putting those already built into a thorough state of repair and efficiency. Nothing however was said about the army. Sensible people looked abroad, but saw no enemy in view; while foreign powers were rather amused than panic-stricken with such announcements. After a short time, quiet was restored, as nobody offered to fight; the trials of the Transvaal raiders were leniently conducted, and with due forms of law; a few were condemned to brief terms of comfortable imprisonment ; the officers holding commissions were cashiered, but recommended to look abroad for future promotion ; and thus all the ends of justice were supposed to have been accomplished. While the Chief Governor, High Commissioner, and Commander-in-Chief of South Africa had slept on his post during the Transvaal raid, the Premier of Cape Colony, Right Hon. Cecil John Rhodes, had conducted himself in an intermeddling and naughty manner, and was summoned duly to a private conference with the Secretary of State for the Colonies—the newspapers said to receive an indignant reprimand and to answer for his transgressions. Shrewd persons have thought, they then smoked together the calamut of good-fellowship and peace ; planned confidentially future operations in reference to the Boers ; and like the confederate brothers of our tale, whose object was to deceive their customers, men of state and politicians can stoop to many discreditable projects, and even more effectually screen themselves from detection, while sailing under false colours and professing to have in view only the promotion of public interests.

Moreover, like the pretended opposition of those confederates already mentioned was that difference of opinion, stated by the press to have arisen between Lord Salisbury and Mr. Chamberlain, when the former found it politic to lower his high-handed pretensions in reference to Venezuela, and his earlier misjudging diplomatic correspondence, which ruled him out of court with the United States. Not from the force of circumstances, but owing to the expediency of having to break the fall, in a manner more graceful, it was necessary to disguise the foreign pressure, and to feign a changed resolution, by yielding to the supposed persuasion of colleagues in the Cabinet. This plan had the advantage of deceiving the general public—apt enough to take plausible statements for truths—also of saving personal credit when seriously damaged, and of serving the purposes of party alliance, by giving the Opposition a false scent in hoping for discord, when in reality a ready agreement to differ and coalesce tuned the harmonic chords between political tricksters—perchance most distrustful of each other, but not forgetful of their own particular interests and official position, even when misdirecting national concerns and compromising national honour.

No. XXX.

The Storm Spectre.

LEGEND OF THE MULLET, COUNTY OF MAYO.

"For see all around him, in white foam and froth
The waves of the ocean boil up in their wrath."
—T. Crofton Croker's *Lord of Dunkerron.*

"The winds the sullen deep that tore
His death song chaunted loud,
The weeds that line the clifted shore
Were all his burial shroud;
For friendly wail and holy dirge
And long lament of love,
Around him roared the angry surge,
The curlew screamed above."
—Gerald Griffin's *Wake without a Corpse.*

IN the remote north-western part of the barony of Erris, in the County of Mayo, lies the almost insulated district known as the Mullet. The isthmus which unites it to the mainland is occupied by the rather modern town of Belmullet, between Broad Haven on the north, and Black Sod Bay to the south. These approach within 400 yards of each other, and could be united by a ship canal, at no very considerable cost, so as to form a completely land-locked harbour, with ready ingress and egress for vessels, as the winds varied their direction. Within that peninsula, the Irish-speaking inhabitants have had little intercourse with the outside world, and they are a simple race, subsisting for the most part on the poorest fare, drawn from a barren soil on land, and from the sea those fishes which are taken in their nets. They are still addicted to many usages and superstitions, unknown to the peasantry in other parts of Ireland.

Like the Highlanders and inhabitants living in the Western Isles of Scotland, the Mullet people believe in a "second sight," and in strange apparitions—especially as foreshadowing calamities about to happen at sea. Thus before furious tempests, which result in shipwrecks and loss of life, shooting stars and preternatural gleams of light are seen in the skies, and reflected again in the waves of the Atlantic Ocean. A still more appalling prognostic is the monstrous and vapoury form, that rises from the deep and hides its head in the clouds, when it suddenly vanishes. Somewhat resembling a gigantic human figure, it rushes onwards for a time with great velocity and of irregular shape. It is probably but the ordinary movement of a water-spout. However, this is regarded by the natives, as an evil spirit, which calls upon the whirlwinds to rage, and it is known to them as The Storm Spectre.

Within the memory of many still living is that destructive cyclone, which happened on the night of January 6th, 1839, and which travelling from a western direction threw vast sheets of water and yeasty spray over the cliffs along the Atlantic coasts. The Islands of Aran and several of the smaller islands out in the ocean were flooded by rivers of the salt-waves, that rolled over the steeps, which were highest near the exposed points, and then down the slopes entering the sea at the eastern shores, the waters washed away much of the light mould, created through the industry of the islanders. These people are accustomed to carry loads of sea-weed and fine sand, from the shallows to the upper levels on the naked rocks, and there spreading them in alternate layers on little plots of ground to form an artificial soil, on which their scanty crops of potatoes and oats are sown. Their chief means of subsistence, however, were the fisheries, then carried on by the well appointed hookers and the small craft of canvas-covered boats called currachs.

The evening before that disaster alluded to occurred, several of the Mullet peasantry observed far out on the western horizon the ocean waves, which seemed to swell upwards, until they assumed the magnitude of a great mountain. Then, from its summit the spirit of the winds suddenly arose, lifting as it were a columnar and misshapen figure to the very clouds, in which its head was finally veiled. Meanwhile, two gigantic arms kept waving wildly on either side, and at their extremities were hands of fire, flashing like lightning, while the features of a frightful ogre were visible in the column, and luminous through the evening gloom. In fine, the Storm Spectre dissolved, as the shades of night approached, and those who witnessed the phenomenon were filled with terror, as, seeking their respective homes, they formed presages of evil believed to be almost immediately impending.

When the next morning dawned, all the sea-faring people

on land, and the families of others still at sea, anxiously watched the foul weather forecasts, and strained their eyes in the direction of the Atlantic, most eager to see the distant fishing smacks return to harbour, while day-light still lingered. The desires of some were gratified, as certain vessels and their occupants reached the land in safety; however, as night set in, the full fury of the gale beat upon the coast, and the tempest howled unceasingly, driving every thing before it, while no eye was closed in the fishermen's huts that so thickly lined the shores. Not only were the straw thatch, and the transverse ropes of hay pegged down to secure it, blown away from their roofs; but, even the stone-built cabins were levelled in various cases, while the crash of hookers and of small boats beaten against the rocks, with the doleful cry of the drowning sailors, carried dismay to the hearts of all who heard those dreadful sounds, and who were utterly powerless to render any assistance.

Of those out at sea on that night of fearful storm, few escaped with their lives; yet, for days after it abated, many dead bodies were recovered, and recognised by widowed wives, orphaned children, or loving brothers, sisters and relations. Although decomposed in several instances, the wake was held as usual and the *caoine* chaunted, before the mangled remains were consigned to the grave. Even in the case of those whose bodies could not be found, according to the invariable custom of their families surviving, a sort of humble pall or shroud was spread over some frame-work resembling a coffin, and mourners duly attended for two days and two nights; while, in the grave plot of his people, a cenotaph or head-stone was set up as a memorial, by the lost mariner's sorrowing relatives. So great was the loss of life and of boats at the time, that the fishery industries around all the western coasts of Ireland received a shock from which they never since recovered; nor is it likely such operations shall be fully revived and developed, until companies be formed with sufficient capital and enterprise, having steam-vessels suitably equipped, and with curing premises readily accessible through railway communication at convenient stations.

THE END.

Works by the Same Author.

1. Abridgment of the History of Ireland, from its Final Subjection to the Present Time—1849.

Patrick Donahoe, Boston, U.S.A., 1849, 18mo.

Price 10 Cents.

---

2. The Irish Emigrant's Guide for the United States.

Patrick Donahoe, Boston, 1851, 18mo.

Price 25 Cents.

"There is published, of late, a very important and complete Emigrants' Guide, by a Catholic Clergyman, Rev. John O'Hanlon, which is the best assistant that can be procured to direct the emigrant."—*The Nation* (1851.)

---

3. The Life of St. Laurence O'Toole,

Archbishop of Dublin, and Delegate Apostolic of the Holy See for the Kingdom of Ireland.

John Mullany, 1 Parliament Street, Dame Street, Dublin. 1857. 18mo. Cloth, gilt.

Price One Shilling and Sixpence.

"This graceful little memoir of one of Ireland's sainted bishops, from the pen of a well-known ecclesiastical scholar and antiquarian, will be an acceptable boon to the readers of Irish Hagiology; and it is all the more welcome, because it is but the prelude to a more extensive work, which is to embrace the Lives of all the Irish Saints. The work before us displays an amount of care and historic research highly creditable to the author."—*The Celt.*

"Though Father O'Hanlon has been anticipated by others who laboured in the same field, it must be acknowledged, to his credit and critical acumen, that his biography of St. Laurence is by far the best that has appeared as yet, and that the copious annotations he has collected from the most recondite sources throw additional light on that dark and dismal era, when 'Lorcan, son of Maurice,' prayed and toiled—alas, in vain!—to unite his countrymen in one grand defensive league against the invader."—*Nation*.

"'The Life of St. Laurence O'Toole,' by the Rev. J. O'Hanlon, is one of the most accurate, critical, and important biographies of our sainted and patriotic bishop ever published."—*Catholic Directory and Registry for* 1858.

"We have lingered with delight over its pages, stood in imagination by the Saint's side, and listened during his distinguished reception by Pope Alexander III., when that bright pillar of the Holy See appointed him Legate of all Ireland—an office filled, even in our day, by a saintly Prelate, on whom the Father of the Faithful has conferred a similar distinction. In our mind's eye we have beheld the heavenly calm on his smiling countenance, as he sank down to the sleep of the blessed, whilst a transcendent brilliance illumed the heavens over the Chateau d'Eu; and at length, closing the deeply touching records, we are transported to the church dedicated to the glorious saint."—*Catholic Telegraph*.

"A flood of light is thrown on the ecclesiastical antiquities of Dublin and Glendalough, which is exceedingly interesting and valuable. But it is his able detection of the false statements hitherto put forth respecting Archbishop O'Toole which renders this memoir one of peculiar utility to the present and future student of history. To perform a task so beset with difficulty, Mr. O'Hanlon must have read deeply and perseveringly, and we can appreciate the laborious research which the various objects of his work necessitated."—*Weekly Agricultural Review*.

"This book is valuable in itself as a repertory of rare and original information as to the early history of the Island of Saints, especially as regards the ecclesiastical antiquities of Dublin and Glendalough. It is also to be prized as the first of a promised series of volumes, containing a complete history, to be presented for the first time to the public, of the Lives of the Saints in Ireland. This great undertaking has been ably and spiritedly commenced by the Rev. Mr. O'Hanlon, whose rare acquirements as a scholar and an Irish archæologist seem to fit him peculiarly for the task. This volume is brought out in a neat and elegant manner, and its value is enhanced by a series of careful annotations and authorities. It will be found amply to repay perusal, and to furnish a pleasing addition to the treasures of a domestic library. We shall look forward with interest to the publication of the forthcoming volumes of the series."—*Freeman's Journal.*

"Our author's volume is not a large one, but it is skilfully put together; and he has produced a work not merely of local but of general interest. There is something in it to attract every reader. In the elaborate and copious notes, the ecclesiologist and antiquarian will find a fund of information, as he has carefully and indefatigably consulted every available authority—Ussher, Ware, Colgan, the Bollandists, Lanigan, etc.—and has derived considerable assistance from the labours of Dr. O'Donovan, Professor Curry, and the Rev. Dr. Todd."—*Irish Literary Gazette.*

"This work was the more urgently required, that much ignorance prevailed respecting the life of St. Laurence, owing to the wanton misrepresentation of hostile, careless, and faithless chroniclers. Father O'Hanlon has laboured successfully to refute the false views which were propagated by political or religious malevolence, and to set the character of the illustrious subject of his work in a true light before the public. To effect this, he has read diligently and deeply; and we are happy to observe that his researches have placed in his hands, or put him on the track of, materials for a series of sacred biographies, which will comprise the Acts of over 500 of our National Saints. Such a task could not be undertaken by any one more competent for its perfect execution; and there can be little doubt that the merits of the series, combined with the moderate rate at which it will be issued to the public, will secure it a large amount of popular favour and support."—*Dublin Evening Post.*

"We hope to see Mr. O'Hanlon's book extensively circulated in this country. It is a work which displays a large amount of learning and research, and is, therefore, a very valuable contribution to our literature."—*New York Tablet.*

4. The Life of St. Malachy O'Morgair,

Bishop of Down and Connor, Archbishop of Armagh, Patron of these several Dioceses, and Delegate Apostolic of the Holy See for the Kingdom of Ireland.

Dublin: John O'Daly, 9 Anglesea Street. 1859. 8vo. Cloth, gilt.

Price Six Shillings.

"His publication shows not only an acquaintance with the classical works upon his subject, but much collateral reading ; while he has availed himself both of the writings and suggestions of contemporaries. His notes, in particular, show great diligence, and a most praiseworthy minuteness and accuracy. We do not pretend to criticise him in detail, but we are safe in saying, that he has written as a scholar ought to write, and as a biography ought to be written."—*The Rambler.*

"This volume will be found to contain authentic reference for every matter of fact which it sets forth. The numerous miracles wrought by St. Malachy in Ireland will be found affirmed by reliable authorities. The chapters which describe the state of the Church, the habitudes of the people, and their political and social status, during the life and mission of St. Malachy, are illustrated by copious notes and references, which will be duly appreciated by the historical reader. We repeat that this volume of the 'Acta Sanctorum' of our native land more than realises our warmest anticipations."—*Freeman's Journal.*

"But no complete Life of the Saint appeared till the present, by Father O'Hanlon, who has brought to his task a strong love for Irish antiquarian lore, and a clear and vigorous style of composition. The book is also enriched with copious notes, illustrative of the state of the Irish Church in the tenth and eleventh centuries, which, in themselves, are exceedingly valuable."—*New York Tablet.*

"The Irish Church owes no trifling debt of gratitude to the literary labours of the author of the Life of St. Malachy O'Morgair. The Rev. Mr. O'Hanlon brings to his task all the requisites that constitute a profound hagiologist, and we are therefore presented, in this Life of one of the most illustrious of our National Saints, with everything necessary to make such a biography complete, interesting and thoroughly reliable."—*Telegraph.*

" A book thus made up commands our respect for the author's unwearied diligence ; and, as we turn over its pages, we are strongly reminded of Diocletian's Nicomedian palace, which was built out of the fragments of many a stately edifice, and whose architect earned fame for working into one harmonious whole the capitals, shafts, friezes, and relievos of his predecessors and contemporaries."—*Nation.*

" The Rev. author is also well known in Irish literature generally. His life of St. Malachy O'Morgair evinces his acquaintance with the rarest muniments of the Government offices in Dublin, as well as an extensive reading in every department of Irish History."—*Kilkenny Moderator.*

" Mr. O'Hanlon's biography of the Saint is entitled to praise for his conscientious research and painstaking accuracy."—*Tablet.*

" The author's rare acquirements as a scholar and archæologist peculiarly qualify him for the study and illustration of Irish Hagiology; and we are gratified to perceive that his researches have placed in his hands materials for a series of ecclesiastical biographies, comprising the acts of five hundred Irish Saints. If the Rev. Mr. O'Hanlon but half complete this great design, he will have earned for himself the distinctive appellation of 'the Alban Butler of Ireland.'"
—*Weekly Agricultural Review.*

5. The Life of St. Dympna, Virgin, Martyr, and Patroness of Gheel;

With some Notices of

St. Gerebern, Priest, Martyr, and Patron of Sonsbeck.

Dublin : James Duffy, Wellington Quay.
1863. 18mo. Cloth, gilt.

Price One Shilling.

"As for ourselves, we consider it quite a relief, as, no doubt, it will be a pleasure and advantage to others, to know that the legend of St. Dympna and the history of Gheel are, happily, at last within the reach of all, even the least opulent readers, and may be found in a pretty little volume, the fruit of abundant care and laborious research, entitled, 'The Life of St. Dympna,' by the Rev. John O'Hanlon. So henceforth, inquiring spirits need not be, with a significant wave of the hand, referred to the Bollandists, reposing, in all but inaccessible state, on the shelves of great libraries—a sealed book to the multitude. Adventurous tourists, who do visit Gheel, may not any more, through sheer want of information, pass by unheeded the most interesting objects; and tarry-at-home travellers may very comfortably, if they will, make themselves up on a snbject interesting alike to the curious in legendary lore, the antiquary, and the moral philosopher."—*The Lamp.*

"In a short notice like this, it would be impossible to give anything like a sketch of this almost romantic history of the Life of the Saint, and we must refer our readers to the work itself—a work upon which the greatest care has been bestowed, and which may fairly take its place with those famous 'Lives' issued from the saintly hands of the Oratorians. * * * * A work of this kind, written by a Rev. gentleman, who is already distinguished in this species of literature, by his 'Life of St. Laurence O'Toole,' and 'Life of St. Malachy O'Morgair,' Archbishop of Armagh, must be a treat indeed."—*Kilkenny Journal.*

"This very elaborate and gracefully written Life of an Irish Saint, little known in Ireland, is well worth perusal. The notes and criticisms show that the author has devoted great labour to this memoir, and taken great care to bring together all circumstances which bear upon St. Dympna's life."—*Irishman.*

"Every courteous feeling towards the author—with every respect for his zeal, and every appreciation of the ability with which he treats his subject."—*Dublin Builder.*

"When, in addition to this kind of merit, we find that it beautifully instils one of the most sublime virtues which lead to Christian holiness, it undoubtedly possesses strong claims on the attention of a Catholic public. The pious author seems to feel fully sensible of the delicate and poetical character of his theme. He has spared no pains in attending to every circumstance which might naturally tend to increase the interest of his felicitously chosen subject. He has joined the erudition of the scholar to the zeal of the minister of the Gospel, and is fully entitled to the approval and support of all the true lovers of Irish literature."—*Tipperary Free Press.*

"The Rev. author has not taken his information from ordinary or questionable authorities. He has gone to the sources of traditions of glorious heroes and heroines of the Irish Church, and he has visited abroad and at home the spots that have been honoured by their names and sanctified by their virtues. All this he has performed with that care and energy which zeal ever brings to a work of patriotism, faith, and love. Under an unpretending exterior the 'Life of St. Dympna' contains the result of deep research and patient study, and it is one of those truly good books to which we have before alluded, and calculated to make the study of the lives of the true heroes of humanity popular with all who admire what is really great, and love what is truly good. Mr. Duffy has produced this little emerald gem with his usual care, and we have much pleasure in recommending it. In conclusion, we sincerely hope that the Rev. author will soon give us another of those *fleurs du ciel*, and we wish him the success ever deserved by those who act up to the great maxim—*Dieu et patrie.*"—*Freeman's Journal.*

"The Rev. author has added another to the many obligations which the National Church owes him, in thus rescuing from obscurity, or rather oblivion, the memory of two Saints, the odour of whose sanctity has been diffused, not only over the land in which it first became known, but throughout the Catholic world. Their present biographer, whose labours in the antiquities and ecclesiology of his country have already gained for him a most decidedly high repute, has by this last 'labour of love,' as he so happily terms it, shown how zealous and untiring he continues to be in the service of his Divine Master and his Church. Uniting in himself, in an eminent degree, the requirements of a sincere patriot, a good priest, and an eminent writer, Father O'Hanlon stands before us as an ornament to his order, and a truly faithful shepherd of the flock which he so wisely and vigilantly guides and directs. No Catholic family throughout the length and breadth of the land should be without this admirable memoir of the two Saints who flourished in those early ages when a portion of Ireland was still inhabited by pagans."—*Catholic Telegraph.*

"A very neat little volume, brought out with much taste,

and highly creditable to the enterprising publisher. The author, the Rev. Mr. O'Hanlon, R.C.C. SS. Michael and John, Dublin, is well known in connection with our local Archæological Society, for his great industry in calendaring the papers and memoirs of the Ordnance Survey; thus rendering the investigation of those valuable documents of comparative facility to the students in Irish topographical and historical research. * * * * The 'Life of St. Dympna,' now before us, is, properly speaking, a book of devotion, and will, no doubt, be read with much interest by the members of the writer's own communion. With its sentimentalism or dogmas, we cannot be supposed either to sympathise or agree. * * * * We cannot withhold from his labours the meed of our approbation, though we may not chime in with his views nor coincide in his conclusions."—*Kilkenny Moderator*.

"A very interesting work."—*The Month*.

"The biography of the Irish Saint and Martyr, St. Dympna, reads like a romance. Her name is still cherished here in Ireland, and on the scene of her trials and sufferings, in legend and fireside story. It is needless to say that the volume is quite as entertaining as it is edifying—that it contains as much interesting matter in the romantic story of St. Dympna's adventures, trials, sufferings, and martyrdom, as it does good and holy lessons of purity, piety, and constancy."—*Nation* (First Notice).

"In fact, it was not till the publication of the Rev. John O'Hanlon's 'Life of St. Dympna' that detailed and reliable information could be got. That comprehensive and erudite little book has supplied a serious want, and visitors to Gheel will find it their advantage to take it with them as a pocket companion in future."—*Nation* (Second Notice).

"We have been exceedingly edified by, and deeply interested in, the perusal of the 'Life of St. Dympna,' a 'martyr both to the faith and to chastity,' and slaughtered by her own father's hand."—*Boston Pilot*.

6. Catechism of Irish History, from the Earliest Events to the Death of O'Connell.

John Mullany, 1 Parliament Street, Dublin.
1864. 18mo.

Price Two Shillings.

"The reverend author of the little work under notice has entered on his task of compiling a Catechism of Irish History in a most commendable and candid spirit, setting nothing down in malice, nor putting himself forward as an apologist or advocate, but the narrator of fact and events in their unadorned and simple truth. The plan of the work is at once familiar, perspicacious and elegant. There is no attempt made at fine writing, nor effect sought to be obtained by word painting or exaggeration. The author proposed to himself to write a hand-book of Irish History for the use of schools, and with that view he has divided the work into lessons, and at the end of each lesson or chapter the questions to be answered are placed in admirable and consecutive order. At a time like the present, when every effort is being made to make Irishmen forget the past of their country, which influenced, more than any other in western Europe, the destinies of mankind, the appearance of the Rev. John O'Hanlon's historical catechism is most opportune. He has discharged his important duty as a Christian minister, a gentleman, patriot and scholar; he gives offence to none in the evidence which he produces, nor has he descended to the meanness of making a book for the instruction of the young a medium for conveying ill-natured statements, or for engendering hostility or ill-feeling between those who conscientiously differ from one another in politics and religion. He has not overdone his work, but has strictly adhered to a rule which he has carried out to the end. His catechism should be generally used in all schools where young Irishmen are instructed, no matter what creed they may profess."—*Freeman's Journal.*

"We would call attention to a little Catechism of Irish History, by Mr. O'Hanlon, the writer of those pleasant papers on Irish Folk-Lore Mythology, that have recently appeared in these pages. The papers, we think, prove that he can treat his subject attractively, and the following extract from his Preface is equally conclusive evidence, that he possesses the other and more important qualifications of the historian."—*Gentleman's Magazine.*

"The quantity of historical matter is immense, clearly assorted, and very judiciously selected. We are glad to see manifested an impartiality, without which history is not merely valueless, but absolutely poisonous."—*Irishman.*

"We are anxious to see this History of Ireland at once in the hands of the members of our Young Men's Societies throughout Ireland, in use in our schools, and in the library of every Irishman."—*Sligo Champion.*

"The publication of this excellent volume, at the low price of two shillings, should be regarded as a boon by that large class of Irishmen, who, by the cost of preceding works on the same subject, have been prevented from acquiring a knowledge of their country's history. They should procure this book for themselves; they should put it into the hands of their children. * * * * For young men who have not previously bestowed attention on this subject, Father O'Hanlon's work will form an excellent commencement. Should leisure and inclination enable them to pursue the study, they can learn from this volume where to seek for the fullest information relative to any given period of Irish history. At the outset of each chapter, Father O'Hanlon gives a list of the authorities which may be consulted in reference to the events of which he writes; and such an index is, of itself, a valuable directory to Irish students."—*Nation.*

"It presents a continuous stream of narrative—unbroken by those abrupt paragraphs which the teacher's queries and the pupil's replies usually necessitate. With an humble title this is an ambitious book."—*Irish People.*

"It gives a most clear, intelligible, and at the same time, concise epitome of national events from the very earliest period to the death of Ireland's illustrious Liberator, Daniel O'Connell. This is a book peculiarly suited for junior classes in our schools, because it is furnished with questions to which corresponding answers are referable in each lesson. Again, its plan makes it a most useful book for reference even for the most advanced and ripe scholars, since at the opening of each lesson we find a list of historical authorities relating to the exact period of which it treats. The book has been drawn up with much care and impartiality, while, at the same time, there is no want of sympathy with the people whose story is so well related."—*Leinster Independent.*

"Avoiding the mythical, eschewing the problematical, and placing vividly in the foreground all that appeared to him essential to the student and the antiquarian, the philosopher and the lover of his country—he has elaborated all the elements of a nation's history in the shape of an elementary treatise—a manual clear to the simple understanding and comprehension of a child, as it is ancillary to the higher knowledge required by those who aim at acquiring a thorough acquaintance with the subject, and employing the information gained for more elevated purposes. It is, indeed, astounding to find so much that cannot be dispensed with comprised within so small a space."—*Carlow Post.*

"A book which should be in the hands of every Irish schoolboy."—*Dublin Saturday Magazine.*

"Welcoming the appearance of this excellent book—excellent for the work of author, printer, and publisher alike—we beg very cordially to recommend it to the public." *Dublin Evening Post.*

7. Catechism of Greek Grammar.

John Mullany, 1 Parliament Street, Dublin.
1865. 18mo.

Price One Shilling.

"This judicious and compendious little Grammar of the Greek language takes the catechetical form, as being one best suited to lead the tyro into the mysteries of its philological constitution and its peculiarities of construction. The science of grammatical analysis, in a language so difficult of masterly attainment, is greatly simplified by this succinct and clear treatise. But, while it is mainly intended to aid junior students in a facile acquisition of the Greek declensions, conjugations, syntax and prosody, it will be found sufficiently comprehensive, as a manual, for more advanced scholars."—*Tuam News.*

"This grammar is the neatest and cheapest we have yet seen, and comprised within a limited number of pages, its rules and examples are thoroughly complete. The publication will be of great utility and advantage to the teacher in facilitating his pupil's progress. The clear and most accurate typography reflects great credit on the united care and capability both of author and publisher. This little work is critically and elaborately compiled. The introduction, or preface, gives a learned and an instructive historical account of the Greek language and writers. The work may well be recommended to the attention of teachers and pupils."—*Drogheda Argus.*

"The Catechism of Greek Grammar is elegantly bound and correctly printed; special attention having been bestowed on the proof-sheets to insure accuracy of typography and the correct placing of the accents. The rules are plain and practical throughout, and the examples are familiar and easy of translation. Its pages seem to contain every instruction necessary for making the student acquainted with the Greek language. It can safely be recommended for the use of colleges and classical schools, being an improvement in many respects on grammars once in vogue. The rules and exceptions are put in a shape easy to be remembered. The notes on the margin are explanatory of the text in the body of the book, and therefore they help rather than encumber the teacher's and the scholar's memory."—*Leinster Independent.*

8. Devotions for Confession and Holy Communion.

Thomas Richardson & Son, London, Dublin, and Derby. 1866. 18mo.

Price Two Shillings.

"The title of this devotional work is very unpretending, and by no means conveys a just idea of its valuable contents. It appears, by its modest title, to be but an ordinary book of prayer; but, on carefully examining and reading its pages, it will be found to combine many advantages not to be met with in books hitherto published on the same subjects. It contains a great number of most beautiful and soul-moving prayers, extracted from the writings of the Holy Fathers. In the examination for confession, the reverend author enters minutely into the duties of people of all classes and professions in life."—*Westminster Gazette*.

"This is a most excellent work, indeed the best we recollect to have ever seen on the two sacraments on which it treats. It is entirely devoted to Confession and Holy Communion. It should be in the hands of every Catholic, for no one can read it seriously and think lightly of confession and communion. It shows the absolute necessity of approaching these two great sacraments, if men want help on the way to eternity, and deserve the bliss of the saints in the next world."—*Dundalk Democrat*.

"The instructions are most excellent, and suitable to every age and condition of life; the devotions themselves are all that could be wished for, and the pious acts which follow the communion have been distributed in sections, so as to serve as time or opportunity may allow for select devotional reading or meditation, either before or after confession or communion. For spiritual retreats, times of special missions, as well as on ordinary occasions of approaching the sacraments, this volume is invaluable."—*Weekly Register*.

"In all Catholic prayer-books some pages are devoted to instructions and devotions suitable for the faithful who are preparing for the great Sacraments of Penance and the Eucharist; but when we consider the immense importance of those sacraments, and the incalculable interests involved in their worthy reception, it becomes at once evident that the subject, if it is to be fully and appropriately treated, requires a volume to itself. Such a volume is that which we have just received from the pen of the Rev. John O'Hanlon, whose works in various departments of Catholic and national literature are held in deservedly high estimation by the public. The reverend author, in his work, goes carefully through the whole process of ministering to a soul diseased; he supplies a series of reflections and meditations well calculated to excite in the mind of a sinner a sense of his misfortune and of his danger, and to awaken within him the desire of a speedy reconciliation with God. By means of prayer and meditation and all suitable devotions, he leads on the soul until he brings it cleansed and purified to the Holy Sacrament of the Altar; and then there are thanksgivings and prayers, instructions and good counsels, and devout exercises, intended to assist in preserving the soul in a state of grace. The volume appears to us to be in every respect admirable, and we feel sure that, as an aid to Catholic piety, it will be largely availed of by the faithful."—*Nation*.

"The book is divided into two parts, the first of which contains General Instructions regarding the Sacrament of Penance; Instructions regarding the principles of our Moral Actions and their practical application to ourselves; the obligations of Different States of Life; Prayers before and after Confession and Absolution; Regulations for a Christian Life, etc.; and Part II. contains Devotions for Holy Communion, with all necessary instructions; Explanation of the Liturgy; Ceremonies and Objects seen at Mass; Acts before and after Communion; Prayers to the Blessed Virgin and all the Saints; a most instructive lesson on the Holy Viaticum and Extreme Unction; and all through, the prayers are arranged with suitable instructions in reference to the immediate subjects. The book—which is embellished with a beautiful frontispiece, and got out in a style worthy of the eminent publishers—should add another wreath to the chaplet so well earned by the Rev. John O'Hanlon."—*Sligo Champion*.

"This admirable work is designed, as we learn from the preface, to provide persons who are desirous of approaching the two great sacraments, which Catholics most generally receive, with a complete manual of instruction and prayer adapted to general and particular requirements. This object is well carried out in the work before us. Whatever station of life the reader belongs to, whatever may be the nature of his avocations, he will find something peculiarly applicable to his circumstances in these pages. The instructions given are clear and precise, and the devotional exercises are pervaded by a spirit of deep and fervent piety. We trust this publication will obtain a wide circulation."—*Weekly News*.

9. The Life and Works of St. Aengussius Hagiographus, or St. Ængus the Culdee,
Bishop and Abbot at Clonenagh and Dysartenos, Queen's County.

John F. Fowler, 3 Crow Street, Dame Street, Dublin. 1868. 8vo. Wrapper, lettered.

Price One Shilling.

" None of the Irish Saints deserve more lasting gratitude and veneration from the students of Irish ecclesiastical history than St. Ængus the Culdee. Here, within a few pages, have we an interesting account of his Life and various writings, in prose and verse, from one of the most accomplished Archæologists of the day. The Rev. Mr. O'Hanlon has entitled himself to the thanks and gratitude of every lover of Irish history by the production of this learned and interesting work."—*Wexford Independent.*

" The writings of St. Ængus are among the most important contributions to early Irish ecclesiastical literature. Were they lost, much of it would be a perfect blank. The life of this early writer must therefore have an interest, in a special manner, for Irish ecclesiologists. With the Life we have here a review and analysis of these ancient historic treatises."—*Armagh Guardian.*

" In the labour that the collection of necessary facts entailed upon Father O'Hanlon, we can estimate his devotion to the cause of Irish literature. * * * * To rescue from the cold shades of oblivion the fame of Ængus, was a task worthy of the piety and scholarship of Father O'Hanlon."—*Quebec Irish Sentinel.*

" The amiable author tells us that it was originally written by him in the shape of a lecture, which he was asked to deliver for the benefit of a charitable institution in the parish in which he ministers. We in Ireland know what the life of a missionary priest must of necessity be, and how scant and how scattered are the intervals that a clergyman, who devotes himself so assiduously and so untiringly to all his duties as Father O'Hanlon does, can dedicate to literary pursuits. * * * * The career of the saint is very strikingly told, and the narrative is interspersed with many curious morsels of interesting lore. The portion of Father O'Hanlon's essay that treats of the writings of St. Ængus is peculiarly valuable, and displays great critical acumen, and no inconsiderable research. The style, from beginning to end, is clear, vigorous, simple, and well sustained, and admirably appropriate to the subject the Reverend author proposes to himself to treat."—*Freeman's Journal.*

"Father O'Hanlon has devoted many years of his useful life to the Hagiology of Ireland. His 'Life of St. Laurence O'Toole, Archbishop of Dublin;' 'St. Malachy O'Morgair, Archbishop of Armagh,' the friend of the great St. Bernard, and 'St. Dympna, Virgin,' are, we hope, known to many of our readers. 'The Life of St. Ængus, the Culdee,' will be hailed with satisfaction by all lovers of Ireland and her saints."—*The New York Tablet.*

"The Life of this holy and learned Irishman reflects great credit alike on the research and the talent of the Rev. gentleman who has undertaken the task—by no means an easy one, when we consider the difficulties which attend the study of Irish Hagiology. We cordially recommend the publication to every educated Irishman, as well as to all for whom the records of the past have any interest—and, lastly, to all who love to read of the Saints who have, from time to time, illumined the Church."—*The Weekly Register.*

"In Irish Archæological and Hagiologic lore, Father O'Hanlon is not only profoundly read, but, in his handling of the subjects which he takes up, clearness, and a certain degree of freshening vivacity, are conspicuous—features rarely found in productions confined to records of events that have occurred in the remote periods of history. * * * * This valuable contribution to Irish Hagiology will possess additional interest to the generality of our readers, inasmuch as the saint appears to have lived near the celebrated Rock of Dunamase, a few miles from Maryborough, and in the monastery of Clonenagh. But, irrespective of all local interest, the general Catholic reader will delight in tracing the life and the sketch of the works of a native Saint, whose rare excellencies of head and heart are thus described by his admiring biographer."—*The Carlow Post.*

"We have already exceeded our limits in our notice of Father O'Hanlon's admirable book. * * * * Ængus has been left nearly 1,100 years in manuscript. This is a disgrace to a Celtic and a Catholic country. We trust that

OPINIONS OF THE PRESS.

Father O'Hanlon, who has done so much for Irish sacred history in his 'Life of St. Malachy,' 'Life of St. Laurence O'Toole,' and the present interesting publication, will, by rescuing the Celtic martyrologist from the obscurity of manuscript, for ever link his name as a Hagiologist with the Wards and the Colgans. The critical acumen and deep research displayed in the present little work prove how well he is fitted for the task of disentombing such long-neglected treasures in aid of the regeneration and progress of historic investigation."—*The Ulster Examiner.*

"Father O'Hanlon has dedicated this little work to the Very Rev. Monseignor Moran, D.D., Professor of Irish History in the Catholic University. The work itself relates the history of one of Ireland's Saints, St. Ængus. * * * * He was also a writer of considerable ability. But for an account of his labours, we must refer the reader to the work itself, which is creditably printed."—*The Dundalk Democrat.*

"The history of an Irishman living some ten centuries ago, whose sanctity of life and whose deep erudition acquired for him an extensive reputation, is most susceptible of embellishment in the course of time; and that, as our author shows, it should be occasionally clogged by fictions and romances, arising from a succession of exaggerated accounts, is no more than is to be expected. In order to discriminate between the simple truth and the more brilliant versions of particular facts, it is requisite that the biographer should be strong-minded enough to reject the beautiful for the rude and truthful. This Father O'Hanlon has succeeded in doing, with all due moderation; and certain astonishing incidents are quietly toned down by brief and judicious remarks."—*The Westminster Gazette.*

"M. O'Hanlon avait originairement publié dans *l'Irish Ecclesiastical Record*, cette biographie de Saint Ængus; après quelques retouches il a présentée aujourd'hui sous forme de brochure. Il a dans ce travail mis à profit les meilleures sources, et il en montre une parfaite connaissance dans des notes nombreuses et instructives."—*Revue Critique d'Histoire et de Littérature.*

"The particulars known regarding the life of an Irish Saint, who died more than one thousand years ago, must be necessarily brief, still the Reverend author of this interesting little work has woven a very readable narrative out of the available materials, and shows the industry which must have been expended upon the task. * * * * We understand the author is about to publish the Lives of the Irish Saints, amongst whom our King and Bishop of Cashel, St. Cormac McCullinan, is counted as one. From the specimen before us, we believe the onerous task could not be in better hands."—*Cashel Gazette.*

"Mr. O'Hanlon's 'Life of St. Ængus' is full of erudition, which is pleasingly varied by touches of nature in his description of the lovely scenery with which the country abounds. The pedigree and early life of the saint, his studies and austerities, his visions and their purpose, his humility in forsaking the life of a choir monk for that of lay brother, his miracles, his literary labours, his life at Tallaght, and the complete list of his works, are given with a fidelity devoid of dryness, and most inviting to the reader."—*The Carlow College Magazine.*

"La savante étude que vient de faire paraître sous ce titre M. O'Hanlon présente, à divers titres, un véritable intérêt. A la vie de St. Ængus l'hagiographe se rattachent en effet plusieurs questions importantes pour l'histoire ecclésiastique et surtout pour l'histoire littéraire de l'ancienne Irlande. L'auteur s'est attaché à éclaircir ces questions sans se flatter pourtant d'avoir fait sur ce point un travail définitif, qui n'est pas encore possible dans l'état actuel de la science hagiographique irlandaise. Il reconte tout ce que l'on peut savoir jusqu'ici de la vie de son héros, depuis sa naissance, vers le milieu du viiie siècle, jusqu'à sa mort, dont la date la plus probable paraît être l'année 824. Il donne surtout des détails sur le séjour de St. Ængus dans une solitude du Queen's County, appelée depuis *Dysartenos*, (*Desertum O'Aengusa*), ensuite à l'abbaye de Tallagh et plus tard au Monastère de Clonenagh, dont il devint abbé. Les œuvres de Saint Ængus sont particulièrement l'objet de l'examen de M. O'Hanlon, qui analyse successivement son *Felire* ou éloges des Saints pour chaque jour de l'année ; le *Martyrologe de Tallagh*, (publié en 1857 par le Dr. Kelly), dont la première partie a été composée, dit-on, d'après des ouvrages, aujourd'hui perdus, d'Eusèbe et de Saint Jerôme ; le traité Latin, *De Sanctis Hiberniæ ;* un recueil de poèmes irlandais sur les récits de l'ancien Testament, recueil connu sous le titre, commun à plusieurs autres ouvrages, de *Saltair na rann ;* et enfin des fragments de généalogies des Saints irlandais, qui lui sont généralment attribués. Nous ne pouvons que nous associer au vœu qu'exprime M. O'Hanlon de voir mettre au jour par une main compétente une édition critique des œuvres inédites, ou imparfaitement publiées jusqu'ici, de Saint Ængus."—*Journal des Savants.*

"This tract contains notices of the historical works regarding early Irish Christianity, as written by a distinguished ecclesiastic of the ninth century."—*Wexford People.*

"The Life of St. Ængus, though on a small scale as compared with the work on St. Laurence O'Toole, is nevertheless most interesting and attractive as a biographical memoir. In it the author collates and arranges, with great care, all the facts which can be arrived at concerning the life and labours of this holy man. * * * * Scarcely less attractive than the body of the memoir itself are the copious notes which the author appends, and which he has culled with great industry and research from the most distinguished authorities on matters of antiquarian interest. The work is written in a plain, unpretentious, and intelligible style, and is utterly free from that pedantry which affects an unnecessary display of erudition. It is published at a very moderate charge, and from those interested in matters which can throw light on our early ecclesiastical history, will claim an attentive and earnest perusal."—*The Nation.*

"Mr. O'Hanlon is an estimable clergyman of the Roman Catholic Church, and the publication before us worthily sustains the reputation which he has already secured as a learned and zealous worker in the important field of Irish Hagiology. The biography of this monk, who flourished in the eighth and ninth centuries, and who was as highly distinguished for his literary attainments as for his religious zeal, will be read with the deepest interest. It is written in a most agreeable style, abounds in racy incidents, and furnishes various lively illustrations of the habits and usages of early monasticism. The *brochure* throughout affords ample evidence of Mr. O'Hanlon's research and learning, and is fitted to stimulate the reader with an admiration for the piety, patriotism, and ability of the old Celtic race."—*Downpatrick Recorder.*

10. The Life of St. David,

Archbishop of Menevia, Chief Patron of Wales, and Titular Patron of Naas Church and Parish in Ireland.

John Mullany, 1 Parliament Street, Dublin.
1869. 12mo. Cloth, gilt.

Price Two Shillings and Sixpence.

"Then does the writer, who so finely appreciates his task, proceed to the more learned and laborious portion of his work, which is divided into fourteen chapters. These are all replete with varied research. The early ecclesiastical history of Wales is fully revealed, in connection with the Life of St. David. His influence on its progress is recorded in text and notes. The birth, education, ordination, ministry, and episcopacy of holy David are clearly and orderly related to the date of his glorious death, at a very advanced age. This beautiful little work, the latest hagiographical production of its author, admirably illustrates his wonderful industry and talents for writing the Lives of our Irish Saints, with whom St. David holds a very close relationship now, as he was the master and companion of many among them in the olden time, when he flourished."
—*Cork Examiner*.

"Father O'Hanlon's rare reputation as a well-read historian and an accurate and earnest Hagiologist is here indeed most amply sustained. We find the same scholarly culture of style to which Father O'Hanlon's readers are well accustomed, and we do not miss the same expenditure of studious care which give all his books peculiar value. The present biography can be fairly credited with the special merit of being suited to all sorts of readers. For the general public it contains a well condensed and skilful biography of the Saint, embracing the main facts of his ancestry, his education, his works and miracles in the sacred ministry, his relations with various holy Irishmen, and his solemn appointment by the Synod of Brevi to the Archbishopric of Britain. The biography is supplemented by an account of the miracles attributed, after his death, to St. David's merits and advocacy, with a collection of inter-

esting facts regarding the Diocese of St. David's; a copious historical and topographical notice of Naas and its vicinity; and a full description, with exceedingly good illustrations, of the Catholic Church at Naas. These will thoroughly satisfy the general reader, and, for the rest, the most persevering student, ecclesiastical or secular, will find ample guidance in the notes and references, which so strikingly attest the great extent of the learned author's researches."
—*The Nation.*

"The events of his life are clearly and consecutively related, as far as they are known, in the work before us, and the historic authorities are quoted which make such a study valuable to antiquarians. Nor, as in the lives of so many Saints, do miraculous incidents hold a very prominent place. We are more attracted by the contemporaneous events of Church history, and the records of churches, founded in the early times of Christianity, in Wales. The ecclesiologist and the archæologist will alike find something to interest and instruct, while perusing this brief, and yet very exhaustive memoir. The learned author has written it with care and good judgment."—*Kilkenny Moderator.*

"This biography of St. David, from the pen of the Rev. Mr. O'Hanlon, embraces all the chief events known regarding him. It is nicely printed on toned paper, appropriately illustrated with wood engravings of Naas Church, and elegantly bound in cloth."—*Evening Telegraph.*

"Father O'Hanlon is, indeed, doing a noble work. * * * * The opening sentences give a fair conception of the tone of thought, and character of style, which herald the biography of this illustrious saint."—*Quebec Irish Sentinel.*

"He has retold the History of the Church of Wales— too long neglected by those who ought to feel most concerned for its honour—with rare clearness, and a rarer fidelity to proven facts. The work is beautifully illustrated, and the notes with which it is enriched would, of themselves, be no mean monument to the Rev. author's ability and industry."—*Weekly News.*

"The Life of St. David has much to do with the study of early Welsh Ecclesiastical History. It appears the Anglo-Norman invaders introduced his *cultus* into Ireland. Here is a brief record of those acts attributed to him, with a very complete Life, taken from early documents. The printing is very well executed, and the engravings of Naas

Church are very creditable to Mr. Hanlon, of College Green, Dublin."—*Londonderry Journal.*

"This is a little work that must have a special interest for all Churchmen, as the subject of it, St. David, is first said to have established Christianity in Wales. Not only there, on St. David's Day, do Welshmen wear the leek to honour their Patron, but it will be seen that the same usage prevailed in Naas until the close of the last century."—*Irish Times.*

"This neatly produced volume has reference to a very distinguished Saint of the Church. It appears he is regarded as the Patron of Naas parish, and the work is dedicated to the Very Rev. Dean Hughes, its pastor. We glean therefrom that the much respected P.P. enlisted the author's willing services to prepare the book, which is published at his expense. This is an example worthy the imitation of other Irish priests, to make the Patrons of our country better known. The little work is illustrated with elegant engravings of Naas Church, while a compendious history of that town and vicinity makes this biography interesting for historians, topographers, and antiquarians."—*Limerick Reporter and Tipperary Vindicator.*

"Several lives, such as those by Giraldus Cambrensis and Wharton, have been written, and a short one will be found in Alban Butler, at the 1st of March; but a fitting biography of the destroyer of British Pelagianism was still to be desired. The master of so many of our own great Saints has special claims on the affections and interest of all Irish Catholics, and in the present work their wishes will be completely gratified, as it presents to them all that can be now brought to light."—*Northern Star.*

"The Life of this eminent Saint is brief, but it contains the chief historic incidents known regarding early Christianity in Wales. St. David taught many of the old Irish Saints, and hence he was venerated in Ireland, where, after the Anglo-Norman invasion, a church was founded to his honour at Naas."—*Saunders's News-Letter.*

"In the different chapters, the notes are vouchers for the statements to which they refer. The book is elegantly bound and printed. We regret being obliged, from exigencies of time and space, to restrict ourselves to-day to this very brief notice of this the latest of the valuable contributions to our hagiographical literature, from the pen of the erudite and accomplished Father O'Hanlon."—*Drogheda Argus.*

"In following the footsteps of our Rev. biographer, from David's birth to the close of his intensely active life, we feel we are in company with a painstaking and sure guide. We are bound to acknowledge that he has consulted the best authorities, carefully investigated the obscure and doubtful points connected with the Saint's history, and altogether proved himself throughout a conscientious biographer. The foot-notes will prove of great service to the ecclesiastical student, as they contain a fund of really valuable information relating to points of early Church History."—*Freeman's Journal.*

"Father O'Hanlon is one of our quiet workers. He is saying nothing to attract public notice, but he is always engaged in labour of a literary kind. He has published Lives of St. Malachy, Archbishop of Armagh, and friend of St. Bernard ; of St. Laurence O'Toole, of St. Dympna, Virgin and Martyr. He has contributed largely to several periodicals—amongst others to the *Ecclesiastical Record.* His pen has produced several works—a Guide for Emigrants, a History of Ireland, works on language, a Greek Grammar. His 'Life of St. David' is not for the general public. The first edition is bespoken—nay, purchased—by the Catholics of Naas, and of the parish of which the Rev. Dean Hughes, author of the work on 'Ceremonies of Holy Mass,' is pastor. The illustrations are artistic—some of them beautiful. The taste and finish of the written work merit words of unqualified praise."—*Tuam News.*

"How a Welsh Saint should come to be the Patron of an Irish Church—the only one in the country dedicated to St. David is that at Naas—together with a biography of the Saint himself, and a learned disquisition on the Archæology and Ecclesiastical History of the locality, will be found most ably explained by Father O'Hanlon, on whom may fittingly be bestowed the title of the Irish Bollandist."—*The Carlow College Magazine.*

11. Legend Lays of Ireland, by Lageniensis.

John Mullany, 1 Parliament Street, Dublin.
1870. 12mo.

Price One Shilling.

"Not very long since we noticed with much gratification a volume on Irish Fairy Lore, by 'Lageniensis'—a *nom de plume* which does not hide from many the real name of the gifted author, but whose incognito—since it is his pleasure to assume it—we feel bound here to respect. The present work is one of a not very dissimilar character from its predecessor, with this important difference, however, that the myths and traditions which are embodied in it, are conveyed to the reader in verse, whilst the former was in prose. In either, the author has been equally successful, and we have now before us as interesting a contribution to our national literature. The third legend in the book, though a brief one, is peculiarly interesting in this locality. We take the liberty of transferring it to our columns here, with the notes, as they stand in the work."—*The Kilkenny Moderator.*

"La grâce de la versification et le charme des descriptions pittoresques des paysages de l'Irlande ne sont pas le seul mérite des *Legend Lays*. Les notes etendues qui accompagnent chaque pièce de vers renferment des détails instructifs sur les mœurs, les superstitions et anciennes croyances du pays ; et l'introduction signale les emprunts, jusqu'à ces derniers temps trop rares, faits par la littérature anglo-irlandaise au trésor des poétiques traditions nationales."
—*Journal des Savants.*

"This little book introduces to our notice a new Poet—as we are happy to designate him—an Irish Poet, who is not ashamed to choose Irish subjects upon which to exercise his pen. As an introduction to the work, there is a well written essay upon the poets of the present day, and their works. The book is neatly printed, nicely illustrated, and well worthy the perusal of those who admire good poetry. As a specimen, we reproduce a legend belonging to our neighbourhood, which will carry its own recommendation."
Cashel Gazette.

"A nicely got up, well printed work with a preface, and

numerous notes, giving a fund of information respecting the poets and poetry of the sister isle. The low price at which the book is sold, places it within the reach of all who wish to listen to the lays sung by our author, and founded on the fairy tales that have floated down to the present days from the times of old."—*Greenwich & Deptford Chronicle.*

"In this book are presented some two dozen familiar fairy legends of the sister isle, dressed in a very becoming and pleasing poetical garb. We feel tempted to make an extract or two from this entertaining little work. * * * * We can cordially recommend these 'Legend Lays' to the lovers of the romantic traditions with which Ireland is specially favoured."—*Catholic Opinion.*

"It specially behoves a Leinster journal to greet any man calling himself 'LAGENIENSIS,' but particularly so genuine a son of the soil. But, in truth, there is no part of Ireland in which the researches of our author will not come home with familiar interest and application. The entire realm of Fairyland is laid open by a wave of our Wizard's wand, and every page we read only serves to allure us with a more irresistible witching of fascination, deeper and deeper into the enchanted cave, which the sparkling light of his society and the torch of a Cicerone jointly illuminate. It contains views and visions not only specially interesting to young people, but to children of a larger growth also, amongst whom we are not ashamed to class ourselves."—*The Leinster Independent.*

"The Legend Lays of Ireland * * * * a careful versified selection of them."—*Nation.*

"There is true poetic purity and power in these, as in the previous lays."—*Daily Express.*

"'The Legend Lays of Ireland' are admirable specimens, not only of the poet's art, but of the fruits of true inspiration likewise."—*The Catholic Telegraph.*

"These poems, thoroughly rich and 'racy of the soil,' are the first we have seen in a collected form, under the above pseudonym; but they emanate, we are aware, from one, who in other walks of literature is neither unknown or unhonoured. The 'Legend of Donegal' and some half-dozen others we remember to have seen exactly ten years ago in the *Dublin University Magazine,* when it really merited that title; but the bulk of the volume is sparklingly new and refreshing. It is a healthy sign to see the increasing growth of Irish national literature published in Dublin, and free from any traces of a disposition to make it instrumental in the propagandism of any peculiar view of politics—the study of which, a thinker once said, is enough to file the soul out of a man. An exhaustive introduction on the origin of popular superstitions, reminding one of the best parts of Sir Walter Scott's 'Letters on demonology and witchcraft,' inaugurates the sequel. This embraces legends of Killarney, Ormond Castle, Cullenagh, Dunamase, Holycross, Lough Gill, the coast of Clare, the Cove of Cork, Lough Erne, Blarney Castle, and the Glen of Imaile, disclosing to us privileged views of the silver-hoofed steed of O'Donoghue ploughing the blue waters of Killarney; the fairy court of hidden caverns, Leprechauns, fairy hurlers, the white goblin of St. Mullins, vision of the Culdees at Holycross, and weird banshees. It may indeed be said, that this volume combines the substantial interest of Crofton Croker's massive prose, with the pathos of Dermody's muse, the fire of Drennan, and the simplicity of Furlong. The volume is dedicated in five laudatory stanzas to William John Fitzpatrick, the biographer of Bishop Doyle, Lord Cloncurry, and Lady Morgan."—*The Irish Times.*

"The 'Legend Lays' will be hailed with delight in every homestead where the works of Kennedy, Banim, Griffin, Lever, Croker, Lover, and Carleton are prized. It affords fresh proof, that the mine of fairy lore, so much loved in this our land, contains many a yet unexhausted vein, to allure and reward the fearless delver. It is a book to read with pleasure, beneath the shade of a tree in summer, by the noon-tide lounger in the field, and beside the winter hearth, when the young and joyous, tired of the dull monotony of a dreary day, clamour for tales of the wild, the bright, or the wonderful."—*The Drogheda Argus.*

12. Irish Folk Lore:

Traditions and Superstitions of the Country: with Humorous Tales, by Lageniensis.

Cameron and Ferguson, 88 West Nile Street, Glasgow. 1870. Crown 8vo.

Price Two Shillings.

"Nor has Lageniensis confined himself to gleaning from *rare* books, inaccessible to all but a few who have time to spend in large libraries; on the contrary, he has contrived to gather from our ancient manuscripts, preserved in the Royal Irish Academy and elsewhere, historical episodes, tales, and legends which will be perused with satisfaction all the more delightful because heretofore utterly unknown to the people. * * * * An amount of edifying instruction and entertainment far surpassing anything of the sort we have ever before seen will be found in these admirable pages. * * * * Every page of this excellent work teems with information of the most pleasing character, and many of the stories convey a moral lesson which will be found valuable in the every-day business of life. It has been wisely remarked that as long as one is able to read he cannot be entirely unhappy, nor do we hesitate to affirm that the perusal of the work before us will not only amuse the lover of his country, but intensify that holy sentiment."
—*The Nation.* (First Notice.)

"This is one of the most readable and most attractive volumes of its class which we recollect to have ever perused. It also embraces a far more comprehensive range of subjects than any similar work with which we are acquainted, since it deals not only with existing legends, traditions and popular superstitions, but embraces a vast amount of antiquarian and historical information connected with all periods of our national annals, while endlessly diversified with amusing tales and stories drawn from all parts of Ireland, North and South equally. The author displays extensive reading, refined taste, matured judgment, and his descriptive sketches even of popular follies are usually lessons of moral wisdom. He has evidently studied with care the history and antiquities of Ireland at their native sources, and his notices of peasant customs as remnants of original Paganism are often curious and instructive. His interesting episode of Dungal, the learned Irish Recluse of the ninth century, and his account of some Irish Astronomical manuscripts, whose existence is scarcely known even in the learned world, prove his fitness for higher researches than those embodied in the highly-interesting miscellany before us."—*Londonderry Standard.*

"The author of the Old Folk Lore of Ireland writes from the fulness of a genial heart, and a well stored head. He is evidently an enthusiast about his theme, and labours earnestly and lovingly to make his reader as interested as himself. He has spared no pains to produce an interesting volume, and we feel a hearty pleasure in congratulating him on the successful result. His task was far from being a light one. True it is, the materials existed in abundance, but it was not always easy to reach them. Many of the oral traditions of ancient manners and customs lay buried in some cottage in the bog, or on the hill-side, and it must have been at the cost of much personal comfort, and at the sacrifice of considerable time and patience, that 'Lageniensis' succeeded in rescuing them from obscurity. The written materials for his work were scattered about in unfrequented nooks and corners of solemn and peaceful libraries, and we can reverentially admire, without the smallest hope of having the courage ever to imitate, the conscientious industry, the unflagging zeal, and the affectionate devotion with which he pursued his interesting, but fatiguing explorations. He has gathered together his varied researches, and presents them to the world in the volume whose title is prefixed to this notice of it."—*Freeman's Journal.*

"Independent of these legendary and mythological subjects, there is contained in this volume very valuable papers on more purely antiquarian matters, such as the early voyages and discoveries of Irishmen and others to remote islands and lands in the chapter entitled 'Hy-Breasail, or the Blessed Island;' and on the religion and ceremonial of the Druids in a chapter devoted to tracing the mysteries of that singular and mysterious belief. These chapters, as also some others not exactly cognate, though bearing on and illustrative of each other, and all illustrative of our ancient peoples, exhibit the most extensive reading and research, patient industry, and scrupulous attention to authorities, with, at the same time, a breadth of view which comprehends within its limits every discordant element, and brings it into one harmonious whole. We would gladly make some extracts from this charming book, at once so entertaining and instructive, but that we fear we would be doing the author an injustice by rudely separating from the context isolated passages, which would fail to convey an adequate impression of its varied and valuable contents. Every admirer of Irish fiction, humour, pathos, and folk-lore, who wishes to understand the people through the medium of their own traditions, as told and recorded by themselves, should possess himself of a copy. He will there find the stories and legends of the past, as told at the pattern and by the fireside, and all breathing the wild simplicity and genuine flavour of the Irish mind."—*Northern Star*.

"Still, a writer versed in Celtic literature, and acquainted with the habits and customs of the peasantry of the generation which is now passing away, can yet, as the author of the present volume shows, present the generic peculiarities, the broad, general features of Irish folk-lore. 'Lageniensis' is certainly well qualified for the task he has undertaken. He unites to a wide and deep knowledge of Irish literature and Irish history an intimate acquaintance with peasant life, especially as it exists in the midland and eastern counties of Ireland. His enthusiasm carries him into nooks and corners of Irish literature and history which have never, or rarely, been visited by antiquarians before; while his power of felicitous expression enables him to throw around the old stories of the people a charm which, it may be said without any disparagement to previous labourers in the same field, is calculated to win for this branch of study more attention than it has as yet been deemed worthy of receiving."—*The Nation*. (Second Notice.)

"There is no book in any language that we know like this charming volume. It is perfectly *sui generis*, unique, and original, and yet it treats of themes which are familiar to all Celtic ears from childhood upwards, but which none of us have ever before seen selected with such felicitous taste, or combined in such charming variety. Traditions, superstitions, humorous and pathetic tales, ancient Celtic idolatries, romances of history, local memorials, popular notions, sprite frolics and peculiarities—these are some of the miscellaneous contents of a book which no Irishman should be without, and no reading man should be ignorant of, if he would be well posted on the multifarious and highly amusing and interesting subjects to which this welcome volume relates."—*Limerick Reporter and Tipperary Vindicator.*

"Of the illustrative tales and legends which accompany these subjects, they are told with infinite humour and graphic effect, and altogether, we have here an Irish work which promises to be held throughout time in high esteem, not alone amongst Irishmen, but wherever the genuine taste for fairy lore and Celtic idiosyncrasies exist."—*Kilkenny Moderator.*

"Two Tales, 'The Fomorian Warrior, Balor of the Evil Eye,' and 'Mr. Patrick O'Byrne in the Devil's Glen.' The former is an interesting legend of Old Ireland—the latter is a humorous sketch of Irish character. * * * * Both are well told. The description especially of Mr. O'Byrne's conversation with the Echo, or 'The Voice of the Rock,' is very ingenious and amusing. The rest of the volume is chiefly devoted to brief chapters on Irish superstitions and customs."—*North British Daily Mail.*

"'The Wizard Earl of Kildare' is a bold sketch well thrown off, and 'Dungal the Recluse' is a very useful and creditable paper; whilst 'Mr. Patrick O'Byrne in the Devil's Glen' is worth the whole volume ten times told."—*The Irishman.*

"Besides these graceful or amusing superstitions, there is the melancholy though poetic faith in the banshee, and the belief in the fetch or doppel-ganger which seems common to all countries. Then we find a universal trust in the tradition of Hy-Breasail, or the Blessed Island, Thierna-Oge, the land of the youthful and happy. * * * 'Lageniensis' speaks of the merrow-maiden and the merrow-man, corresponding to the English superstition of the mermaid. On the south coast of Ireland the mermaid is to the present hour fully believed in, and the writer of this article has frequently while sea fishing listened to detailed narratives of her appearance. * * * * The national schools have seriously encroached upon the haunts of the fairies, have dispelled the sheeted banshee, and silenced the chant of the cluricaun and the tap of his tiny hammer, as he cobbled at his shoe-leather. The hills are no longer hollow, burrowed with diamond-lit caves, the earth holds no crocks of gold, and no sunset reveals a happy island on the far dim verge of the sea. These things are no longer the simple and common properties of the people, they are almost unknown to the up-springing generation. * * * * The fairies are as dead as great Pan is in Greece, and the tribute that 'Lageniensis' pays to their memory is probably the last that we shall have of them in print."—*The Pall Mall Gazette.*

"Much that is historically interesting is being altered, and the old-world stories are rapidly becoming forgotten. Yet there is hardly one of them in which there does not lurk something worthy of immortality—something to which the antiquarian of the future will not be able to point as an illustration, or the historian refer as a landmark, actually fixing the date of some event or action, stretching far back into the past. For which reason the labours of 'Lageniensis' in collecting his *Irish Folk Lore: Traditions and Superstitions of the Country* (Glasgow: Cameron and Ferguson. 1870,) are beyond all praise."—*The Carlow College Magazine.*

"We must refer the lovers of old floating stories—or bits of stories, for they are often no more—about Banshees, sprites, ghosts, fairies, wizards, and the like, to the volume itself. One of the most interesting traditions prevalent of old in Ireland was that which related to an unknown and a most beautiful island far to the west, which went by the name of Hy-Breasail, the Blessed Island. The belief concerning it was probably a shadow of some early knowledge of America. A chapter in the present work (chap. xv.) collects the traditions on this subject."—*The Month.*

"The reader will find both amusement and instruction in the pages of the book now under review. The author has happily blended the facts which his industrious research has gathered, together with the amusing fictions which pass current among the imaginative sons of the Emerald Isle. We conclude our remarks by commending the book to our readers' notice, as a capital collection of Irish folk lore, and as a reliable history of the curious customs and observances which, from an early period, have prevailed in Ireland, and the origin of which is involved in much obscurity."—*The Guernsey Mail and Telegraph.*

"L'Irlande est par excellence le pays des légendes et des traditions. Nulle autre contrée en Europe n'offre une mine plus riche, peut-être même aussi riche, de poétiques trésors et d'antiques souvenirs, le peuple qui l'habite étant privilégié, comme on le sait, sous le double rapport des facultés imaginatives et de la fidélité à la tradition. Déjà cette mine a été explorée dans diverses directions, et les récits populaires, aussi bien que les monuments connus de l'ancienne littérature nationale, ont été mis à profit, un peu par les érudits, et surtout par les romanciers et les poëtes. Toutefois il reste encore, non-seulement à glaner, mais à moissonner largement dans un champ aussi fécond ; et il faut se hâter, car les sources de la tradition orale tendent à se tarir tous les jours. On doit donc savoir beaucoup de gré à l'auteur d'avoir, en publiant cet intéressant volume, sauvé de l'oubli un grand nombre de récits, de légendes et de superstitions populaires qui auraient pu tomber dans l'oubli, et qui ont une grande importance pour l'ethnographie et la mythologie comparées. Il en a emprunté les éléments à deux sources différentes : à la tradition orale pour la meilleure part, et aussi aux nombreuses œuvres de la littérature moderne de l'Irlande, où se trouvent dispersées une foule de précieuses indications. Le volume est divisé en trente-cinq chapitres, consacrés chacun à une des faces si multiples du sujet. Il renferme aussi plusieurs 'récits humoristiques' spirituellement contés. L'auteur n'a pas eu la prétention de donner un ouvrage complet sur les légendes et superstitions irlandaises, et il serait par conséquent injuste de lui reprocher le peu de développement qu'il a donné à chacun de ses chapitres ; mais, après avoir lu ce qu'il fait connaître, on doit souhaiter qu'il puisse, grâce à de nouvelles recherches, donner au public dans un ouvrage étendu, et exempt cette fois d'ornements accessoires, un recueil aussi complet que possible des croyances et des traditions populaires de l'Irlande."—*Journal des Savants.*

"It is unnecessary for us to go over the other chapters, and we need say nothing more than that the book is most valuable as a record of the 'folk-lore' of other days. The respected author has done Ireland much service in preserving those interesting tales and legends from oblivion. The book should be in the hands of every Irishman."—*The Dundalk Democrat.*

"Decidedly, this is the most entertaining book the year

has brought forth. It abounds with humorous and pathetic legends. * * * * The chapters which relate to fairy lore are highly interesting, and we feel certain that the *pater-familias* who pooh-poohs when his children eagerly relate the marvels they have read in their new book, will himself peruse it with much avidity ' on the sly,' when the youngsters have retired for the night. He can remember the charm such legends cast over his own life's morning hours ; and after his battle with the hard, cruel world, he will be ready to exclaim, with an admired song writer :—
> 'There are many less innocent things I ween,
> Than dreaming of fairies now.'"

—*The Leinster Independent.*

"L'ouvrage de Lageniensis (pseudonyme sous lequel se cache un ecclésiastique distingué de Dublin) a surtout pour but de faire apprécier au grand public le côté poétique et pittoresque des traditions irlandaises. L'auteur les passe toutes en revue dans des récits d'une lecture agréable et qui donnent une idée assez fidèle de l'ensemble du *Folk Lore* irlandais, mais qui n'approfondissent pas le sujet."—*Revue Celtique.*

"This is an unpretending little volume, but it forms a welcome addition to the stock of materials which are possessed by folk-lore students. * * * * The more collectors we have like 'Lageniensis,' who will set forth in simple style what they have gathered from the lips of the country people. the better will it be for the author of the comprehensive work which yet remains to be written on the folk-lore of our islands. In one respect, in particular, it is to be hoped that those who labour in Ireland will follow his example, and that is in avoiding over-facetiousness. In his book the 'humorous tales' do not occupy more than their appropriate share of space ; and the grave reader is not depressed by too great an exhibition of the boisterous high spirits in which Irish writers so often deem it necessary to indulge when they are describing the manners and customs of their countrymen. * * * * The folk-lore of Ireland has been so carefully studied and so fully illustrated by Mr. Crofton Croker, that 'Lageniensis' has not thought it necessary to build up anything like a mythological system, but has merely gossiped, and that agreeably enough, about certain of its more prominent points. The most valuable parts of his book are, of course, those additions to our stock of information on the subject which his own experience has enabled him to contribute. * * * * Before taking leave of this pleasant little volume, we ought to call attention to the kindly tone which pervades its pages. When so many authors are in the habit of hewing away at their brother writers as ferociously as if they were ancient Israelites smiting Amalekites, it is pleasant to find one of the irritable race who dispenses kind words around as lavishly as 'Lageniensis.'"—*The Athenæum.*

"The humorous tales in 'Folk Lore' demonstrate that Irish wit and Irish jokes are devoid of that coarseness and horseplay which is so essentially John Bullish; the pathetic legends will show the tenderness of the Irish nature; the fairy tales, their superabundance of faith, and the riotousness of their imagination; whilst the peeps into archæological and religious subjects, such as are to be found in the chapters devoted to the 'Traces of Druidism in Ireland,' 'Lake Habitations and Spirits,' 'Divinations, Astrology, and Nostrums,' 'Dungal Recluse, a learned Irishman of the Ninth Century,' and many others, will amply repay the time spent by the antiquarian in reading them. It is a work without which no college, monastic, or conventual library can be considered complete, and one which ought to be studied as well by the archæologist as the general reader."—*The Weekly Register.*

"The cheapest and pleasantest shilling's worth of the season. It is really wonderful to see such a work produced for such a price. For a course of three hundred pages and upwards the reader is wafted, as if in a balloon, to that cloud-land of magic and fairyism, in which the imagination of the young delights to revel. The fairy changeling—the mermaid—the merman—the hidden treasure—the banshee —the lake spirit—the water sheerie or bog-sprite—the enchanted island of the blest—the warrior of the evil eye— divinations—enchantments—sprite frolics—in short, the whole realm of Fairydom is flung open to view. But the graceful writer has waved o'er the scene a torch-glare by which it was hitherto unillumined. Scattered throughout the interesting volume will be found valuable analogical remarks which connect those apparently childish legends with the pagan lore held in estimation by our forefathers before the sun of Christianity arose. Thus the volume is rendered one which may be safely placed at recreation hours in the hands of pupils of Convent Schools and Colleges, and for older persons will often pleasantly beguile a leisure hour."—*Catholic Opinion.*

13. The Buried Lady:

A Legend of Kilronan, by Lageniensis.

Joseph Dollard, 13 and 14 Dame Street, Dublin. 1877. Crown 8vo.

Price Four Pence.

"While the story is told in flowing verse, the notes are given, of course, in plain prose; and curious it is to observe the wealth of historic, traditional and miscellaneous lore crushed into about three pages of small type appended to the poem."—*The Irish Monthly.*

"'Lageniensis' has been pressed to publish in one volume a selection from the charming poems which he has written from time to time during the last twenty years. * * * * All appeared anonymously, if the *nom de plume*, Lageniensis, by which he is as well known in literary circles, as the poet, antiquarian and hagiologist, as by his own name, can be called an anonymous signature. One of his longer poems, 'The Buried Lady, a Legend of Kilronan,' has recently fallen under our notice. * * * * We trust that he will include in the forthcoming edition this little poem, which breathes, throughout, all the spirit of tenderness and piety, so appropriate to the venerable Church of Kilronan,—the burial place of Carolan, the last of our Irish bards—where the scene is laid."—*The Leinster Leader.*

14. The Life of St. Grellan,

Patron of the O'Kellys and of the Tribes of Hy-Maine.

James Duffy & Sons, 14 and 15 Wellington Quay, Dublin. 1881. Crown 8vo.

Price Sixpence.

15. Report of the O'Connell Monument Committee.

James Duffy & Co., Limited, 14 and 15 Wellington Quay, Dublin. 1888. 8vo.

Not Sold.

16. Life and Scenery in Missouri,

Reminiscences of a Missionary Priest.

James Duffy & Co., Ltd., 14 & 15 Wellington Quay, Dublin. 1890. 18mo.

Price One Shilling.

"The handy but comprehensive little volume under notice, nicely printed and brought out by Duffy and Co., does not fall short of any previous cognate work. Indeed is it on the contrary, for the quantity and variety of knowledge contained within its three hundred clearly printed pages indicate not only an immense amount of pertinent information on the part of the talented, facile, and reverend author, but display an amount of personal experience, garnered by close observation and characterised by an ability of arrangement, combined with a great facility of graphic description and perfect narrative, which few authors have approached in historical or topographical record. The reader is introduced to St. Louis in the autumn of 1843, and the settlement, growth, and development of the great State of Missouri, of which it is the capital, during nearly forty years, until it has reached a point of civilisation second to none of its sister States of the Union. This is recounted with a fidelity, completeness and power of description and narrative all absorbing to the general reader, and it is a source of delight to the student or *littérateur*. * * * Besides the personal sketches, the chapters abound with several beautiful pieces of scene painting, recitals of stirring incident, solid reflection, and effective moral, all punctuated here and there with humorous episodes. As affording a good insight to the history of North America the work will be most valuable as a book of reference. As a history of Missouri it is probably unequalled."—*The Weekly Freeman's Journal.*

"The book has naturally much to say of the illustrious and singularly gifted prelate, the Most Rev. Dr. Kenrick, who has directed the spiritual affairs of St. Louis with such splendid success, and through so many years of trials and vicissitudes. * * * * The incident of his Grace's Golden Jubilee cannot fail to be of interest to Irishmen here at home, as his Grace is a native of the city of Dublin, and has always shown a deep concern for the welfare of the land of his birth."—*Irish Ecclesiastical Record.*

"The neat little volume, whose title we have given above, is sure of a prompt and an extensive welcome, and it is well entitled to it. It consists for the most part of letters written many years ago, and whilst the observant and genial author of them was in the very centre of the 'Life and Scenery' he so gracefully and graphically records, and contributed to the *American Celt,* then edited by the able and lamented Thomas D'Arcy M'Gee. * * * * 'The missionary priest' has turned all his opportunities to the best account, and has succeeded in producing a very readable book, full of information, replete with admirably drawn sketches of character and of incidents that impart to it great life and variety. A good deal of the rev. author's missionary career was spent in St. Louis, and he has much that is full of interest to tell us of the growth of that city, of its Catholicity, and of its social and political life."—*The Freeman's Journal* (Daily).

"An interesting little book, entitled 'Life and Scenery in Missouri,' is published by Messrs James Duffy & Co., Dublin. It contains the reminiscences of a missionary priest—now a Canon of the Dublin diocese, the Very Rev. J. O'Hanlon—who has had exceptional opportunities for observation and inquiry throughout all the country which this volume covers. Some of the sketches originally appeared in an American paper, but they have been recast, with many additions and corrections, and in their present form they constitute an agreeably descriptive handbook of the scenery, the mineral resources, and the manners and customs of an important district in the Far West."—*The Daily Telegraph.* (London.)

"The book is divided into forty-two chapters, and from the opening lines to the very last page the interest is sustained throughout. * * * * We hope to have sufficiently indicated the scope of the work to recommend it to the reader, who cannot fail to derive from its perusal a fund of instruction on many points, and especially a deep insight into the free institutions of America, that great haven of the Celtic race, the greater Ireland beyond the waves."—*The Leitrim Observer.*

17. The Irish Emigrant's Guide for the United States,

With Coloured Map and Railway Connections.

First Irish Edition, revised, and Information brought down to the present Year.

Sealy, Bryers and Walker, Middle Abbey Street, Dublin. 1890. 18mo.

Price One Shilling.

"Canon O'Hanlon was a resident of the American Republic forty years ago, and he knows something about this matter. For ourselves, we must say that we entirely agree with him when he sounds a note of warning against promiscuous emigration; for we are very much inclined to think that the last state of many of our countrymen when they 'go West' turns out to be very much worse than the first. Be that as it may, however, those who have made up their minds to try their fortune in America will find in Canon O'Hanlon's volume the information which it is absolutely essential they should be in possession of, if they mean to have their wits about them in taking the serious step of going to a strange country. The first issue of the work was published in 1851 in Boston. It had then a very extensive circulation, and has since passed through a number of editions. This is the first edition produced in Dublin, and it has been revised throughout, and its information and directions brought up to date. An excellent feature of the book is a very good map of the United States."—*United Ireland.*

"There is a brief review of the historical progress and development of the United States, and the constitution of their several governments, each State treated separately. Advice is also offered on the obtaining of employment, wages, farming, the climates, and many other interesting matters. An appendix gives the constitution of the United States, and full particulars about each of the Transatlantic steamship companies."—*Evening Telegraph.*

"It has been compiled from the most trustworthy sources, and the learned author's personal knowledge and experience have been largely drawn upon. * * * * To the general reader the book affords most interesting and instructive information, and it may be read universally with profit. It is produced in a very attractive and handy form."—*Irish Times.*

"The uneducated peasant leaves Ireland very often in the hope of securing immediate employment, and with a few years' labour a competency, but that hope is seldom realised in the case of the man or woman who does not count the cost, or goes out unprepared for any emergency that might arise on landing. To avoid any such misfortune in the case of future emigrants, this handsome and most instructive little book, which has been compiled with much care and forethought by the Rev. Mr. O'Hanlon, is now offered at a reasonable price to all who desire to become acquainted with America and its resources."—*Irish Society.*

"The Irish Emigrant's Guide for the United States, by the Rev. John Canon O'Hanlon, P.P., Dublin, Sealy, Bryers and Walker, is an excellent book, well worth its price of a shilling, and it would be great advantage to the numerous emigrants from this country if they consulted its pages before leaving home."—*Cashel Gazette.*

"The impression before us is the first Dublin edition, and the author states that it is the outcome of careful revision, in order to bring its information down to the present date."—*Morning News.* (Belfast.)

"The information is detailed in short chapters, each combined to its own special circumstances. Accompanying the present work is a large and finely drawn and coloured modern map of the United States, representing the different lines of railway and their directions, as also the boundaries of the various States and Territories, which will prove especially useful, as it has been specially designed to illustrate the information given in the Guide."—*Armagh Guardian.*

WORKS BY THE SAME AUTHOR.

" The eminent position Canon O'Hanlon occupies in the literary world gives guarantee that anything emanating from his facile and energetic pen will, as well, be most entertaining and useful reading as reliable and accurate in information. * * * * This guide was first issued in 1851, at Boston, while Canon O'Hanlon was a resident of the United States, where he sojourned several years, and it had then a very extensive circulation ; but the one under notice is the first Dublin edition, which has been revised throughout, and the exact information brought down to date ; some special remarks pertaining to the wants and conditions of Irishmen being adapted by the Very Reverend author, which really take the form of practical instruction on emigration. An excellent map of the United States is attached to the handy volume, which should be had and carefully studied by every Irish Emigrant."—*Weekly Freeman.*

" The reverend author writes of America and the Americans from a lengthy personal experience, and his manual touches every department of knowledge useful to emigrants."
—*The Bookseller.*

18. Essay on the Antiquity and Constitution of Parliaments in Ireland.

By Henry Joseph Monck Mason, LL.D., and M.R.I.A.

With a Life of the Author, and an Introduction by Very Rev. John Canon O'Hanlon.

James Duffy & Co., Ltd., 14 & 15 Wellington Quay, Dublin. 1891. 18mo.

Price One Shilling.

" A re-issue of this able Pamphlet by Canon O'Hanlon comes at an opportune moment. It is a valuable addition to the literature on the great question of Irish Home Rule. There exists a tendency in certain quarters to ignore the great fact that Ireland possessed a Parliament entirely independent of the Parliament of England from the very beginning of such institutions, down to our own times.

(40)

* * * * Mr. Mason explains the powers and privileges of each. * * * * We heartily recommend it."—*Dublin Review.*

"The Very Rev. John Canon O'Hanlon has issued this new edition of Dr. Mason's valuable essay, with an introduction and life of the author. The introduction so supplements and completes Mr. Mason's work as to give the reader a complete view of Irish Parliamentary history. The historical period covered is from the first Irish Parliament under Henry II. to the Parliament of 1800. Dr. Mason's original work had been long out of print and had grown very scarce. In bringing out this edition of it as 'a work indispensable for the elucidation of the Irish Home Rule question,' the editor has added greatly to its value by his own original writing in connection with it."—*St. Louis Daily Republic.*

"There is something significant in the spirit of brotherhood that is abroad among the various religious communions of the Ireland of to-day in the fact that Canon O'Hanlon has edited this new edition of the pamphlet which Mr. Henry Joseph Monck Mason published seventy years ago, in defence of the ancient prerogatives of the Parliaments of Ireland. Mr. Monck Mason was in his time a sturdy, if not an aggressive upholder of Protestant principles."—*The National Press.*

"The author demonstrates that Irish Parliaments succeeded each other with undeviating regularity, that they were legislative and popular bodies, that they enacted all the statutes necessary for the governing of the country, and most important of all, that as a nation, Ireland was altogether independent of the English Parliament, and was in no way bound by its enactments. What have those who found fault with the provisions of Mr. Gladstone's Home Rule Bill, and who based their opposition to it on the erroneous argument that Ireland for centuries did not possess Parliaments distinct from those of the Saxon, to say to this? Enough has been said to show the high appreciation in which both the antiquarian and politician should hold Dr. Mason's choice collection of historic records and literature. Canon O'Hanlon has done more for the new edition than capably editing it. His facile and gifted pen has adorned it with a brief, lucid preface, a deeply interesting, and even elaborate biography of the author, and a voluminous, scholarly, deeply-thought, and closely-reasoned introduction."—*Freeman's Journal.*

"The work has been long since out of print, and no more useful literary labour has been undertaken by anyone during the last few years than that which gives to the public, in the cheap and handy form in which this book is now issued, a work with which every man who means to take any part in the settlement of the Home Rule question should be acquainted. Canon O'Hanlon has prefaced Mr. Mason's essay by an introduction of considerable value, in which he shows a profound knowledge of Irish history. * * * * Altogether the little book, which has been turned out very neatly by Duffy, is, as it stands, a distinct gain to the Irish political literature of the day."—*United Ireland.*

"Henry Joseph Monck Mason's 'Parliaments of Ireland,' long a standard work, appears in a new edition prefaced by an introduction and a life of the author by the Very Rev. John Canon O'Hanlon, who dedicates the work to Mr. Gladstone. The book itself needs no notice, but the 'Life' is both interesting and curious. The book is simply bound and is intended to be within the means of all buyers."—*The Boston Pilot.*

19. The Case of Ireland's Being Bound by Acts of Parliament in England Stated,

By William Molyneux.

With Preface and Life of the Author, by the Very Rev. John Canon O'Hanlon.

Sealy, Bryers and Walker, Middle Abbey Street, Dublin. 1892. 8vo.

Price Two Shillings.

"A new edition of this valuable and exhaustive book has just been published with a preface and life of the author by the Very Rev. Canon O'Hanlon, P.P., M.R.I.A. Like all works with which Canon O'Hanlon is connected, it is marked by erudition, knowledge, and care. The life is extremely interesting, and authorities are quoted for all statements contained in it. The aim of the editor was to render the present edition more desirable and satisfactory than any other which preceded it, and in this he has succeeded. It is a most useful work for all who desire to be acquainted with the real facts of the connection between this country and England, and no Irishman's library is complete without 'The Case of Ireland Stated.'"—*The Evening Telegraph.*

"The publishers have conferred a great boon on Irishmen by securing the services of Canon O'Hanlon for the editing of this new edition of Molyneux's famous book, and the very rev. gentleman merits our cordial acknowledgment of the manner in which he has completed his task. The Preface and the Life of the Author of the 'Case Stated' are invaluable as helping to awaken fresh interest in our past history, and at this stage in our political fortunes, we cannot doubt but that the work will be widely read by all who are desirous of understanding the problems attending the Legislative Union."—*Belfast Morning News.*

"We have to thank the enterprise of a Dublin publisher and the careful, patriotic scholarship of Canon John O'Hanlon, for filling this vacant place on the popular bookshelf. They have given us a handy, readable, and scholarly edition of Molyneux's famous work. Canon O'Hanlon has prefixed to it a brief but industriously compiled and complete account of the author."—*National Press.*

"It is a couple of centuries since this work first appeared, and was, after due condemnation in Parliament, burned by the common hangman. The present edition is chiefly remarkable for the very interesting life of the author prefixed."—*Monthly Literary List.* (New York.)

"An attraction upon which the learned Canon lays stress is a reproduction of a likeness of Molyneux from a picture in the Theatre of Trinity College, Dublin, and from a beautiful stipple and copperplate line engraving by the celebrated Brocas, published by R. E. Mercier, in Dublin, many years ago. * * * * Our only regret is that the publication of this glorious vindication of Irish liberty has been delayed so long."—*The Weekly Examiner and Ulster Weekly News.*

20. The Poetical Works of Lageniensis.
With Portrait of Author.

James Duffy & Co., Limited, 15 Wellington Quay, Dublin. 1893. Crown 8vo, cloth.

Price Five Shillings.

"The first poem, which has well-nigh attained the dimensions of a great epic, consisting as it does of six cantos, or nearly two thousand lines, written in Spenserian verse, deals with a subject admitting of the highest poetic embellishment, and often presents graces of thought and felicitous turns of expression that prove the author's thorough conversance with the noblest poetry of the language. * * * * Nor will any one who reads this poem deny that the distinguished author has discovered abundance of poetic material in his theme, and has expressed it in language that lends to the 'Land of Leix' an interest it had never hitherto possessed. * * * * The second part of the volume is entitled 'Legend Lays of Ireland,' and expresses in poetic form, as the author informs us in his erudite preface, some tales selected from a treasury of folk-lore which is practically inexhaustible. * * * * The poems are for the most part replete with life and movement, and encircle the incidents to which they give expression in all the weird glamour of an Irish fairy-land. * * * * We congratulate Canon O'Hanlon on his admirable book, and beg to express a hope that he may continue long to labour in this and the other fields of our Irish national literature, in which the harvest is so abundant, and the labourers so few."—*The Irish Ecclesiastical Record.*

"A warm welcome must be extended to the newly-collected 'Poetical Works of Lageniensis,' which have been published by James Duffy and Co., of Dublin. The author is a very reverend gentleman, who prefers to issue his verses under the name which first made his compositions popular, although it is an open secret that his real name is Canon John O'Hanlon. He wields a graceful as well as an enthusiastic, learned, and patriotic pen, and many besides his fellow-countrymen in Ireland will like to peruse not only his longer poem, 'The Land of Leix,' but the interesting 'Legend Lays of Ireland' and his scholarly sonnets." —*The Daily Telegraph.* (London.)

"The Very Rev. Canon O'Hanlon's name was for long associated with the graver pursuits of Irish hagiology and archæological research. He now comes before us as a poet and folk-lorist, and it would ill become us—poet-priests are rare—to pass by one whose pen has served the literary world so well. * * * * The learned poet—for poet he is—has given us 'The Land of Leix' in six cantos, covering 125 pages, and in it deals with the history, antiquities, battles, ruins, etc., which always, alas! alas! have such a pathetic interest for us. Whether unfolding a vision of prehistoric times, or making allusion to the grave of a friend of early years, the Canon's pen moves with ease and elegance. * * * * After 'The Land of Leix' comes 'The Legend Lays of Ireland'—a variety of legends in a variety of verse. * * * * Miscellaneous verses and sonnets bring the collection to a close."—*The Dublin Review*.

"These poems are accompanied by long and valuable archæological notes, which greatly enhance their value and make the book a contribution not only to the treasures of Polymnia, but also to those of her graver sister Clio."—*The Catholic Times*. (Philadelphia.)

"In the 'Poems of Lageniensis' the distinguished Dublin priest leads captive the hearts of his compatriots. * * * * That lovely region, archaic Leix, is here delineated with exhaustive minuteness of detail. The fascinating panorama unfolds in chequered vicissitude nature's varied charms, glittering in the blended tints of gorgeous imagination and elegant scholarship. Numerous foot-notes comprise a miniature museum of quaint tit-bits in history, philology and poetry—a choice mosaic worthy an honoured member of the Royal Irish Academy."—*The American Catholic News*.

"The first pages of the present volume are occupied by an epic, the 'Land of Leix' a district which embraces the greater portion of Queen's County, and one which has many personal associations for the author. * * * * The next division of the volume consists of a number of 'Legend Lays of Ireland,' many of which are, metrically, most effective and original. There are in them repeated instances of that musical rhythm which characterizes so much genuine *Irish* poetry. A patriotic enthusiasm is exhibited in every line, and a natural spontaneous poetry actuates almost every image and expression. It is gratifying to find an instinctively national writer adopting home-grown subjects for his theme, and treating them with so much inspiration and effect. The remaining poems, which include some admirable sonnets, are deserving of a careful reading, and are sure to be found full of merit. They are a decided addition to the national poetry of Ireland; and it is to be expected that with the revival of interest in Irish literature and history they will become popular. The author is entitled to the gratitude of his countrymen, for having unearthed so many old-time events and fictions, and for having presented them in such agreeable form. All who take an interest in literature as a national product must be attracted to this book and will read it, we are sure, with great satisfaction."—*The Month.*

"It is a volume which has many claims upon many readers; for almost every page is enriched by learned notes, or reminiscences of the writer's early days, which contain a wealth of information not to be neglected by students of Irish topography, hagiology, folk-lore, history, social customs and traditions. * * * * There is a poem in the Spenserian stanza, upon the famous principality, so celebrated in history and tradition, through its great line of chiefs, the house of the O'Mores. * * * * The poem flows from theme to theme, somewhat in the manner of 'Childe Harold,' mingling history and love of nature with deep personal feeling. * * * * No review can give a just impression of the wealth of stirring and beautiful tradition in this poem, which springs from a great storehouse of learning indeed, but is far more than merely learned. * * * * 'The Land of Leix' is a true service to Irish literature. * * * * Upon the miscellaneous poems and sonnets there is not space to dwell, they are religious, memorial and patriotic, all of no little deep sentiment and kindly grace: *pius vates* and *de Hibernia bene meritus.*"—*The Academy.*

"His 'Land of Leix' is a long poem in Spenserian stanza, describing minutely that part of Ireland which may be said to be our present Queen's County. Every hill, river and castle is lovingly commemorated, with all the historical associations and many personal and local particulars which are often interesting and valuable."—*The Irish Monthly.*

OPINIONS OF THE PRESS.

"Canon O'Hanlon divides his book into several sections, beginning with a lengthened contribution in six cantos of Spenserian stanza, entitled 'The Land of Leix,' which is a delightful picturesque manual to all that is stirring in the ancient territory of the O'MORES—that noble district of central Ireland—and then follows a graceful collection of legendary lays. * * * * 'The Land of Leix' was particularly interesting to us, for we are familiar with every inch of the ground treated of by the bard, and were personally acquainted with many of the characters of a later generation to whom he alludes. In truth, we felt an especial attractiveness in his plain and copious footnotes describing many spots, famous, like the Dun of Clopoke, the Round Tower of Timahoe, and the Rock of Dunamase."
—*The Universe.*

"We are glad to welcome a volume of the collected poems of the author of the 'Lives of the Irish Saints.' * * * * It contains the 'Land of Leix,' the well-known legendary poems of the author, and also a considerable collection of reflective and miscellaneous poems. The 'Land of Leix' is a production of great beauty, and remarkably original in conception. It is not always easy to invest a poem dealing with local history and characteristics and scenic attractions with the interest which it is comparatively easy for a versifier of any talent to give to matters which afford room for more discursive treatment. But in the hands of Canon O'Hanlon the theme has been treated with great power. There is melody and grace in the poem from beginning to end, and, full as it is of sentiment which is altogether Irish, it could not fail to be read with the deepest pleasure by anyone who loves the old land, her traditions, and the heroism of her past, and who has ever learned what a great part the ancient territory of the Land of Leix played in the battles for freedom in modern times as well as in the exploits handed down in the records of the dim ages of Ireland's glory. The poet touches with a facile genius upon the history, antiquities, legends, and ancient remains, and his poem is studded with beautiful and chaste reflections to which his theme gives rise. * * * * The collection of Irish legends in poetry, which fills a goodly number of pages, is a work that will be grateful to the soul of every Irishman. * * * * We have read Canon O'Hanlon's legends with the greatest delight. We feel sure the delight they occasioned in the reading was nothing to the pleasure which their composition gave the reverend writer. He handles them reverently, and with a glow of pride in the ancient records which unfortunately is not always felt by Irishmen. The legends are collected from north, south, east, and west. The lakes, the mountains, the raths, cromleachs, and duns, and round towers—all furnish their quota. Some of them are weird Pagan traditions; a good many of them have cast around them the softening influences of Christianity which had so marked an influence upon all the literature, custom, and character of the impressionable Irish."—*The Evening Telegraph.*

"Those who love to hear of the old tales and legends, and to learn more of the poetry and history, the biography and romance, of the land of their fathers, will find, we think, in those poems, and in the wealth of historical, biographical and topographical notes, with which they are illustrated, a real fund of enjoyment and profit."—*The American Catholic Quarterly Review.*

"The abundant notes which are appended to the poems are, in themselves, most interesting and instructive illustrations of Irish history and topography, and of Irish legendary lore."—*The Austral Light.*

"Messrs. James Duffy and Co., Limited, Dublin, have published a volume of poems termed *Poetical Works of Lageniensis.* It is strong and elegantly bound, while in type and paper it will compare with the best issues of first-rate London houses. * * * * All who peruse the book will find it palpitating with the true tender sympathy of the meditative poet, who, devoid of the fateful passions of the ordinary mortal, muses with a melancholy tinge of twilight romance over the real and mystic glories of his beloved native land."—*Irish Society.*

"He tells of the legends and folk-lore of that central district where battles were fought in the heart of Ireland when the great chieftains were still holding out a fierce resistance to the Crown and to each other. Long before these conflicts and far further back does he go to bring a picture before his readers of the historic interests connected with what is now the Queen's County. Such work has an especial value beside the poetic, and this work is added to by the number of notes and authorities which the author gives. More than half the contents of the volume is devoted to the old territory of Leix, and the rest deals with legends of other parts of Ireland. The care which Canon O'Hanlon has displayed upon this collection of his metrical works is worthy of all acknowledgment, and the work is one which will be treasured by those who take an interest in the legends and the lore of this country."—*The Daily Express.*

" Ce volume est aussi remarquable par le charme de la poésie, la hauteur de vues, le sentiment patriotique, que par la valeur traditionniste des notes nombreuses qui l'accompagnent et qui en font un vrai livre de Folklore irlandais."
—*Dictionnaire International des Folkloristes Contemporains.*

"At a time when Irish literature and legend is being revived around us, no more admirable volume could be published than Canon O'Hanlon's poems, thoroughly racy of the soil as they are. We bespeak for them a very wide circulation, and wherever they go they are sure to carry on in a rich stream the love of faith and fatherland. The volume is gracefully dedicated to the Countess of Aberdeen, and is adorned with a good portrait of the rev. author."—*The Freeman's Journal.* (Daily.)

" Many of these compositions have been long out of print, especially the 'Legend Lays of Ireland,' which have often been sought for by collectors and students of Irish national folk-lore. 'The Land of Leix' was unprocurable in any form, until its several parts had been extracted from different periodicals, and placed in the order of cantos and stanzas they now occupy in this very readable volume, which is enriched with very valuable footnotes exhibiting the writer's extensive acquaintance with Irish history."—*The Catholic Times.* (Liverpool.)

" Canon O'Hanlon's many friends and admirers will most gladly welcome the above collection in book form of his legendary and other verse. * * * * Taken altogether it is a book which needs no recommendation to the Irish reader. The name 'Lageniensis' is a sufficient guarantee for the high value of its contents. Those who are already familiar with the 'Legend Lays of Ireland' and the stray poems published in the different periodicals, will be delighted to meet their old favourites in this collection, while those who are so unfortunate as to be unacquainted with the reverend author's charming verse, will have an opportunity of enriching their minds and libraries

WORKS BY THE SAME AUTHOR.

by a store of melody at once elevating, entertaining and instructive. We heartily welcome this new volume, added to the varied list of books, for which Ireland owes a debt of gratitude to her distinguished son."—*The Weekly Freeman.*

"The volume now under consideration is a collection for the most part of descriptive and legendary verse, divided as follows: 'The Land of Leix,' descriptive and historical; 'Legend Lays of Ireland,' containing stories illustrative of folk-lore in almost every county; and quite a number of miscellaneous poems, many of which appear here in collected form for the first time. In his poems Father O'Hanlon displays almost as much variety of form and excellence of manner as in his varied prose writings. The rhythm is always smooth and the diction elegant, while the word-painting presents a literary landscape that is not often surpassed by the foremost masters in the art, the poets reputed to be possessed of real genius."—*The Catholic Standard.* (Philadelphia.)

IN THE PRESS, AND PREPARING FOR PUBLICATION.

21. Irish-American History of the United States.

With Coloured Map of the great American Republic. By Very Rev. John Canon O'Hanlon.

Sealy, Bryers and Walker, Middle Abbey Street, Dublin.
8vo.

"The Rev. Canon O'Hanlon, of Dublin, the erudite Irish historian and hagiologist, whose great work on 'The Lives of the Irish Saints' is gradually approaching completion, is at present engaged in a work entitled 'An Irish-American History of the United States,' in which he will show the extent of influence of the Irish settlers of America. His introductory chapter will deal with St. Brendan's pre-Columbian voyage to the Continent."—*The Daily Chronicle.*

ALREADY PUBLISHED.

DUBLIN: JAMES DUFFY & CO., LTD., 15 Wellington Quay.

To be completed in Twelve Royal Octavo Volumes, and in 120 Parts, of 64 pages each Part.

LIVES OF THE IRISH SAINTS,

Compiled from Manuscript and other Sources,

With the Commemorations and Festivals of Holy Persons,

NOTED IN

Calendars, Martyrologies, and Various Works, Domestic or Foreign,

RELATING TO

The Ancient Church History of Ireland,

BY THE

REV. JOHN CANON O'HANLON, M.R.I.A.

Price, ONE SHILLING each Part to Subscribers; ONE SHILLING & SIXPENCE each to Non-Subscribers.

VOL. I. For the Month of January, containing 13 Parts, comprising Introduction, pp. i. to clxxii., and pp. 1 to 624, cloth, gilt, and gilt edges, bevelled, in highly ornamental Covers, Price to Subscribers, 16s.; to Non-Subscribers, 22s. 6d.

VOL. II. For the Month of February, containing 12 Parts, pp. 1 to 736, do., Price to Subscribers, 15s.; to Non-Subscribers, 21s.

VOL. III. For the Month of March, containing 16 Parts, pp. 1 to 1,036, do., Price to Subscribers, 19s.; to Non-Subscribers, 27s.

WORKS BY THE SAME AUTHOR.

VOL. IV. For the Month of April, containing 9 Parts, pp. 1 to 576, do., Price to Subscribers, 12s.; to Non-Subscribers, 16s. 6d.

VOL. V. For the Month of May, containing 10 Parts, pp. 1 to 624, do., Price to Subscribers, 13s. ; to Non-Subscribers, 18s.

VOL. VI. For the Month of June, containing 13 Parts, pp. 1 to 832, do., Price to Subscribers, 16s.; to Non-Subscribers, 22s. 6d.

VOL. VII. For the Month of July, containing 8 Parts, pp. 1 to 520, do., Price to Subscribers, 11s. ; to Non-Subscribers, 15s.

VOL. VIII. For the Month of August, containing 8 Parts, pp. 1 to 512, do., Price to Subscribers, 11s.; to Non-Subscribers, 15s.

₊ Binding in Cloth, gilt, and gilt edges, each Vol., 3s.; plain, each Vol., 2s. 6d. ; in best morocco, extra, 12s. ; in any Variety of Colour ordered. The rich style of Cover design, the *Opus Hibernicum*, specially adapted, only furnished from the Bookbinding Establishment of Messrs. James Duffy and Co.

☞ Cloth Cases, in a Variety of Colours, with richly gilt Sides and Back, and in a Style to match for each Volume, can there be obtained at 2s. each, or free by Post, 2s. 3d.

TERMS OF SUBSCRIPTION.

☞ The printed Numbers are sent to Home Subscribers, who shall have paid FIVE SHILLINGS in advance, thus securing five successive Parts, *post free*. From Subscribers in the United States, the British Colonies, and abroad, ONE POUND in advance is required to receive twenty successive Parts, *post free*.

Money or Postal Orders to be drawn on the General Post Office, Dublin. Cheques (*crossed*), to be drawn on a Dublin Bank, to save the cost of collection. Address: Rev. John Canon O'Hanlon, P.P., Star of the Sea Church, Irishtown, Dublin.

NOTICES OF THE PRESS.

The following notices are selected from many other reviews that have hitherto been published :—

"It was, we believe, in 1857, when publishing his 'Life of St. Laurence O'Toole,' two years previous to that of 'St. Malachy O'Morgair,' that Father O'Hanlon first publicly announced his intention of bringing out the 'Lives of the Irish Saints.' But it was the dream of his early youth, one which haunted him from the dawn of his missionary career, in Ireland, in the great cities and savannas of America, and after his return to his native land. It was a work necessarily of immense labour, requiring untiring exertion, and unlimited access to printed and manuscript sources of information, and when these were secured, then was absolutely necessary the hand of a skilful master, one of clear judgment in the selection and arrangement of the material accumulated, and possessed of the highest critical faculty in discriminating evidence. We are happy to say, that so far as the present work has proceeded, Father O'Hanlon has fully realized, if not exceeded, his antecedents. His Lives of Saints Laurence, Malachy, and David, had marked him as one of the most eminent of modern Irish hagiologists, as one standing alone in a great and glorious effort to recall and render imperishable the labours of the saints of Erin. Colgan only accomplished three months of the ecclesiastical year, and to the general public his work was in a sealed language, out of print, and almost impossible to procure. The same might almost be said of the mighty tomes of the Bollandists and Benedictines of St. Maur. Nowhere was to be had an express work on the lives of the saints of Ireland, or of their missionary children who christianized the greater part of Europe. * * * We have no doubt therefore, that the public will receive the present instalment of Father O'Hanlon's admirable undertaking with feelings of no ordinary gratification, not only to those who honour and revere the saints of God, who shine as lights in the brightest as well as in the darkest eras of the Church's history, but to those who love and wish to learn the story of their country's strange vicissitudes, its peaceful disenthralment from the slavery of idolatry, its progress in faith, its struggles against the usurpation of the invading Norse, who desire to know the holy places sanctified by those saints, as their abodes in life or sanctuaries after death—all will turn to those pages with yearning interest and eager inquiry. In them they will find the result of long continued and patient research, the record and biography not only of distinguished holy men, but of many others, partially obscure and half forgotten, save in those remote places where their memories are still cherished, and their graves and humble baptisteries are still pointed out by a grateful people. To discover those half-forgotten and holy wells, draped with ivy or marked by the solitary thorn, has been no easy operation; but once found out, it is pleasant to see how joyfully and piously we linger round them, and pour forth the silent prayers of thanksgiving and supplication. Around these sacred monuments of Irish faith and devotion, Father O'Hanlon guides us in quiet pilgrimage, pouring out his varied information, and describing the place and the adjoining scenery with true poetry and loving devotion of mind."—*Ulster Examiner.*

"A book called the 'Lives of the Irish Saints,' with many hundred wood engravings of old Irish Churches, by the Rev. John O'Hanlon, is being prepared for publication, and is expected to throw much light on Irish Christian antiquities."—*Public Opinion.*

"The labours of the Bollandists, whose writings, 'the Acta Sanctorum,' have extended over more than a century, have passed into a proverb, and it is well known that the great Dictionary undertaken many years since by the French Academy has still years of labour before it; but here we have one man undertaking a work, which to judge by the first part now before us, holds out the prospect of a labour almost as gigantic. It will not, however, we feel sure, be for want of encouragement on the part of the Catholic press, if Father O'Hanlon should never realise the accomplishment of his purpose; and we can assure him, that our best wishes will follow him, as he brings out each succeeding number. The first part contains so much as is known of the several Irish Saints for the four first days of January, with the beginning of the fifth; and the facts of each Life appear to be put together in a most readable form, interspersed with picturesque descriptions of scenery and plenty of pious reflections. Each page contains copious notes of explanation, or reference to authorities quoted in the work, and there are occasional illustrations, such as ruins of ancient churches, and spots rendered interesting from association with some Saint of old."—*Weekly Register.*

"An original and a voluminous work."—*The World.* (U.S.A.)

"The Rev. Mr. O'Hanlon, a zealous and active Catholic missionary priest in one of the parishes of the metropolis, has devoted the best part of his life to the accumulation of materials bearing on the sacred and historic incidents of Irish hagiology. He has been a living and enthusiastic explorer amongst the bright past days of Christian Ireland, and has spared neither time, nor health, nor money, nor toil, to reach the best and surest sources of information and of authority on the subjects to which he has devoted such constant—we had almost said—such affectionate study and attention. The materials out of which he had to construct his narratives were, no doubt, ample and abounding, but it was this very fact, their amplitude and their number, that, perhaps, constituted his chiefest difficulty. They were scattered about in various places, and the same lives were often written by different hands. It was, therefore, a matter of necessity, that all of them should be got at, and all of them carefully read. For Father O'Hanlon proposed to himself, that his work should be a full one, or that at least no important incident in connection with the Irish Saints should be omitted from his biographies of them. In fulfilment of his purpose, he has left no available source unexplored, and has been careful to make his 'Lives' a work that will be fit to take rank amongst the worthies of genuine hagiology. He has brought us in the first number of his great book, from the Saints of the first of January to those of the fourth, and has in all presented us with lives of more than thirty Saints. Some of the lives are, as might naturally be expected, longer than others, and there are a few of the Saints of whom, with all his research, our reverend author could find but the simple record that they lived and that they died. He has succeeded in making his narrative very interesting, and some of his descriptive bits of Irish scenery display a considerable amount of literary skill. The number is admirably brought out, and the printing of it does the greatest credit to the workmanship of its native printer, Mr. Dollard, of Dame Street. It is

largely illustrated with really excellent woodcuts, which as works of art—apart altogether from their great value as accurate and interesting representations of cherished sacred historical spots—impart much attractiveness to the work."
—*The Irish Times.*

"At last the name and the fame of the holy ones of our Island of Saints are to be brought from out the dim, religious shadows of monastic libraries, and set up before our people in the light of our national literature. It was not to our credit as a literary people, that so little was popularly known of our Irish saints; nay, in quarters where better things might have been expected, Irish hagiology was a region unexplored, and our Irish saint-lore an unopened volume. * * * This, however, only intensified the difficulties against which Father O'Hanlon had to struggle, and made, as it were, thicker and more palpable the hagiological darkness through which he had to grope the way. It was only a patriotic as well as a religious enthusiasm such as his, coupled with and sustained by an almost heroic patience and perseverance, that could have borne him onward through a task so overwhelming in the variety as well as in the comparative obscurity of its details and its materials. Yet he has triumphed over them all, and now beholds, we are sure, with pleasure, as well he may with pride, the first public beginning of a noble work, which we earnestly trust he may live to see auspiciously crowned with a worthy and successful completion. No. 1 of the book is now before us, and we sincerely congratulate Father O'Hanlon and all concerned with him in its production on the most creditable and artistic appearance which the work presents. We congratulate them all the more heartily that all of it is the work of Irish hands, and all of it has been done at home in our city. The number contains sixty-four pages of matter, and is enriched with about a dozen of clear and beautifully executed illustrations. It opens with the hagiology of the first day of the year and the life of the saint whose name appears first on the calendar. No less than nineteen saints are noted for the 1st of January; and Father O'Hanlon exhausts all the sources that could throw light on their lives. Some of them are known, and nothing more; and of others the recorded incidents are but few and fragmentary. He devotes to each saint a separate 'article' —each article, of course, varying in length according to the supply of the materials—and this division will, when the work is finished, be found admirably convenient for easy reference. * * * * * We have said nothing of the notes with which it is enriched. They are most learned and most valuable. They contain the reference for every biographical, historical and topographical statement in the context, and are completely exhaustive of the subject about which they treat. We have said that the illustrations are excellently done. They embrace a set of subjects little known through photographic reproductions, and are, therefore, of all the more interest for the scholar or the intellectual tourist."—*The Freeman's Journal.*

"The Irish Saints by a painstaking and scholarly writer."—*The Sacristy.*

"The engravings are finely executed, and the paper and press-work are of the very best. The approbation and encouragement given to the author by the Irish hierarchy ought to be a guarantee for the excellence of the text. The Lives of the Irish Saints are less known than the Saints of almost any country in Europe. Even the Irish people themselves are not acquainted with the lives of many, and with even the names of some. Three centuries of persecution explain this destruction of these holy remembrances; but now, when Catholic Ireland raises her head and repairs her past misfortunes, she must also revive these the purest of her glories."—*The Boston Pilot.* (U.S.A.)

"The great, the almost sacred, labour of a lifetime is fast nearing its completion, and the people of Ireland are soon to have placed within their reach the rich and abounding records of the illustrious dead, who in times gone by achieved for our country its title and its fame of the Island of Saints."—*The Castlebar Telegraph.*

"A great work on the Irish Saints, which ought to be in the possession of every Catholic family."—*The Monitor.* (San Francisco, U.S.A.)

"The first profusely illustrated number of Rev. John O'Hanlon's 'Lives of the Irish Saints' is expected to be published in Dublin shortly after Easter, and to be derived from original sources, both as to literary materials and artistic subjects."—*The Irish Builder.*

"The claims of St. Fursey have been put forward by Canon O'Hanlon in his 'Lives of the Irish Saints.' He thinks there can scarcely be a doubt, that Fursey's Vision furnished Dante in a great measure with the idea and plan of the Divine Comedy, and he quotes several passages of it which so closely resemble passages in the Vision, that it seems impossible to regard the coincidence as fortuitous. * * * Fursey's Vision is set out in Canon O'Hanlon's Life of the Saint."—*Irish Daily Independent.*

" It is a subject of no small congratulation, that the task, so long delayed, has fallen into the hands of a student so conscientious, a scholar so accomplished, an antiquary so enthusiastic, and an ecclesiastic so capable of appreciating the great features in the great characters of the Irish saints as Father O'Hanlon. It would be needless to enlarge upon the difficulty and laborious research involved in the work. A glance at the first number is sufficient to indicate, though not fully to reveal, the pains which have gone to the accomplishment of this *magnum opus*. * * * To call a work learned is calculated to frighten some people, especially in the present day, when only the lightest of light literature is thoroughly favoured. But we beg to assure our readers that it is quite possible to be learned and at the same time pleasing, and Father O'Hanlon has mastered this art, desirable even in one who deals with so grave a subject as the lives and character of the Irish saints. The minds of the sainted ones of our race appear to have been tinged with something of the poetic character of the land, and their career abounds in the picturesque. Father O'Hanlon has not gone out of his way to search for such graces of narrative. On the contrary, he has exercised a very rigid severity in the rejection of untrustworthy and incredible legends."—*Cork Examiner.*

"This learned work is a fund of sacred instruction and devotional reading."—*The Ave Maria Magazine.* (U.S.A.)

"A book called the 'Lives of the Irish Saints,' with many hundred wood engravings of old Irish churches, by the Rev. John O'Hanlon, is being prepared for publication, and is expected to throw much light on Irish Christian antiquities."—*The Northern Whig.*

"It is beautifully printed, well illustrated, and will furnish future writers on the history, ecclesiology and topography of Ireland with a most valuable storehouse of information."—*The Athenæum.*

" There is no living writer better qualified for the arduous task he has undertaken than Father O'Hanlon, and we cordially commend his labours to the notice of the clergy and archæologists of the city and county of Kilkenny."—*Kilkenny Journal.*

"His work is a substantial repast, not for one day, but for every day throughout the year. The first part of Vol. I. is just out. It is first-class in its history, in the authorities cited, in the learning displayed, and above all in the extraordinary research of the writer, and the pains he has manifestly taken to know all and every thing connected with the subject matter regarding which he writes."—*The Tuam News.*

"There can be no doubt, therefore, that the work will be accomplished with all the accuracy that zeal, industry and erudition can bring to the task."—*Saunders's News-Letter.*

"A complete work of Irish Hagiology."—*Northern Star.*

"A project which will truthfully reveal the piety, the devotion, the God-like knowledge which preserved the blessing of the Faith to Erin."—*Tipperary Free Press.*

"Lives of the Irish Saints, to the number of over 3,000 separate articles, with many hundred wood engravings of old Irish churches, is preparing for immediate publication."—*The Morning Mail.*

"We have much pleasure in recommending the above work to the antiquarian and the literateur, and in congratulating its learned and revered author on the success that promises to crown his labours."—*Wexford Independent.*

"We know of no one more competent in the Irish Church to do justice to this magnificent undertaking. * * * Father O'Hanlon has given good earnest in the many learned works already written by him, that the forthcoming work will be worthy of his high literary character and his inspiring subject. What curious and precious glimpses into the ideas and habits of early Irish life, especially the religious life, may be expected from the 'Lives of the Irish Saints.'"—*Clare Advertiser.*

"None but a man of indomitable perseverance could have carried to a successful completion a task beset with so many difficulties. The scholar of Irish history knows the intricate and obscure paths he has to tread when trying to trace out the story of his country in a political point of view; but the labour is vastly increased if it be the sacred history or lives of Ireland's 3,000 saints that he endeavours to depict. The materials are often scant, the *data* uncertain. Many holy persons of the same or similar names lived frequently in the same period. In the lapse of years their acts became so blended together as to render it a hopeless task to be able to distinguish between them. The manuscripts which could elucidate what is often so uncertain now have either been entirely destroyed or are scattered far and wide through the libraries of Europe. The 'Lives of the Irish Saints,' in the Rev. J. O'Hanlon's twelve large volumes, will have a great deal of interest for us on this side of the Channel."—*The Tablet.*

" His work is at last complete. He has surmounted the obstacles that at first seemed unconquerable ; he has verified sites of saintly dwellings that seemed lost in doubt or in obscurity ; he has availed himself to the full of the more than kindly generosity and hospitality with which Belgian monasteries and their invaluable libraries were thrown open for his use, and he has exhausted every record that has lain for years unexplored in private and public collections of manuscripts and printed memoirs of libraries here at home. Therefore it is that Father O'Hanlon's ' Lives of the Irish Saints ' will rank as a standard work, not alone of Irish hagiology, but of Irish history and of ancient Irish topography—for he has identified every locality, and confirmed every reference by the aid and the light of researches, the value and authority of which it is impossible to dispute. The work was a huge one, beyond all question ; and it needed a courageous and an enthusiastic spirit to dare it. Nearly three thousand saints are mentioned in our Irish calendars and martyrologies, and it was a necessary portion of his task to leave not a source unexplored, whence he could hope to draw even the tiniest supply for his vast undertaking."—*Dublin Evening Post.*

" The second part of Vol. I. of this magnificent edition of the Lives of the Irish Saints has just been issued by the publishers. The wonderful labour, the exhaustless patience, the deep and constant research, and varied learning of the gifted author, are seen in every page of this splendid work, which promises to be a monument worthy of the theme, and unspeakably creditable to the author's indefatigable perseverance and those other qualities, which fit him for a task so herculean in all its proportions."—*The Limerick Reporter.*

"The first number of Father O'Hanlon's *magnum opus*—'The Lives of the Irish Saints'—is before us; and we are glad to say it fully realizes the promises of the Prospectus, and the high expectations which had been formed of the work. * * * The several smaller works of a kindred character previously published by Father O'Hanlon were evidence of his competency for the task he had undertaken. He possessed, in fact, all the qualities suitable for a labourer in that peculiar field of ecclesiastical literature—a love for his subject, unwearying patience and industry in the collection of materials, and a careful and conscientious habit of using them. * * * * The compilation of this valuable work has occupied the reverend author's spare hours—and many hours that could ill be spared from needful rest and relaxation—during twenty-five years of his missionary life. We congratulate him now on the beginning of the end—in other words, on the commencement of the issue of his work from the Press; and we congratulate the Catholic people of Ireland on the same fact."—*The Nation.*

"It can hardly be conceived that Ireland, the Island of Saints, is at present the only Christian country that does not possess a history of its own men—that the land which has given so many saints to the world has not worthily recorded their good deeds. This disgrace is about to be lifted from us."—*Tralee Chronicle.*

"Il obtint accés dans les grandes bibliothéques de Dublin et devint l'ami des hautes personnalités littéraires de la ville. Depuis il n'a cessé d'ecrise une foule d'ouvrages, tandis qu'il preparait son magnifique travail: *Lives of the Irish Saints*, qui abonde en legendes recueillies dans les anciens *Actes.*—*Dictionnaire Biographique des Membres du Clergé Catholique.*

"The work could hardly be in better hands."—*Cashel Gazette.*

"Since the days of Colgan no effort has been made to collect together the history of the three thousand and more holy personages whose lives won for Ireland the title, 'Insula Sanctorum.' Certainly the person who has had the courage and the zeal now to undertake this herculean task deserves well of his country and of posterity."—*Catholic Opinion.*

"Le savant auteur * * * longs et importants travaux d'histoire hagiographique, dont il est a souhaiter que le public soit bientot mis a même de profiter."—*Journal des Savants.*

"Alone and single-handed, with but scant and precarious resources, he bravely projected, and has brought within measurable completion, one of the monumental works of this century, not simply on the Gaelic Church, but in respect of European Christianity."—*The New York Catholic News.*

"As a monument of Irish typography it shall be unsurpassed."—*The Bookseller.*

"Such a work, no matter from what point of view it may be regarded, must abound with matter of deepest interest to every one who cherishes a taste for our national history and antiquities; and, most assuredly, for carrying it out, no one could possibly be better fitted than the Rev. gentleman who has now undertaken the task."—*Kilkenny Moderator.*

"The forthcoming work by the learned and gifted Father O'Hanlon will literally unlock a hidden treasure."—*Clare Freeman.*

"This extensive work, now quite ready for publication, only awaits a full list of one thousand subscribers to issue from the press."—*Catholic Times.* (Liverpool.)

"The terms of subscription have been marvellously moderate, and payment of it made as easy as could by possibility be expected."—*Galway Vindicator.*

"Father O'Hanlon has earned the gratitude of all Catholics in his efforts to resuscitate the records of the lives and labours of Ireland's long roll of saints, and his work deserves the appreciation of a liberal patronage in this country as in the old."—*The Irish World.* (U.S.A.)

"It is quite unnecessary for us to say anything about Father O'Hanlon's qualifications for the pious task he has undertaken; for his name is too familiar both to the Irish and American public to need any further introduction to them."—*Leinster Independent.*

"'The Lives of the Irish Saints' is a publication, which has already reached its eighth octavo volume, and it has won too much praise from the erudite to need any fresh commendation."—*The Catholic Times.* (Philadelphia.)

"He has accomplished his portion of a solemn duty, and it rests now with the pastors and people of this country to accomplish theirs."—*Waterford News.*

"The work is published in numbers to suit the convenience of subscribers. It is beautifully illustrated, and highly recommended by our patriotic Archbishop. For sale at the 'Ontario Catholic Book Store,' 16 Francis Street, Toronto. Price per number, 40 cents. Sent free by mail."—*Irish Canadian.*

"The press of the United Kingdom speaks of the work with the highest respect and commendation, and in America its appearance has been hailed with marked favour."—*Wexford People.*

"The first part of Mr. O'Hanlon's *Lives of the Irish Saints* gives promise of a book of great research, learning, good taste and archæological interest."—*The Union Review.*

"We have gone through this volume very fully, and have found it interesting and instructive. Of course we do not look upon its contents in the same light as our Roman Catholic countrymen do, and our religious belief forbids us receiving many statements in connection with the lives and labours of Irish Saints, whom we, as Protestants, claim as having been of a faith more in harmony with our own than with that of the Roman Catholic Church. But, apart from these considerations, Irishmen like ourselves look back with pleasure and with pride upon that period when Ireland was emphatically the 'Island of Saints,' when in her monasteries, great public colleges, the virtues of religion were cultivated and grouped with the study of literature and art, preparing missionaries and commissioning them to carry the Gospel to England and Scotland, and to very many parts of the Continent of Europe. These being our feelings, formed from the authentic testimony of history, we have no scruple about reading the work of an educated Roman Catholic clergyman, whose labours attest great scholarly attainments, deep and varied research, and patient perseverance in a department of literature over which few would be disposed to pore, and fewer still be qualified to collect and arrange the materials. * * * Now, as to the Introduction itself, it occupies clxxvii closely printed pages royal octavo, and it is a valuable repertory of hagiology, proving the richness, the abundance, and the distribution, of the materials from which the Saint History of Ireland must be written. What the Menologias did for the Greek and the Acta Sanctorum for the Latin Church, Calendars and Martyrologies and other records did for the Irish Church. In the fifth, sixth, and seventh centuries there were, and still are, writings of St. Patrick, Benignus, and many others. In the eighth, ninth, tenth, and eleventh centuries, the writers were numerous. * * * * We now come to notice fuller details than we have seen before of the eminent persons who founded religious houses in Ireland. And first in the list is St. Fanchea, Abbess of Ross Oirther, or Rossorry. She was daughter of Conall Dearg, Prince of Oriel, and was born at Rathmore, in the vicinity of Clogher. * * * * That our country formerly possessed many eminent persons —eminent for their piety and learning—cannot be denied. They may not have been, and very likely were not, all that their admirers say; but they were pre-eminent in their day, and they earned for our country the title of 'Island of Saints.' Their memory is done justice to in the volume before us, which is very neatly got up, and bears evidence to the research and ability of the Rev. John O'Hanlon, to whom the labour must have been a labour of love, or he never could have got through it so successfully."—*The Belfast News-Letter.*

" Mr. O'Hanlon's labour and research give him claim to the support of Celtic antiquaries, without difference of religion."—*The Graphic.*

" Mr. O'Hanlon is well known as an eminent hagiologist, and some of his previous works have been reviewed most favourably by French as well as home reviewers."—*Bedfordshire Times.*

" But one opinion can be formed on the subject, that Father O'Hanlon will supply a want, which, while there has been an excuse for not supplying before, it would be a disgrace to have neglected any longer."—*Catholic Review* (U.S.A.)

" This valuable work will prove that many English and Scotch Saints, eminent for learning and piety, went to Ireland, and became so famous there, that both churches and parishes bear their names to the present day; whilst Irish saints, in still greater number, came to England and Scotland, planting the Faith, and founding churches and great educational establishments in those kingdoms."—*Westminster Gazette.*

" Many of the readers of the *Catholic Union*, doubtless, are aware that the great Catholic and National work undertaken by Rev. John O'Hanlon, M.R.I.A., is in course of publication in Dublin. Some thirty odd numbers of the 'Lives of the Irish Saints' have already appeared, and the work promises to be one of the most important contributions to the ecclesiastical and antiquarian literature of Ireland. * * * Besides its hagiological value, it will also prove a copious mine of information on the subject of the history, antiquity, topography, and traditions of the 'Island of Saints and Scholars.'"—*Catholic Union* (U.S.A.)

"Rev. John O'Hanlon, who will be remembered by many of our Catholic readers as an earnest and devoted missionary, at one time stationed in this State, but now an active minister in the archdiocese of Dublin, and a distinguished ornament of the Irish priesthood, announces the early completion of an elaborate and important work, on which he began in St. Louis, over twenty-five years ago. It is entitled the 'Lives of the Irish Saints,' and embraces a complete history of Irish hagiology."—*Missouri Republican.* (U.S.A.)

"Many things are required to constitute a good standard work in the ordinary acceptation of the term, foremost among which is, of course, the subject and mode of treating it ; and next, the perfection attained by the publisher in printing, illustrating, etc. That the subject chosen by Mr. O'Hanlon is of the last importance to Irishmen at home and abroad no one will deny ; and that the publishers have done much to raise the character of this country for beauty and accuracy of type, and for most superior engraving, a glance at the present number will sufficiently prove. The engravings are particularly beautiful, and what is of interest to us, are the work of Irishmen. Indeed we do not remember to have seen so perfect and elegant a publication issued at any previous time from the Irish Press. * * * * To chronicle the Lives of the Irish Saints is a task beset with peculiar difficulty ; because, in the first place, the manuscripts that could elucidate these lives have to a great extent been destroyed, or are scattered at wide intervals through the libraries of Europe ; and in the second place, because that in the long dark night of our country's miseries, fable and legend became frequently entwined with true history, rendering it now a herculean labour to separate the chaff from the wheat. The delicacy and tact displayed by our author in dealing with this portion of his work are worthy of every praise. He does not push rudely aside the venerable fable with a sneer at the credulity of bygone ages, as the clever and caustic Cæsar Otway would have done; but he treats it as we are wont to treat reduced gentlemen in society—with a certain air of respect for sake of the prestige they once enjoyed. * * * * In turning over the pages of the 'Irish Saints,' we can comprehend how our country was formerly known as the 'Insula Sanctorum,' for every mountain and valley, every city and hamlet, every desert and solitary place, boasted of a saintly hermit, a holy abbot, a spotless virgin, or a zealous bishop; and now, as under our author's guidance we turn to gaze through the shadowy bygone ages, the prophet's vision of the valley of dry bones seems realised again, and the Saints of old appear once more to live, and look, and watch, and pray, as they did in Ireland's golden past. Nor does Derry rank last in the bead-roll of sainted celebrities. In the present number we find an interesting sketch of one of its early religious, one, too, who has stamped his name in an indelible manner on our local history, in giving title to an entire parish. Among the engravings is one of the old church of this Saint at Tamlagh Finlagan."—*The Derry Journal.*

"It includes likewise the acts of early British, Saxon, Cymri, and Scottish Saints, who are venerated as patrons in Ireland, as connected with their Irish missionary career." *Catholic World.* (U.S.A.)

"Canon O'Hanlon has just issued the 85th part of his 'Lives of the Irish Saints.' It brings his great work down to the 18th of August, the feast of St. Daigh or Dega, of Inniskeen, in Co. Louth."—*The Irish Monthly.*

"Already eight volumes of the 'Lives of the Irish Saints' have been published, and as the plan of the work has included acts and notices of the Saints, and commemorative of their several festivals, given in the Irish Calendars and Martyrologies, and drawn from various other sources, according to the usual arrangements found in the great collections of *Acta Sanctorum;* so each of Canon O'Hanlon's volumes takes in a whole month, and he proceeds in the mensual order of days, from the first to the last, while the life of each Saint is registered on that of his chief festival, and his minor festivals are again distinguished, in like manner, whenever they occur. This work is therefore a systematic and complete cyclopedia of Irish Saint-History. The first volume takes in the month of January, and it comprises an Introduction to the whole, in

172 large and closely printed royal octavo pages, and afterwards follow the different biographies under the heading of numbered articles for each subject, from pp. 1 to 624—thus constituting it a very thick volume. In a similar way, the month of February—saints and festivals—is continued in a volume of 736 pages. Volume the third, for the month of March, as containing the most extensive and exhaustive Life of St. Patrick hitherto published, is the largest of all, containing no less than 1,036 pages. The month of April contains 576 pages; the month of May, 624 pages; the month of June 832 pages—many under the Life of St. Columbekille; the month of July, 520 pages; and that of August—the last completed—512 pages. These eight volumes are elegantly and strongly bound in cloth, bevelled, gilt, and gilt edges, at the published price for the whole set, £7 17s. 6d., or with plain edges, £7 13s. 6d. As a work of general reference for the ecclesiastical history, antiquities—and above all—biography, of the Irish Church, this voluminous compilation is indispensable for public libraries, and it has secured a large circulation at home and abroad. Nor is its interest confined to Ireland alone, since in the early ages of Christianity, Irish missionaries spread over England, Scotland, and the different countries of Europe, where their acts and fame have caused them to be venerated in various localities as special patrons. Thus incidentally the 'Lives of the Irish Saints' serve to elucidate the ecclesiastical history of nations far apart, and add largely to the bead-roll of their native hagiology."—*Sunday World.*

Omitting various favourable references to the Author's biographies of Irish Saints, since their issue, and to be found in standard works hitherto published, Father Victor de Buck, the very celebrated and learned Bollandist writer, thus closes his most interesting treatise. " L'Archéologie Irlandaise" (Paris, 1869. Royal 8vo). From the original French these passages have been faithfully translated:—

" It is an undoubted fact, that if Mr. O'Hanlon's collections were published entire, an immense service must accrue, not alone to the Irish nation, but even to religion. Ireland is now the only Christian country in the world which has not yet issued its complete History of the Saints; although she has had a host innumerable of holy confessors, and, owing to their example and teaching, Scotland, England, the Low Countries, the north of France, with parts of

Germany, have been Christianised, while she has given saintly bishops to the whole of Europe—even to Italy herself—thus deserving the glorious title, *Island of Saints*, which still signalises her Catholic instincts among all other nations on earth—and, in fine, she cherishes a sentiment and conviction towards manifesting hereafter a proud position in the annals of Holy Church ! Russia, Greece, the Scandinavian Provinces, Germany, the Low Countries, England, Scotland, France, Portugal, Spain, Italy, etc., have their Saint Histories, oftentimes in multiplied editions. Ireland has scarcely anything of the kind—especially she has nothing of a perfect character. There is no other nation in which the *Officia Propria Sanctorum* are so scantily provided; in several of her dioceses the patron saint's festival is celebrated with only common lessons for the second nocturn. How many of her national saints do the Irish people know, even by name, not to speak of their acts? How many patrons of her parishes are completely unknown? In a word, where has national Hagiography been so thoroughly ignored as in Ireland? Three centuries of persecution explain this destruction of holy remembrances; but now, when Catholic Ireland raises her head, and repairs her past misfortunes, can she consign to forgetfulness her purest of all glories? Will she suffer Mr. O'Hanlon's labours—which should exalt her ancient grandeur before God—most unfortunately to perish? Whosoever knows how imperfectly Ireland's printing and publishing business has been organised will have much reason to fear such a result, if the successors of the O'Reillys and Flemings do not extend their patronage to an humble priest, and the author of a collection of Irish Saints' Lives. * * * *

"The Irish Saints' biographies present advantages altogether special for men of the same race. In those acts may be found the story of their clans, of their mountains, of their lakes, of their rivers, of their parishes, of their crosses, of their chapels—often of their habitations—with all that can cherish, exalt, and even hallow patriotic sentiment. Let us hope, at least, that patriotism and religion will speak as effectually in the nineteenth as in the seventeenth century, and that, if in the generosity of two prelates Colgan found means for the publication of his two inestimable volumes, Mr. O'Hanlon will not be left abandoned altogether to his own personal exertions."

www.ingramcontent.com/pod-product-compliance
Lightning Source LLC
Chambersburg PA
CBHW031814230426
43669CB00009B/1132